MILTON, SPENSER AND
*THE CHRONICLES OF NARNIA*

# Milton, Spenser and
## *The Chronicles of Narnia*

### *Literary Sources for the C.S. Lewis Novels*

ELIZABETH BAIRD HARDY

McFarland & Company, Inc., Publishers
*Jefferson, North Carolina, and London*

LIBRARY OF CONGRESS CATALOGUING-IN-PUBLICATION DATA

Hardy, Elizabeth Baird, 1971–
    Milton, Spenser and The chronicles of Narnia : literary
sources for the C.S. Lewis novels / Elizabeth Baird Hardy.
        p.     cm.
    Includes bibliographical references and index.

    ISBN-13: 978-0-7864-2876-2
    ISBN-10: 0-7864-2876-7
    (softcover : 50# alkaline paper)

    1. Lewis, C. S. (Clive Staples), 1898–1963. Chronicles of Narnia.
2. Spenser, Edmund, 1552?–1599 — Influence.   3. Spenser,
Edmund, 1552?–1599. Faerie queene.   4. Milton, John, 1608–
1674 — Influence.   5. Milton, John, 1608–1674. Paradise lost.
6. Lewis, C. S. (Clive Staples), 1898–1963. Settings.   7. Christian
literature, English — History and criticism.   8. Evil in literature.
9. Spirituality in literature.   10. Christianity in literature.
I. Title.
PR6023.E926C5335 2007
823'.912 — dc22
                                                    2006033192

British Library cataloguing data are available

Cover images ©2006 Clipart.com

Manufactured in the United States of America

*McFarland & Company, Inc., Publishers*
    *Box 611, Jefferson, North Carolina 28640*
    *www.mcfarlandpub.com*

For my parents,
who encouraged my love of reading;
for my husband,
who wouldn't let me give up on this project;
and for Nathaniel,
in anticipation of many journeys
to Narnia and other fantastic realms.

# *Acknowledgments*

This project would not have been possible without the kind assistance and encouragement of a number of fine individuals. I am particularly indebted to Drs. Roger Stilling and Emory Maiden, who guided me through the early stages of research and drafting. Though this project might have been considered an unconventional scholarly choice, they encouraged me and provided valuable support and feedback. The Mythopoeic Society allowed me to present part of this book at its 2003 conference, propelling me into finally completing it, and the Watauga County Library allowed me to present programs on Lewis that inspired me with the interest and encouragement of fellow Lewis scholars and of children clutching their dog-eared copies of the *Chronicles*. My fellow teachers at Mayland Community College and at the Watauga Campus of Caldwell Community College and Technical Institute gave me much-needed encouragement, and the excellent library staffs at these colleges and at Appalachian State University helped me hunt down and dig up sources. My intrepid readers Daphne Baird, Lynn McKinney, Ralph Lentz II, and, most importantly, Michael C. Hardy, aided me in shaping and refining the text. I am also deeply indebted to the anonymous individual who once decided that a copy of *The Lion, the Witch, and the Wardrobe* would make an excellent second-place prize in my local Girl Scout Cookie–selling contest. I am very grateful that, in that particular race, I did not place first.

# Table of Contents

# *Preface*

    This project began long before I ever realized that literary scholarship was in my future. When I was nine years old, I received my first copy of *The Lion, the Witch, and the Wardrobe*. It was a plain trade paperback, and though I didn't know the first thing about C.S. Lewis, I did recognize the title from having seen bits of the animated film on television while I recovered from a tonsillectomy the previous year. After devouring the first of the Pevensies' adventures, I was enchanted to learn that there were six more *Chronicles* when a family friend gave me the entire set. Over the years I wore out two complete sets of the *Chronicles* with my frequent re-readings and was delighted to discover other facets of C.S. Lewis's writing. I had been both spiritually moved and challenged by the *Chronicles,* so I was not surprised to see Lewis in his role as Christian apologist. When I began my university literary studies, I was thrilled to find my old friend, the creator of Narnia, offering insights on authors I was studying in class, and it was with particular fervor that I discovered his writing on two authors to whom I was devoting considerable academic and personal interest: John Milton and Edmund Spenser. I had met both before, albeit in abbreviated form. As Lewis himself suggested was best, I had first come to know *The Faerie Queene* in a beautifully illustrated children's book, forever making Trina Schart Hyman's St. George the one I picture when I read of Redcrosse and his quest. Milton I had met in high school, when, like Lewis, I wondered why people saw Satan as heroic. Yes, he was proud; but pride is a sin. He did not impress me as worthy of admiration, and I was reassured to find that Lewis felt much the same way.

    As my studies in Milton and Spenser grew more focused, I began to notice familiar threads. I knew that Lewis was an author who

1

absorbed everything from his experiences and his vast reading and that those influences might surface in any of his writing: fiction, criticism, or apologetics. The more I read, the more I began to see how Lewis's love for and understanding of *The Faerie Queene* and *Paradise Lost* had shaped his creation of the stories I had loved since childhood. I began to suspect that my interest in the works of Spenser and Milton might have been partially fueled by meeting some of their characters, settings, and themes before: in Narnia. Perhaps I admired Britomart so because I had first met her in Lucy Pevensie and Jill Pole; perhaps Milton's Eden resonated so deeply for me because I had seen it before, in *The Magician's Nephew*. After beginning my college teaching career, and often feeling pangs of sympathy for Lewis the teacher as I tried to convey my own passion for literature to students who saw poetry as a form of torture rather than a form of communication, I found that I could convey to students the importance of authors like Milton and Spenser by showing them where they had met snippets of their work before. Just as a poem became more accessible if some musician had recorded it as a rock song, themes and characters of literature were less daunting to students when I showed them where such elements may have cropped up in their reading. Thus, I returned to my analysis of the influence of Milton and Spenser upon Lewis's *Chronicles* and began to shape this book.

In researching this project, I found that some scholars had analyzed some aspects of the Chronicles that connected with *The Faerie Queene* and *Paradise Lost*. However, these were limited studies, focusing on specific elements or episodes. This research was helpful in the development of the project but also showed me how much more remained to be done. In addition to close textual analysis of *The Faerie Queene*, *Paradise Lost*, and the *Chronicles*, I relied on Lewis's own words about his own writing and the epic poems that he treasured throughout his life. Fortunately, Lewis did not hesitate to express himself on all matters of importance to him: religion and literature being the foremost of these issues. In his characteristically disarming writing style, he analyzes works of literature and his own process for writing without pretense or what he would call "gas." This straightforward style has inspired me in my writing and teaching to strive for clarity while avoiding pretension, to understand that a work of criticism does not have to be intentionally complicated in order to be intellectually complex, and to use humor and good plain sense to help others understand even the densest of literary works. Lewis's own writing about his work and the writing of Milton and Spenser was also remarkably helpful in the evolution of this analysis.

Despite the critical tendency to dismiss any literary work that seems to be written for children, the *Chronicles* have received some excellent scholarly examination. This is likely due in part to Lewis's own stature as a scholar. While many of his contemporaries seemed a bit embarrassed by his children's writing, later critics tend to treat the Narnian stories with a measure of respect not usually afforded to "juvenile literature" because Lewis himself was clearly an important and brilliant scholar whose work on many levels remains relevant and vital.

The *Chronicles* have also received more serious attention because of their spiritual depth. Lewis's well-known work as a Christian apologist whose writings have encouraged, uplifted, and inspired generations of readers also gives him a measure of credibility seldom lavished on children's authors, in part also due to Lewis's aversion of heavy-handed preaching. While the overly sentimental and often maudlin works of late Victorians like George McDonald have fallen out of fashion, the *Chronicles*, with their solid spiritual foundations that never get in the way of the entertaining and thrilling stories, continue to find new readers with each generation.

A good deal of the scholarly interest in the books, though, comes from the fact that they are wonderful stories, stories that enchant, delight, and enthrall children and adults year after year, while, at the same time, haunting us with the possibility that there is more there than meets the eye. One lesson quickly learned by any child reader of the *Chronicles* is not to take things at face value: that delicious candy may be enchanted, that animal may be able to talk, that seemingly ordinary little girl may become a hero, that old wardrobe may be a gateway to another world. Because of this, scholars, like myself, are returning to the stories we have loved since childhood and using our skills to produce a growing body of scholarship on Lewis's stories that treats them not as mere trifles, as Mr. Beaver would say, but as valuable and vital pieces of writing whose complexities we have only begun to explore. Perhaps this work, and others like it, will aid both scholars and casual readers of the *Chronicles* as they continue exploring the depths of these books to find even more of their secrets to share with the world.

# A Note on Citations

In this text, references to the primary sources — *The Chronicles of Narnia*, *The Faerie Queene*, and *Paradise Lost* — are noted with parenthetical citation. Secondary sources are noted in chapter end notes.

Within citations, the books in *The Chronicles of Narnia* are abbreviated thus:

*The Lion, The Witch, and the Wardrobe* . . . . . *LWW*

*Prince Caspian* . . . . . . . . . . . . . . . . . . . . . . . . . *PC*

*The Voyage of the "Dawn Treader"* . . . . . . . . *VDT*

*The Silver Chair* . . . . . . . . . . . . . . . . . . . . . . . *SC*

*The Horse and His Boy* . . . . . . . . . . . . . . . . . *HHB*

*The Magician's Nephew* . . . . . . . . . . . . . . . . . *MN*

*The Last Battle* . . . . . . . . . . . . . . . . . . . . . . . *LB*

# Introduction

"Any children's story," wrote C.S. Lewis, "that can be read and enjoyed only by children, is a bad children's story." "Jack" Lewis, known in a variety of contexts as Oxford don, Christian apologist, literary critic, and novelist, was well aware that didactic or heavy-handed children's stories, laden with things children "should" like, insulted the intelligence of any reader over ten years old and held little appeal even for younger readers. When Lewis set out to create his now vastly popular *Chronicles of Narnia*, he did not map out morals for his young readers, then wrap them in attractive packages of adventure and fantasy. Rather, he sought to create the kind of stories he liked, consciously and unconsciously including in them elements of the Christian faith which he embraced as an adult and defended in his nonfiction, fiction, and radio broadcasts. Instead of forcibly teaching Christianity, these elements familiarize the reader with Christian concepts such as love, sacrifice, repentance, and forgiveness. In this way, readers who encountered these concepts later in life would already have a connection to them. In Narnian terms, they would know Christ better for having known Aslan:

> "Dearest," said Aslan very gently, "you and your brother will never come back to Narnia.... You are too old, children ... and you must begin to come close to your own world now."
>
> "It isn't Narnia, you know," sobbed Lucy. "It's *you*. We shan't meet *you* there. And how can we live, never meeting you?"
>
> "But you shall meet me there, dear one," said Aslan.
>
> "Are — are you there, too, Sir?" said Edmund.
>
> "I am," said Aslan. "But there I have another name. You must learn to know me by that name. This is the very reason you were brought into Narnia, that knowing me here for a little, you may know me better there" [*VDT* 215–216].

However, Aslan is not the only Narnian element that readers can "know better" from reading the *Chronicles*. Lewis, like most educators, was sometimes frustrated in his work as a teacher, but remains long beyond his death a very good instructor on a variety of levels; in Narnia, he teaches his readers both about Aslan and his "other name," and about much else that was important to him spiritually, personally, and professionally, particularly about the literature that he respected and enjoyed. A close reading of the seven-book series reveals the strikingly effective influences of literary sources as diverse as George MacDonald's fantastic fiction and the courtly love poetry of the High Middle Ages. In *Christian Fantasy from 1200 to the Present*, C. N. Manlove describes a Lewis who "looked for sources as he looked for friends; he is essentially gregarious in his vision." Despite his elevated academic position, Lewis was no literary snob. He enthusiastically enjoyed reading Chaucer and H. Ridder Haggard, Jane Austen and Beatrix Potter, Shakespeare and Arthur Conan Doyle. Lewis's *Experiment in Criticism* remains one of the most refreshing and rational examinations of how we should judge the value of literary works, rather than simply falling back on the academic "canon" and the "right" books. "At his memorial service, Austin Farrer called Jack 'the best read man any of us is ever likely to meet.'" Everything he read and enjoyed, no matter its literary weight, was likely to be woven into his fiction. This range can be readily seen in the *Chronicles,* in which E. Nesbit's children's stories are just as likely to receive a nod as are the plays of Shakespeare. Works with which he was both personally and professionally involved were even more likely to be powerful influences: "When Lewis began to write fiction, much of the inspiration was set moving by the academic studies on which he was engaged or which were still fresh in his mind." The more he treasured a work, the more likely it would become a serious influence.[1]

Though it is unlikely that anyone, even Lewis himself, could readily identify every text that finds its way, in some form or another, into the *Chronicles of Narnia*, two of the most influential sources for the series are clearly Edmund Spenser's *The Faerie Queene* and John Milton's *Paradise Lost*. Although he certainly thought that everyone should read and appreciate Spenser and Milton, Lewis did not include material from these classic works of Western literature merely in order to indoctrinate young readers with blatant literary criticism nor even to ensure that the crucial works of Western literature and thought received adequate attention. Just as his books are Christian in nature because Lewis was himself a Christian, and because his books feature British protagonists because Lewis was himself British, the *Chronicles* echo Milton and Spenser naturally as a result of Lewis's lifelong appreciation of their work.

Lewis was famously opinionated, once experiencing a moment of connection with a child when he declared "rather too loudly, 'I loathe prunes.' 'So do I,' came an unexpected six-year-old voice from another table. Sympathy was instantaneous. Neither of us thought it funny. We both knew that prunes are far too nasty to be funny." Lewis didn't publicly announce that he hated prunes because he wanted to make others hate them or because he wanted to promote the advantages of prune-hating; rather, his spontaneous reaction elicited an honest and sympathetic response. His writing, particularly the *Chronicles*, displays this same attitude. Lewis did not include detailed descriptions of meals ranging from hearty dwarf breakfasts of sausage and omelettes to sumptuous royal feasts with elaborate presentations merely because children like food or to make other people like food; he included so much food because he liked to eat:

> In my own first story I had described at great length what I thought a rather fine high tea given by a hospitable faun to the little girl who was my heroine [*LWW* 13]. A man, who has children of his own, said, "Ah, I see how you got to that. If you want to please grown-up readers you give them sex, so you thought to yourself, 'That won't do for children, what shall I give them instead? I know! The little blighters like plenty of good eating.'" In reality, however, I myself like eating and drinking. I put in what I would like to have read when I was a child and what I still like reading now that I am in my fifties.

Lewis actually admitted that he did "not enjoy the company of small children "and recognized this as a 'defect' in himself." Yet children, like that sympathetic six-year-old, find immediate resonance with the *Chronicles*, hearing in them a narrator who doesn't try to give them "what they want," or force something unwanted upon them, but who, despite lacking children of his own, was still very aware of his own childhood experiences and who included in his books the things he liked himself, including the literature he most enjoyed, such as *The Faerie Queene* and *Paradise Lost*. In the process, the *Chronicles* both overtly and subtly display the influence of these two texts on Lewis and perhaps provide a gateway for readers to look to Lewis's sources for themselves.[2]

Tracking every element of any literary work back to each possible influence is all but impossible. It is, however, possible to see how Lewis, in his deep admiration, understanding, and literary grasp of these monumental texts, draws upon them to create books that resonate with literary as well as spiritual power. Because Lewis was influenced by *The Faerie Queene* and *Paradise Lost* both consciously and unconsciously in the composition of the *Chronicles*, their impact is visible in all seven of the Narnian books.

Many readers immediately associate Lewis with his thoughtful and perceptive Christian apologetics, but he went through a period in which he rejected Christianity, only converting to theism, admitting that "God was God" in 1929 at the age of 31. It would be two more years until he fully accepted Christianity in 1931 while riding to the Whipsnade Zoo in the sidecar of his brother Warren's motorcycle: "When we set out I did not believe that Jesus Christ is the Son of God, and when we reached the zoo I did." Yet even in the years when he denied Christianity, Lewis did not reject Christian authors, actually finding himself alarmed that many of the writers he admired and enjoyed most were those whom he saw as "tainted" by "'Christian mythology' ... [but] authors who might be claimed as the precursors of modern enlightenment seemed to me very small beer and bored me cruelly." One favorite that challenged, inspired, but never bored Lewis was his "longtime friend" *The Faerie Queene*, which was important to him from the time he first encountered the six-book compliment to Queen Elizabeth I. Before age eighteen, he reveled in his reading of the epic poem "regretting that it was not longer." In fact, late in his life he "expressed a wish that when he reached the Next World he might find that Spenser had written another six books of *The Faerie Queene* for him to read"; not a surprising sentiment for a man who always believed that "[I] couldn't get a cup of tea large enough or a book long enough to suit me." This passion for the poem led to some of the most acclaimed Spenser criticism in any age. His *Allegory of Love*, the posthumous *Spenser's Images of Life*, his monumental *English Literature in the Sixteenth Century Excluding Drama*, and the collection of lecture essays in *Studies in Medieval and Renaissance Literature* are all manifestations of his profound interest in and understanding of *The Faerie Queene*. His critical work on the text remains some of the most insightful ever produced. Lewis was the first scholar to truly explore the symbols and iconographic implications of much of the poem. *The Allegory of Love*, often considered "one of the most influential literary histories of the century," is still respected, even by scholars who disagree with his conclusions. Both critics who concur with his analyses and interpretations and those who believe that he was incorrect in some of his assertions or overstated his case in regard to poem's opposition of art and nature, must acknowledge that "his boldest generalizations have incited some of the best subsequent reading of Spenser" and that "The positive side of this [*The Allegory of Love*] was that it made medieval and Renaissance literature, Spenser, Dante, and numerous others, appear necessary to our self understanding and not at all anachronistic." N.S. Brooks prefaced his refutation of many of Lewis's statements regarding *The Faerie Queene* by asserting that "There are few books on the student's shelves which command more admiration and respect [than Lewis's does]." However, for Lewis, Spenser's tales of knights and ladies and daring deeds were more than great literature; they were great fun to read:

> Beyond all doubt it is best to have made one's acquaintance with Spenser in a very large — and preferably illustrated — edition of *The Faerie Queene*, on a wet day, between the ages of twelve and sixteen; and if, even at that age, certain of the names aroused unidentified memories of some still earlier, some almost prehistoric, commerce with a selection of "Stories from Spenser," heard before we could read, so much the better.

Although highly idealized, this scene clearly reflects Lewis's delight in the text, as well as his recognition of its importance. Ironically, he also asserted that it "is perhaps the most difficult poem in English. Quite how difficult, I am only now beginning to realize after forty years of reading it." It is not surprising that Spenser's work, encountered so early in his intellectual development and so clearly rooted in his scholarship, deeply influenced Lewis's fiction as well as his academic writing, for it would not let him go. Scholars who want a closer look into Lewis's motivation and thought life often turn to *The Faerie Queene*. In *The Scientification Novels of C.S. Lewis: Space and Time in the Ransom Stories*, Jared Lobell uses the epic in his attempt to untangle Lewis's unfinished *The Dark Tower* and even to predict how Lewis would have completed the story based on his references to the Faerie Queene and parallel elements between the epic poem and the fantasy manuscript.[3]

Yet, *The Faerie Queene* was not the only epic poem that took root in Lewis's imagination and his scholarship. It is clear that in his mind, as well as in his writing, he linked Edmund Spenser with John Milton. In a letter to his friend Arthur Greeves, Lewis uses Milton and Spenser rather as ends of a spectrum for placing a recently read poem's difficulty and style. *The Faerie Queene,* the first three books of which were published in 1590, predated Milton's 1674 publication of *Paradise Lost* by nearly a hundred years, and it is quite certain that Milton himself was influenced by Spenser, but both authors clearly influenced Lewis in patterns that are often unique and separate from one another. Ever since the publication of *Perelandra*, the second installment in Lewis's Deep Heaven trilogy, critics have noticed evidence of the influence of *Paradise Lost* on that novel. Even readers with no knowledge of Lewis's Milton scholarship recognize the natural parallels, since *Perelandra* revolves around a prelapsarian Adam and Eve (Tor and Trinidil) who, on Venus, succeed where Milton's (and the Bible's) primal couple fails. Because of the subject matter, Lewis logically relied on *Paradise Lost* as well as on the Bible and Judeo-Christian traditions. Miltonic threads are woven even more deeply into the Lewis canon, partly because of his early, unfaltering interest in *Paradise Lost.* On March 5, 1908, Lewis noted in his diary that he had read *Paradise Lost* and made notes on the text. He was nine years old. Nearly forty years later, he would publish his *Preface to Paradise Lost,* which "originated in a series of eleven lectures given at Oxford during Michaelmas Term 1939, before being delivered as the Ballard Matthews Lectures at University College, North Wales, in 1941." Although frequently criticized and re-examined, the *Preface* remains a distinguished and well-established piece of Milton criticism. In fact, "No other book on Milton that old has remained continuously in print to the present day." Lewis openly attacked and refuted the theory that Satan is the hero of the poem, while also examining structural, theological, and textual issues. Lewis's boldness in claiming his Christian beliefs, rather than making excuses for them, has also been cited as a refreshing and impressive aspect of the *Preface*. Although Milton was, for some time, out of favor among the literary elite, Lewis rejoiced that "Milton, hanged, drawn, and quartered by two or three influential critics — and their disciples all said Amen — seems to have revived." His analysis set out to correct a number of commonly held misconceptions and misunderstandings about the poem, and subsequent works of Milton scholarship rely on Lewis, both concurring with his conclusions and contesting them. Even T.S. Eliot, whose point of view is excoriated in the *Preface*, told Lewis that "he considered *Preface* his best book." The fact that Lewis, even during his "atheist" period, did not abandon either *Paradise Lost* or *The Faerie Queene* is evidence of the power they held over him. It was a power Lewis himself recognized, for he knew that much of who he was, and what he himself created, was the result of what he had read:

> Those of us who have been readers all our life seldom fully realise the enormous extension of our being which we owe to authors ... in reading great literature I become a thousand men and yet remain myself. Like the night sky in the Greek poem, I see with myriad eyes, but it is still I who see. Here, as in worship, in love, in moral action, and in knowing, I transcend myself; and I am never more myself than when I do.

These two texts, so important to him on a variety of levels, were absorbed into the very essence of who Lewis was and what he wrote.[4]

By the time he began composing the *Chronicles* in the late 1930s, like both Milton and, to some degree, Spenser, Lewis sought to "justify the ways of God to man" (*PL* I.26).

Though some of the works' similarities stem from the authors' common goals and from biblical and Christian traditions, there are patterns of similarity that reveal even deeper and more subtle connections. While many researchers and critics have been intrigued by the *Chronicles* and by Lewis's work on *The Faerie Queene* and *Paradise Lost*, less emphasis has been placed on examining the masterpieces of Spenser and Milton as direct or indirect sources for the Narnian *Chronicles*. In part, this may be a result of a critical temptation to treat the *Chronicles* as self-explanatory and simplistic. Considering the complexity of Lewis's *Till We have Faces* and apologetic material, this oversight is somewhat understandable. Many a startled young reader has come up short against texts like *The Abolition of Man* after happily reading through the entire *Chronicles* in a few weeks' time. Lewis himself was also aware of the scholarly tendency to disregard any piece of writing that a child might enjoy or that any reader might find pleasurable or fantastic: "No one that I know of has indeed laid down in so many words that a fiction cannot be fit for adult and civilised reading unless it represents life as we have all found it to be, or probably shall find it to be, in experience. But some such assumption seems to lurk tacitly in the background of much criticism and literary discussion." At one level, the *Chronicles* are indeed a set of simple stories relating the truths of a greater story. However, their depth and complexity should not be ignored. Many critics, particularly those who, as children, enjoyed the *Chronicles* for pleasure reading, have closely analyzed the deceptively simple stories of Narnia and her heroes, usually focusing on the Bible and Christian tradition as sources: "It is true that there is little original material in Lewis's books for children. He tapped many literary sources for the fanciful frameworks of his stories." Critics have explored Lewis's Platonic references and his fairy tale sources, but Milton and Spenser have only recently begun to be as thoroughly examined as sources. Some excellent scholarly attention has been paid to isolated connections, such as the similarity the maze-oriented opening sequence of *The Faerie Queene* bears to the excursion into the wardrobe, or the resemblance *The Silver Chair*'s Green Lady/Witch bears to Errour in Book I of *The Faerie Queene*. However, there are far more connected issues and more complex ways in which *The Faerie Queene* and *Paradise Lost* overlap and intertwine in Lewis's *Chronicles*. Certainly, there is little chance of cataloging every possible reference or influence of these, or any other works, upon the *Chronicles*. Considering Lewis's habit of drawing material into his stories from any source that came to his hand or into his mind, such an attempt would be doomed to failure. Instead, several major areas help reveal some of the most powerful resonances. Important interweavings can be seen in the depiction of evil, of female characters, of fantastic and symbolic landscapes and settings, and of the spiritual concepts central to all three texts. In addition, it is important to see why Lewis so clearly echoes *The Faerie Queene* and *Paradise Lost*, and how all these elements work together to convey similar meanings.[5]

In order to analyze how the depiction of evil in Narnia has much of its history in *The Faerie Queene* and *Paradise Lost*, both "evil" characters and actions must be examined. Narnia certainly has no shortage of villains, many of whom are both externally and internally similar to Spenserian and Miltonic antagonists. Other elements of evil, such as deception, manipulation, and misuse of power, are apparent in all three texts, and manifest themselves in protagonists as well as in negative characters. Lewis certainly was interested in how one could depict evil as realistically insidious without making the negative look too appealing: "In all but a few writers, the 'good' characters are the least successful." Lewis, who campaigned so mightily against the heroic reading of Satan's character in *Paradise Lost*, was painstaking in his depiction of his villains as evil, unappealing, and occasionally ridiculous. This is also how he interpreted many of the villains and monsters in *The Faerie Queene* and *Paradise Lost*.[6]

Lewis's depiction of women is at least as complex as his depiction of evil, and possibly more enthralling to readers. While some of the females fall under the category of evil characters, there is still a plethora of human, Narnian, and nonhuman females within the *Chronicles* who are generally positive or neutral. Examining Spenser and Milton as sources for Lewis's depiction of females reveals how varied and surprising the roles of women in Narnia often are. While the texts are separated by hundreds of years and their accompanying changes in social and political views toward women, there are a number of striking parallels in the roles played by females. There is also cause to look at the ways in which these female characters deny, conform to, or reshape stereotypes.

Perhaps the most memorable aspect of Narnia is the country itself. Few readers of any age can forget the snowy lamppost where Lucy meets Mr. Tumnus, the fantastic creation of Narnia in *The Magician's Nephew*, or the incredible sights encountered by the crew of the *Dawn Treader* at the end of the world: "Together they [the *Chronicles*] are like a vast descriptive, historical, and geographical account of the strange land of Narnia." In many ways, landscape and setting are crucial to the *Chronicles*, *The Faerie Queene*, and *Paradise Lost* because all three stories take place in settings unreachable by the readers. The setting of Narnia, like those of Faerie Land, Paradise, Heaven, and Hell, requires imagination as well as symbolic power. Frequently, Narnia has a familiar feeling for readers of Spenser and Milton. Those acquainted with Narnia may, in turn, find a similar resonance with Spenser and Milton. This familiarity is partly due to the fantastic qualities of all three settings, but is also a result of the influence of *The Faerie Queene* and *Paradise Lost* on Lewis's composition.[7]

Clearly the most critical area in which the *Chronicles* exhibit the influence of Spenser and Milton is in the depiction of spiritual issues. In portraying innocence, obedience, sin and repentance, salvation, discipline, and other elements of the Christian faith, Lewis draws upon *The Faerie Queene* and *Paradise Lost* almost as faithfully as he draws upon the Bible and Christian traditions. Since Lewis, like Spenser and Milton, sets his stories in a distant and myth-filled environment, he, like they, also must seek to somehow incorporate elements not included in the Bible, while at the same time depicting the truth of Christianity without its jargon. This challenge and a number of other factors, both spiritual and structural, lead to echoes of Spenser and Milton in Narnia. Some of these echoes reveal possible reasons for other intertwinings between the texts.

Taken together, these influences cast a light on Narnia that, like Lucy's lamppost, illuminates the wilds of Lewis's country inside the wardrobe. Rather than simply exposing the *Chronicles'* indebtedness to Spenser and Milton, these influences show the subtle and often profound ways in which the *Chronicles of Narnia* allow readers to know Milton and Spenser for a little while in the world of Narnia that they may know them better in the world on this side of the wardrobe.

# I

---

# The Depiction of Evil:
# Women of Power and Malice

"I expect most witches are like that. They are not interested in people and things unless they can use them; they are terribly practical."
—*The Magician's Nephew* 72

Although the *Chronicles* clearly focus on the positive and powerful force of Aslan and his followers, evil in the series is given a thorough and well-developed treatment that echoes *The Faerie Queene* and *Paradise Lost*. There are a number of major villains in the *Chronicles*, who, both in appearance and in essence, resemble the primary antagonists created by Spenser and Milton to provide struggles for their protagonists. In addition to these reprobates, there is a host of evil minor characters who reflect the influence of Milton and Spenser. Finally, like Milton's Eve and Spenser's Redcrosse Knight, several of the characters in the *Chronicles* are not innately evil; they are simply swayed from the true path by temptation and weakness and become temporary or unintentional antagonists. While some of these characters' failings allow redemption and Christian growth to take place, they often serve to show the negative aspects of characters and even allow "good" individuals to become antagonists. The two types of antagonists—the purely evil and the corrupted good — are also indicative of the seemingly repetitious lines of The Lord's Prayer: "Lead us not into temptation/ but deliver us from evil." These lines, in fact, do not have to be repetitious at all; they may "have different but complimentary intentions, the first asking God to keep us safe from ourselves ... the second asking protection from the outside." These two kinds of moral danger add depth and reality to the peril faced by Lewis's protagonists. The influences of *The Faerie Queene* and *Paradise Lost* thereby give powerful force to villains who must be challenging obstacles for the heroes to overcome while remaining sufficiently uncomplicated and non-threatening to be effective in a work designed, at least on one level, for children.[1]

Some of the similarity between Lewis's villains and those of his sources lies in the archetypal and primal elements that make up these adversaries. Such elements are vital components of any successful villain and resonate in all the "great" villains, from The Big Bad Wolf to Darth Vader. Lewis often feared that his work would be given the "Walt Disney" treatment of cuteness and charm, but he did respect what he called "good unoriginality," or archetype, in Disney's *Snow White and the Seven Dwarfs*. He was unhappy with the dwarfs, as one may imagine based on his own dwarfs, but found parts of the film truly delightful. One of his favorite segments was the scene in which the abandoned and terrified Snow White sees eyes peering at her from the spooky darkness of the forest and believes they are wicked beasts bent upon her destruction. She is happily surprised by the presence instead of friendly, cuddly forest creatures. Lewis liked the scene's balance of expectation and surprise. Snow White, like the heroes of Narnia, is opposed by a sinister villain, whom Lewis praises as "the archetype of all beautiful, cruel queens." Lewis even included the similarly named Queen *Swanwhite* in Jewel the Unicorn's list of rulers of Narnia during years of peace (*LB* 88). Disney's wicked queen occupies a place as one of the supreme villainesses, so frightening that, after years of parental complaints and shrieking children, Walt Disney World's Magic Kingdom finally diminished her terrifying role in the Snow White ride. Lewis, like Disney and his artists, drew upon the primal characters of fairy tales to create his villains. Perhaps the primal nature of such villains is what makes them most frightening. Rather than trying to scare us with the unfamiliar, they evoke fear and power simply because they embody all that in the core of our beings we already fear. Whether they play upon the fear of the dark, of insects (Lewis's particular phobia), of abandonment, or of the perversion of wholesome family relationships, such villains are built on the fears that are part of every human being.[2]

When C.S. Lewis wrote about the composition process he followed for the *Chronicles of Narnia,* he frequently emphasized that *The Lion, the Witch, and the Wardrobe* was born out of images he had been mulling over for years. The great Lion Aslan was an image that came "bounding in" through dreams, while Mr. Tumnus the Faun, carrying his umbrella, had been with him since adolescence:

> All seven Narnia books ... began with seeing pictures in my head.
> At first they were not a story, just pictures. The *Lion* all began with a picture of a Faun carrying an umbrella and parcels in a snowy wood. This picture had been in my mind since I was about sixteen. Then one day, when I was about forty, I said to myself: "Let's try to make a story about it."

It is not terribly surprising that this inspirational image was one framed in snow. From early childhood, Lewis had a longing for what he called "northerness," creating in him a sense of delight and wonder for everything from dwarfs to frozen waterfalls, leading him to rapture at the sight of Arthur Rackham's illustrations or the sound of Richard Wagner's operas, and finding expression in his lasting interest in Norse mythology. Many of the most powerful images in his writing come from the thrill of cold and darkness, often associated with danger. Another image that was crucial to the formation of the *Chronicles* was one draped in snow and seething with danger. This vision was to later take on literary flesh in the *Chronicles* as Jadis, the White Witch. Lewis was inspired by the image of "a queen on a sledge" who grew to become one of the most impressive and iconic villainesses in all of children's literature.[3]

The most successful of Lewis's villains, and the only one to appear in more than one installment of the series, is Jadis, the White Witch. Jadis is most certainly another incarnation of the same bad mother archetype who rears her sometimes ugly head in fairy and folk tales as wicked stepmother and sorceress. Although Lewis was often skeptical of Jungian theory, the "terrible mother" of Jung's analysis is one effort to codify the power of these characters. Rather than nurturing, the terrible mother is deadly. Her power to produce fear lies in her perversion of the associations we have with a good mother: instead of cooking food for children to eat, she cooks or poisons the children, like the witch in "Hansel and Gretel" who uses sweets as bait rather than a reward or treat; instead of having children of her own to care for, she kidnaps other people's children, marries a widower with children and becomes an overbearing or murderous wicked stepmother, or strikes would-be parents barren; instead of offering comfort and hospitality, her house is a death trap. Many contemporary children's stories attempt to negate this powerful and chilling character by making her flat, uninteresting, and not terribly dangerous, but this reduces the power and the resonance that the witch/child-devourer/cruel mother has for readers. Like Snow White's stepmother, Jadis is a powerful archetypal figure: beautiful, vain, cruel, and powerful. Yet, many elements of her character cannot be attributed to Disney's artists nor even to the Brothers Grimm and their predecessors. Spenser and Milton, certainly also drawing upon archetypal sources, created villains who lend a number of characteristics to Jadis.

*The Faerie Queene*'s Duessa, one of Spenser's masterpieces, is clearly an influence in the creation of Jadis. Like Duessa, the White Witch appears with all the trappings of royalty and an usurped name. As Lucy reports, "She calls herself the Queen of Narnia though she has no right to be queen at all.... And she drives about on a sledge, drawn by a reindeer, with her wand in her hand and a crown on her head" (*LWW* 37–38). Duessa, too, wears a stolen name, Fidessa, "Borne the sole daughter of an Emperour" (I.ii.22.7) until she is tried and convicted in Book V: "false Duessa now untitled Queene,/ Was brought to her sad doome, as here was to be seene" (V.ix.42.8–9). Her crown and richly caparisoned steed are props of royalty as deceptive as the Witch's: "Like a Persian mitre on her hed/ She wore, with crownes and ouches garnished, ... Her wanton palfrey all was overspread/ With tinsel trappings, woven like a wave,/ Whose bridle rung with golden bels and bosses brave" (I.ii.13.4–5, 7–9). Interestingly, both villainesses have bells on the harnesses of their animals, reflecting the brashness of their assumed identities, and their deceptively cheerful appearances. The Witch, when she sets about the serious business of pursuing Peter,

Susan, Lucy, and the Beavers, orders her dwarf slave to prepare her sledge using the harness without the bells (*LWW* 94). Her true nature has been exposed, and the pretext of a pleasant sleigh ride is discarded in favor of deadly silence and stealth. Once her hand has been revealed she is no longer concerned about making herself appear royal and harmless. Like Duessa, who makes her "speedy way" (I.v.19.9) to get aid from Night, Jadis is a "terribly practical" (*MNN* 72) person who uses disguise when she must, but who essentially uses whatever means she has at her disposal in order to achieve her aims of power and destruction.

Although Jadis is certainly physically attractive, she is not painted as quite the sexual creature that Duessa is. In his essay, "Sometimes Fairy Stories May Say Best What's to be Said," Lewis attests that one thing he liked about the genre of his stories was that they required no depiction of erotic love. The fact that Jadis is not as alluring as Duessa is clear from the color schemes attached to each character. While the White Witch's reindeer have golden horns and scarlet harness, she is, herself, almost completely without color, especially the sensual reds and purples that dominate the descriptions of Duessa and her garb. The White Witch's "face was white — not merely pale, but white like snow or paper or icing sugar, except for her very red mouth. It was a beautiful face in other respects, but proud and cold and stern" (*LWW* 27). Only the Witch's mouth is red, perhaps a reference to her consumption of the "forbidden" fruit from Aslan's Garden, or to her use of enchanted food, such as Turkish Delight. In addition, her red mouth marks one of her most powerful weapons: words which often twist and distort the truth in order to bring others under her sway. She also uses words in a more tangible way, with her spells of destruction: "she said something which they couldn't understand (but it sounded horrid) ... those high and heavy doors trembled for a second as if they were made of silk and then crumbled away till there was nothing left of them but a heap of dust on the threshold" (*MN* 58). Though her physical strength is astonishing, she only resorts to flinging people across rooms, tearing crosspieces off lamp-posts, and knocking policemen in the head with clubs when she discovers that her ability to turn people to dust with "horrible words ... which had been very real in her own world, was not going to work in ours" (*MN* 80). Indeed, the doomsday weapon with which she wiped out her entire native world of Charn was not a bomb or other conventional weapon: it was the Deplorable Word "which, if spoken with the proper ceremonies, would destroy all living things except the one who spoke it" (*MN* 60). Her mouth, then, is clearly a powerful weapon, and appropriately an alarming color, for red is not only the color of sensuality and lust, but of danger; in her very first appearance in *The Lion, the Witch, and the Wardrobe*, she represents both sensual desire, in the form of addictive sweets and a warm seat on a cold day, as well as a very real threat that Edmund only stops perceiving when his desire overcomes his good sense: "When he had first got onto the sledge he had been afraid that she might drive away with him to some unknown place from which he would not be able to get back, but he had forgotten about that fear now" (*LWW* 34). Other than the one spot of shocking red, Jadis is completely devoid of color.

Duessa is quite another story: "A goodly Lady clad in scarlot red, Purfled with gold and pearl of rich assay.... He [Redcrosse] in great passion all this while did dwell,/ More busying his quicke eyes, her face to view" (I.ii.13.12–3, 26.5–6). The dissimilar color patterns in the two antagonists emphasize the natures of their seductive powers. While Jadis, particularly in *The Lion, the Witch, and the Wardrobe*, lures mainly with words, Duessa uses her whole deceptive person. At a basic level, they are both seducers who utilize magic to achieve their goals. Both tempt protagonists by offering them something physically desirable and sensually fulfilling. In Duessa's case, she offers "the shield, and I, and all" (I.v.11.10) to Redcrosse, an emotionally vulnerable knight who believes he has been betrayed by his beloved Una. Thus, an alluring female offers a real temptation. Edmund, as a child, is lured by the Turkish Delight and by the power the Witch promises to give him over the siblings he resents, particularly Peter: "While he [Edmund] was Prince he would wear a gold crown and eat Turkish Delight all day long" (*LWW* 34). As the third child who resents his older siblings' authority, Edmund is seduced by the opportunity to pay them back for what he perceives as their mistreatment of him. In *The Magician's Nephew*, Digory, struggling with the reality of his mother's terminal illness, has been sent on a mission to retrieve an apple that, once planted, will produce a tree to protect Narnia from the evil Jadis represents. He is tempted by the healing and normalcy offered by Jadis if he keeps the Apple of Protection rather than returning it to Aslan as ordered: "What about this Mother of yours whom you pretend to love so?" ... "Do you not see that one bite of that apple would heal her? Soon she will be quite well again. All will be well again. Your home will be happy again. You will be like other boys" (*MN* 161–2).

On the surface there is nothing intrinsically wrong with desiring healing for a terminally ill loved one, or even with the enjoyment of sweets or female company: "whether the element invoked is gold or luxury or food or feminine beauty, enchantments are always brought on by evil disguised as innocent attractions.... Greed is the first tool of enchantment. The other one, perhaps more important, is the technique of mental confusion and the subjugation of intelligence by emotional persuasion." Lewis, whose own mother's terminal illness most assuredly influenced the creation of Digory and his dying mother, well knew the temptation offered by Jadis, for he knew the agony Digory feels and the longing to make everything right again. Such a longing is not, in and of itself, wrong, but, when manipulated by those whose motivations are power and pride, even the most innocuous human tendencies can turn dangerous. Just as witches have always used what seems innocent — apples, spindles, romantic fulfillment — Jadis and Duessa promise the protagonists what they think most desirable and attempt to convince them that they want it more than anything else. Although these promises are exactly what Redcrosse, Edmund, and Digory most want, they are as false as Duessa and Jadis themselves. Duessa's cry of encouragement is apparently a general one since she has made overtures to both Redcrosse and his opponent, the pagan knight Sans joy, evidently to ensure that whichever knight wins will take her. In addition, as her later defeat reveals, Duessa's beauty and physical charms are illusions covering her hideous true form. Edmund's Turkish Delight is merely bait to bring him and his siblings under the Witch's power. It is also candy without any nutritional value whatsoever. The gelatinous, insubstantial confection is also so enchanted that people "would want more and more of it, and would even, if they were allowed, go on eating it until they killed themselves" (33). Such an addictive quality is even more alarming considering the sticky, cloying sweetness of Turkish Delight, especially in the bizarre (at least to American palates) rose flavor. Even Digory's mother would not experience a true healing from Jadis's proffered apple: "The day would have come when both you and she would have looked back and said it would have been better to die in that illness" (*MN* 175). These villainesses' temptations are no more valid than their identities and titles. Yet despite the deception inherent in both women, their magical powers, however illusory, do have some tangible results.[4]

Both Jadis and Duessa possess a brand of magic that opposes and perverts nature, reflecting the sterility of their characters. Duessa, for all her sexual imagery and appearance as a lusty young woman, is not a fertile being. Under her beautiful disguise, she is old, misformed, and not even human, "Her nether parts, misshapen, monstruous" (I.ii.41.1). Jadis is also inhuman and sterile. Mr. Beaver emphasizes the fact that she is "no Daughter of Eve" (*LWW* 77) but descended from giants and the Jinn, though she pretends to be human. In Mr. Beaver's opinion, this is further evidence of how dangerous she is: "take my advice, when you meet anything that's going to be Human and isn't yet, or used to be human once and isn't now, or ought to be human and isn't, you keep your eyes on it and feel for your hatchet" (*LWW* 77–78). She herself tells Edmund that she has no children of her own, and thus no heir (*LWW* 34). Of course, since she has no intentions of dying, she does not require an heir. She prefers the false immortality given by the forbidden apple she has consumed, rather than the natural immortality achieved by reproduction. To Lewis, sterility, particularly within sexuality, is the antithesis of all that is good or genuine. While his criticism of this brand of empty sensuality appears in much of his literary and apologetic writing, one of his most insightful analyses of sterile and therefore joyless sex lies in his examination of the artifice within the Bower of Bliss in the second book of *The Faerie Queene*: "There is not a kiss or an embrace in the whole island: only male prurience and female provocation." He incorporates this sterile corruption of nature, or cold artifice, into Jadis. Her magic in *The Lion, the Witch and the Wardrobe* is most clearly manifested in her snow spell and her magic wand. The spell, like Duessa's transformation of Fraudubio and Fraelissa into trees, is a perversion of nature. Jadis creates a hundred-year winter without a Christmas, thus extending a small portion of the calendar and suppressing the other three seasons. Not surprisingly, the missing seasons are those of birth, growth, and ripeness. She favors only the nonproductive winter, removing the festal holiday of Christmas with its vibrant reds and greens of blood and growth and its celebration of holy birth, as well as its astrological importance as the winter solstice. Jadis despises change, so Christmas and its emphasis on transformation is most unwelcome. The appearance of Father Christmas, who is "so big, and so glad, and so real" (103) hails the beginning of the end of the winter spell and the return to a natural and normal order. She is terrified of any celebrations or expressions of life, seeking to extend and preserve her illegitimate claim to the throne by silencing the "summer when the woods were green ... and the whole forest would give itself up to jollification for weeks on end" (*LLW* 13). In fact, her fury with the Christmas party is the essential moment when Edmund realized what a bad bargain he has made in joining her, for she resents even the possibility of Father Christmas's arrival, as well as the lively rejoicing that she calls "gluttony ... waste ... self-indulgence" (*LWW* 112). It is, importantly, the baby squirrel's refusal to deny that Father Christmas has arrived and his indignant cry of "He has — he has — he has!" (*LWW* 112) that drive the Witch over the edge so that she draws blood biting her own lip before unleashing the fury of her wand upon the festive group. For the sterile and cold Jadis, reminders of life, particularly from children, must be silenced. In addition, as Wesley A. Kort argues in *C.S. Lewis Then and Now*, "Nothing marks Jadis more than her antipathy toward celebration. She and the evil she embodies are set against them.... Her acts are reductive (turning animals into stone statues), homogenizing (causing the constant winter), [and] intimidating (deploying her Gestapo-like henchmen)." Though she claims to be all-powerful, it clear that such power is not cause for celebration, but a motivation to destroy celebration wherever she finds it.[5]

So too, Duessa contorts nature by her tree enchantment and her manipulation of life and death for the mortally stricken Sans joy. Certainly, counteracting the forces of life and death and turning people into other things is a perversion and corruption of nature. However, by transforming Fraudubio and Fraelissa specifically into trees, rather than into birds or animals, Duessa also makes them unable to marry and mate. All through *The Faerie Queene*, positive characters are those who chastely seek appropriate spouses, then marry, and eventually produce children. Duessa's victims are reduced to a virtually unmoving state in which gender, and therefore mating, is irrelevant. Closely resembling this transformation is the power contained in Jadis's wand. With this object she turns living beings into stone. This is the power of the Medusa, the ultimate manifestation of the "bad mother" archetype. By transforming people into stone, Jadis nullifies their lives, their very identities, and freezes them just as she has the landscape with her snow spell. Jadis's castle courtyard resembles a cemetery more than a yard: "There were dozens of statues all about — standing here and there rather as the pieces stand on a chess board when it is half-way through the game" (*LWW* 91). Both women use different techniques to achieve their ends, but they share the impetus to sterilize and freeze, to contort nature and defy the progress of time.

Even the heritage of the two characters is similar. Duessa is "the daughter of Deceit and Shame" (I.v.26.10). Jadis, according to Mr. Beaver in *The Lion, the Witch and the Wardrobe* is descended from

> "...her they called Lilith. And she was one of the Jinn. And on the other she comes of the giants. No, no, there isn't a real drop of human blood in the Witch."
>
> "That's why she's bad all through, Mr. Beaver," said Mrs. Beaver [77].

Jadis's descent from Lilith is a connection to the Hebraic and Babylonian archetype of Adam's first wife "cast out of Eden for insubordination and doomed to roam the world [as] a malevolent spirit." The Lilith demon is also credited with murdering infants, pregnant women, and lost children. Both Duessa and Jadis, then, are descended from the embodiments of evil traits. These are traits that they themselves possess. Duessa is both deceitful and shameful, tricking everyone she meets and concealing her true, hideous form of which she is understandably ashamed, while the White Witch overturns the true hierarchy of Narnia and attempts to kill children who are lost in the forest. Duessa claims to be the daughter of an Emperor, yet her true parents are not only negative, but powerful as well, placing her in Night's esteem. When Digory views the rulers of Charn in the Hall of Images, it is clear that Jadis is descended from a long line of rulers whose faces progress from good and happy to wicked and happy, and at last to wicked and unhappy. Like Jadis herself, they have remained proud and strong, but at the cost of their happiness and emotional well-being.

Both Jadis and Duessa are members of distinguished but tainted royal families. Their true names ring with this negative, lofty heritage as well: "Duessa" accurately echoes her dual nature, her literal two-faced aspect, and has a distinct hissing sound from the doubled "s," calling to mind a serpent; "Jadis," like many names of Lewis's creation, also has an important sound to it, reminding the reader of jade, with its connotations of being jaded, or cynical, and perhaps of the "false jade," or duplicitous woman, as the thwarted Prince Rabadash calls Susan in *The Horse and His Boy*. This connection is even clearer when the books are read in their original publication order since Jadis's name is only revealed in *The Magician's Nephew*. Lewis had also toyed with the name in his abandoned verse rendering of the Cupid and Psyche myth. In his original concept, Psyche was to have a twin brother, Jardis, and the older sister was to be named Caspian. Lewis eventually used both names in completely different ways. He switched the genders so that Caspian became instead a major male character in the *Chronicles of Narnia*. Appropriately enough for a person named for a body of water, Caspian is a seafarer. Lewis never did complete the Psyche poem but did retain some of his original concepts in creating his remarkable *Till We Have Faces*, replacing Caspian with Orual who, ironically, has many masculine characteristics. The twin brother he removed altogether. Lewis, who enjoyed the sounds of names, was not one to let interesting names go to waste, and so Jardis became Jadis. In addition, the French word "jadis" is usually translated "formerly," or even "once upon a time." This association echoes her aloneness, her chosen "high and lonely destiny" (*MN* 62) as the last queen of her once-mighty world. By her own selfish and cruel choices, she is the last surviving inhabitant of Charn and of her once-noble ruling family. Their names remind the reader that these villainesses are tricksters, and that their heritage, while noble, is also shameful, sub-human, and completely ingrained within their characters. Mr. Beaver's strong opinions about beings that are not quite human would apply both to the supernaturally birthed Duessa and to her disguise, which masks her hideousness and her "foxes taile, with dung all fowly dight;/ and her feet most monstrous/ for one of them was like an Eagles claw/ ...The other like a Beares uneven paw" (I.viii.48.4–6,8). The inhuman nature of both villainesses makes them appropriate antagonists for Lewis's Sons and Daughters of Adam and

Eve, and for Spenser's Una, whose royal parents are typified Adam and Eve figures, the queen and "mighty king of Eden" (I.xii.26.2). Inhuman witches, both descended from corrupt if notable families, contrast completely with fully human protagonists descended from "The Lord Adam and the Lady Eve both honor enough to erect the head of the poorest beggar, and shame enough to bow the shoulders of the greatest emperor" (*PC* 212). Unlike the witches, the human protagonists understand and accept their heritage, both noble and tainted, rather than concealing it.[6]

The fascinating Duessa certainly supplies many of the elements that make Jadis ring with Spenserian echoes. Yet the false queen of Narnia is also powerfully reminiscent of Duessa's queen, Lucifera, and her House of Pride. To Edmund, Jadis describes her house as a boy's paradise with "whole rooms of Turkish Delight" (*LWW* 34). The reality, however, is a cold, dimly lit castle with only the sinister wolf, Fenris Ulf, and a pair of subservient dwarfs as courtiers. Edmund's promised feast is actually a condemned prisoner's portion — bread and water — foreshadowing his planned execution by Jadis. For both the White Witch and Lucifera, the castle or house is a place of deception:

> It was a goodly heape for to behould,
> And spake the praises of the workmans wit;
> But full great pity; that so faire a mould
> Did on so weak foundation ever sit [I.iv.5.1–4].

Redcrosse's view as he leaves the House of Pride gives him an even more graphic view of its true nature:

> Forth ryding underneath the castell wall,
> A donghil of dead carkases he spide,
> The dreadful spectacle of that sad house of pride [I.v.53.7–9].

While Jadis's castle is not nearly as elaborately described, the fact that its towers look like sorcerer's caps (88) is a clear indication that it is not to be trusted. Both palaces are beautiful on the surface, yet both offer only death, literally destroying victims and displaying their bodies as clutter. Lucifera's house "digests" the victims of pride, leaving them to languish in its dungeon as "wretched thralles" (I.v.51.1) or tossed on the "Donghill of dead carcases" (I.v.53.8), in such numbers that "Scarse could he footing find in that fowle way,/ For many corses, like a great Lay-stall/ of murdered men, which therein strowed lay (I.V.53.1–3); Jadis's castle is full of statues, her previous victims, who serve as trophies and as warnings to any who think of crossing the Witch. The statues are eventually restored, but until the return of Aslan, they are as cold and lifeless as corpses. Edmund even mistakes Fenris Ulf, one of the only living creatures in the castle, for a stone wolf (92). Despite his fears, Edmund, like Redcrosse, enters where he really does not belong. Neither character heeds the evidence that chances of escaping the castles are not good. The broad entrance to House of Pride is deceptive, since few who enter ever escape: "Great troupes of people traveiled thitherward/ Both day and night, of each degree and place,/ But few returned" (I.iv.3.1–3). Mr. Beaver's description of the fate of the White Witch's guests is similar: "There's not many taken in there that ever comes out again" (73). Like the entrance to Lucifera's palace, the "great iron gates" of Jadis's castle stand "wide open" (*LWW* 89) since neither woman wants to keep anyone out: it is escaping, not entering, these castles that presents problems. Like any clever predator, both Jadis and Lucifera know that a good trap starts with an open door. The allure of both Jadis and Lucifera masks their true natures and the very real threats they pose, but it is also indicative of their exceptional confidence: a deadly pride that infests both of them. Neither sorceress feels that she can be defeated.

When Digory and Polly discover her in the palace in Charn, Jadis even more strongly resembles Lucifera, for here she actually has destroyed all but herself. Even the Witch's ancestors, frozen along with her in the hall of images, reflect the descent into pride and its attendant misery:

> Both the men and the women looked kind and wise, and they seemed to come of a handsome race ... a few steps down the room they came to faces that looked a little different ... very solemn faces.... When they had gone a little further, they found themselves among faces they didn't like.... The faces here looked very strong and proud and happy, but they looked cruel. A little further on they looked crueller. Further on again, they were still cruel, but they no longer looked happy.... The last figure of all was the most interesting ... with a look of such fierceness and pride that it took your breath away [*MN* 47–48].

Pride is clearly one of the strongest of Jadis's characteristics. While she is already a well-rounded character in her first appearance in *The Lion, the Witch and the Wardrobe,* in *The Magician's Nephew* her coming to Narnia is detailed, and her pridefulness is even more apparent. When Digory and Polly awaken the Witch from suspended animation among her ancestors, she assumes that she has been sent for by some powerful magician, who saw "the shadow of my face in some magic mirror or some enchanted pool; and for the love of my beauty has made a potent spell" (65). The reality, that she has been stumbled upon by two lost children who have been the guinea pigs in the careless experiment of a dabbling magical bungler, is so intolerable to her that she cannot fathom its possibly being true. Her pride creates an interpretation of events that is completely wrong, but noble and flattering. The destroyed condition of Charn is a result of Jadis's pride during her sister's attempt to gain the throne: "At any moment I was ready to make peace — yes, and to spare her life too, if only she would yield me the throne. But she would not. Her pride has destroyed the whole world" (*MN* 60). Ironically, it is actually Jadis, and *her* pride, that wipe out every trace of life in Charn. Rather than surrendering to her sister who technically did win the last war: "the last of my [Jadis's] soldiers had fallen" (61), she uses the power of the "Deplorable Word," an ultimate weapon whose results connect her to the most sinister antagonist available from either *The Faerie Queene* or *Paradise Lost.*

Jadis, so unable to accept defeat that she chooses destruction for her whole world, is reminiscent of Milton's Satan. She certainly prefers reigning in hell to serving in heaven. Her throne, in a dead castle in a dead city of a dead world, is a meaningless one, but it is a throne, one that she prefers to subservience in a living world. The notion of servitude is clearly as foreign to Jadis as it is to Satan, who declares, "To bow and sue for grace/ with suppliant knee, and deify his power who from the terror of this arm so late/ Doubted his empire/ that were low indeed" (I.111–14). When Polly, shocked at Jadis's use of the Deplorable Word, asks about the common people of her world who died, she replies, "I was the Queen. They were all *my* people. What else were they there for except to do my will" (61). Her pride is more than vanity, for, as Lewis attests in *Mere Christianity*, vanity is not nearly so dangerous as Pride: "As long as you are proud you cannot know God.

A proud man is always looking down on things and people; and, of course, as long as you are looking down, you cannot see something that is above you." Jadis looks down on everyone and everything, and not simply because of her impressive height, which Digory estimates at seven feet (*MN* 62). She, like Satan, refuses to acknowledge any power or authority other than herself, but also refuses to accept full responsibility for the events she sets in motion. Though she wants all the power, she wants none of the blame, and she consistently blames others, such as her sister or even Aslan, for her own actions. Satan also does not acknowledge that it is his pride that has led to the downfall of his followers; instead he blames God. Even when he encourages the fallen angels to "Awake, arise, or be for ever fall'n" (I.330), Satan is not concerned about their well-being; he is trying to keep his army intact for a possible future attack. Pride, more than any other sin, is responsible for the downfall of Satan and for the fall of humanity: "That the Fall is disobedience and results from pride is reiterated by every character in *Paradise Lost* from every possible point of view." Both characters, exhibiting diabolical pride, want to be served rather than to serve anyone, and they are not at all concerned with anyone else's suffering in their ascents to power. Jadis further resembles Satan in her perception of herself as a tragic figure with "a high and lonely destiny" (*MN* 62). This clearly mirrors Satan's first appearance in the first book of *Paradise Lost,* which emphasizes his "mighty stature" (I.221) and his form of an "Archangel ruined" (I.592). Lewis's concern over the heroic interpretation of Satan is one of the primary tenets of his acclaimed *Preface to Paradise Lost,* leading to his contention that creating an evil character is much easier than creating a good one; humans all know what it is like to be bad, and it takes little imagination to create a magnification of that. No one, however, can truly fathom ultimate goodness, making evil characters more interesting as well as easier to depict: "We do not really know what it feels like to be a man better than ourselves." By creating female villains, perhaps Lewis does not merely magnify evil propensities he himself experienced; in addition to using wicked characteristics any person could display, he also portrays those characteristics as they are uniquely manifested through the feminine. His female antagonists thus take on the characteristics of his sources rather than of a projection of the evil Lewis could have magnified from his own experience. It is not surprising that Satan has a role in the creation of Lewis's most fully realized and intriguing villain. After all, "Lewis knew intimately Milton's depiction of the newly fallen Satan in the opening books of *Paradise Lost*" and he always contended that Satan was both villainous and unheroic.[7]

Lewis also indicated that Satan cannot be truly heroic because he makes such a fool of himself, much in the same way a spoiled child is foolish in its tantrums. Both Jadis and Satan, although they may be read in some contexts as admirable, become unheroic. Jadis, particularly in *The Magician's Nephew*, is clearly a majestic and impressive creature, a "dem fine woman" (186) as Uncle Andrew calls her, whose beauty and power take one's breath away; but when she slays Aslan — her moment of triumph — she exhibits no heroism or even superior strength. Her adversary is a willing sacrifice whom she has shaved, muzzled, and tied down. She is not a hero, or even an antihero; she is a bully and a coward. Despite heroic interpretations by Romantic authors, including Percy Bysshe Shelley, Satan also picks on the helpless. He does not confront Adam and Eve together, nor does he approach Adam first. He does not use weapons to kill the first humans or force them to do his will. Instead, he sets out to divide and conquer, starting with Eve, whom he perceives as less able to resist him: "behold alone/ The Woman, opportune to all attempts,/ Her husband, for I view far round, not nigh,/ Whose higher intellectual more I shun,/ And strength" (IX.480–3). Satan's comments not only indicate that he has a low opinion of Eve and thinks she is less intelligent than her husband, but also reveal that he is a coward, afraid to face Adam whom he perceives as the more critically perceptive and physically powerful of the two. Clearly Satan does not appear to be the same brilliant general who made war in heaven; rather, he is afraid of confronting anyone whom he perceives may be a match for him, even a newly made human who lacks experience with his kind. Lewis's deep concern with the reading of Satan as a hero is exhibited in his points about the unheroic descent Satan voluntarily undertakes "from hero to general, from general to politician, from politician to secret service agent, and thence to a thing that peers in at bedroom or bathroom windows, and thence to a toad, and finally to a snake — such is the progress of Satan." Jadis goes through a similar descent. When the books are read in chronological order, rather than publication order, Jadis goes from queen to mass murderess, to criminal in London, to lurking evil in Narnia, to witch, and finally to a tormentor of animals, little children, and helpless enemies, no more noble or heroic than Hansel and Gretel's witch with her candy house and oven. "His [Lewis's] discussion of the lightning scarred lord of Milton's Hell indicates that he thought seriously about the amputating power of evil upon the spirit of any creature." Lewis would likewise see Jadis not as a majestic queen, but as a damaged and diminished entity, scarred and transformed by evil.[8]

One of Jadis's most obviously Satanic moments is in *The Magician's Nephew* when Digory encounters her in the mountaintop garden he has entered to fetch the Apple of Protection. The garden is walled, and its only gates bear the inscription: "Come in by the gold gates or not at all,/ Take of my fruit for others or forbear./ For those who steal or those who climb my wall/ Shall find their heart's desire and find despair" (157). After Digory enters properly, he finds Jadis, who has apparently come over the wall and is just finishing an apple that makes "a horrid stain" on her mouth (159). Jadis's vaulting of the wall is almost identical to Satan's entry to Eden in Book IV of *Paradise Lost*: "Due entrance he disdained, and in contempt,/ At one slight bound high overleaped all bound/ Of hill or highest wall, and sheer within/ Lights on his feet" (ll.180–183). Although Jadis's actual entry has occurred before Digory encounters her, he "guessed at once that she must have climbed in over the wall" (159–60). It is important to note that as Lewis created his tempter figure, he even brought her into the garden in the same manner Satan uses. This method of entry also marks both of them as criminals, for, as Jesus indicates in John 10:1, one who eschews the gate and "climbs in by some other way is a thief" (NIV). Both characters move from the violation of a sacred garden to the temptation of a protagonist who belongs there. While Lewis's feminizing of the tempter role can be seen as a blending of Eve's sin and the serpent's guile, it is intriguing that Jadis, a woman, is so clearly Satanic. Such a role, while equating a female villain with the ultimate personification of evil, also casts her in a role of power; while she is dangerous, Jadis, like Milton's Satan, is a highly-motivated tempter rather than merely a mindless, malignant foe.

The biblical temptation scene is, of course, the basis for both Milton's and Lewis's temptation tableaus. However, it is Milton's garden and tree and Satan's temptation that appear in *The Magician's Nephew*. The biblical account mentions nothing about Eden being walled, and the tree is simply described as bearing fruit. Although the apple has long been viewed as the traditional forbidden fruit, there is no specific scriptural identification of the fruit. Lewis follows Milton's lead in using the apple, rather than any other fruit, or even one uniquely Narnian. Even the "specious rhetoric" employed by Satan is mirrored by Jadis. Satan flatters Eve as "Goddess humane" (IX.732) and tries to twist the purpose of the heavenly injunction against eating from the tree to a rule against eating from any tree. One of his most persuasive tropes is that of testimony, since he claims to have eaten the fruit himself and experienced intelligent thought and speech as a result: "Look on me,/ Me who have touched and tasted, yet both live,/ And life more perfect have attained than fate/ Meant me" (IX.686–688). Though it is easy to condemn Eve for falling for the serpent's wiles, his testimony is impressive, since he really is speaking to her. In addition, Eve has never experienced dishonesty and thus has no reason to think the serpent a liar. Jadis appeals to Digory's love for his mother, and even makes the implication that not taking the apple to his mother will make Digory a bad son. She also uses her own experience with the apple to tell Digory of its value: "I have tasted it; and I feel such changes in myself that I know I shall never grow old or die" (161). Unlike Eve, Digory is a child of a fallen world; he has experience with lying and does not merely take the Witch's word for truth, as Eve does with Satan's testimony. He must see Jadis actually eating the apple. While Satan lies about having eaten the fruit, Jadis lies about its results. Although the fruit makes her strong and virtually immortal, it also brings her despair: "For the Witch looked stronger and prouder than ever, and even, in a way, triumphant; but her face was deadly white, white as salt" (160). The apple has such a negative effect on her that the Tree of Protection Digory plants from one of these apples creates in her a horror so great that she cannot enter Narnia for generations. In fact, as Evan K. Gibson notes in *C. S. Lewis, Spinner of Tales*:

> Although Lewis quite clearly did not have the Queen of Charn in
> mind when he created the tyrant who kept Narnia in winter's grip for
> a century, he works backward from the White Witch and ... shows the

corrosion of individuality which evil wreaks upon its possessor. The Empress is figure of evil grandeur. Even as an old man Digory still said she was the most beautiful woman he had ever seen.... But when we meet her as the White Witch, her grandeur is gone. Hers is a holding operation, guarding against the threat of four unfilled thrones at Cair Paravel.... Gone is the glory of the Queen whose troops laid waste the great cities of Felinda, Sorlois, and Bramandin. The White Witch ... is a hollow ghost of the full-bodied woman who uttered the Deplorable Word.

Aslan also confirms that the Witch's claims of the apple's effects are erroneous for one who stole the fruit, telling Digory that had he stolen an apple for his mother "it would have healed her; but not to your joy or hers. The day would have come when both you and she would have looked back and said it would have been better to die in that illness" (*MN* 175). Since the apples, as Aslan says, always work according to their nature, the Witch's lie is partially mixed with truth, making it, like Satan's deception and the twisting of God's word, all the more insidious. The most significant difference in the two episodes is the result. Digory, unlike Eve, is already a fallen human being, a "son of Adam," and by resisting temptation simply resists one sin, while Eve's failure brings about the fall of herself and her descendants.[9]

Though the intended victims respond differently, and thus experience different fates, the two temptation sequences both set in motion drastic changes for individuals and entire worlds. Satan's successful seduction of Eve transforms the newly created Earth from a reflection of Heaven into a flawed, mortal planet. Jadis, while unable to convince Digory to eat an apple, profoundly affects Narnia by her own consumption of the forbidden fruit since the long but miserable life it gives her enables her to outlive the Tree of Protection and to eventually cast her powerful winter spell, marking Narnia forever with her theft of the throne and hundred-year rule of cruelty and cold.

In addition to the role of tempter, Jadis, like Satan, is also an usurper. Since Lewis valued hierarchy, particularly as expressed in Milton's epic, usurping was a disturbance of a moral hierarchy as well as an act of pride and aggression. Like Jadis, Satan also wants to have power over his peers, but he refuses subordination to one who is his natural superior: "He wants hierarchy and does not want hierarchy."

Satan's fallen state is exposed in his assertion that he is not a created being, and therefore not under God's command to worship the Son. Jadis, too, pursues the ultimate goal of pride by usurping power. She refuses to acknowledge Aslan as king, though all true kings of Narnia recognize that the Lion is the High King over them all. In *The Lion, the Witch, and the Wardrobe*, she is clearly not the rightful ruler because she cannot inhabit the true capital of Cair Paravel. Her fortress, which she calls a house, rather than a castle, is clearly inferior to the splendor and beauty of Cair Paravel, but since she is not at all human, and therefore not the rightful Queen, she must rule from a secondary castle. Like Satan, who has lost the glories of heaven and must create an inferior kingdom, but one all his own, Jadis lives in a castle that is a strong fortress, but lacks warmth, comfort, or any amenities one would expect to be accorded a queen. Usurpers, such as Jadis and Satan, inevitably convince themselves that their seats of power, though inferior to the true capitals of rightful monarchs, are somehow superior, just as they are convinced of their own right to power that is not truly theirs.[10]

Like all usurpers, Jadis is also a bully. Once she realizes that Digory's Uncle Andrew is not an all-powerful magician, she makes him her tool and looks for a way to conquer London:

> ...I shall allow you to be my servant.... Listen to your first task. I see we are in a large city. Procure for me at once a chariot or a flying carpet or a well-trained dragon, or whatever is usual for royal and noble people in your land. Then bring me to places where I can get clothes and jewels and slaves fit for my rank. Tomorrow I will begin the conquest of the world [*MN* 71].

As usurpers, both Jadis and Satan hate humanity, which is favored over each of them. Satan views God's newly created beings as replacements for himself and his fallen angel colleagues, and Jadis can never be a true queen of Narnia because "there isn't a real drop of human blood" in her body (*LWW* 77). Because of this, she cannot fulfill the prophecy which states, "When Adam's flesh and Adam's bone,/ Sits at Cair Paravel in throne,/ The evil time will be over and done" (*LWW* 76). She knows that this prophecy's fulfillment will end her life and her reign, and she seeks to destroy all "Sons and Daughters of Adam and

Eve" who enter Narnia in order to ensure a continuation of her already unnaturally long life. Satan feels that humanity has been created to take over his position and that humans are both dear to God and vulnerable to corruption. Satan does not merely seek to destroy humans but to pervert them into objects of grief for God rather than blessings: "on him who next/ provokes my envy, this new favorite/ Of Heav'n, this man of clay, son of despite,/ Whom us the more to spite his Maker raised/ from dust: spite then with spite is best repaid" (IX.174–8). Jadis also attempts this ploy with Edmund, using him as a pawn to bring her his brother and sister: "Because, if you did come again — bringing them with you of course — I'd be able to give you some more Turkish Delight" (*LWW* 33). Edmund, despite being warned by Lucy that Jadis is not the true queen, is fooled by her trappings and her food, lured to treason by her promises to make him first a prince, and then a king under her; however, his true destiny actually is to become king, but a king under Aslan, the true High King over all High Kings, not under an usurper. Jadis's methods are not dissimilar from Satan's temptation of Eve as a design to corrupt Adam and thus all of humanity. Instead of immediately killing humans, the rightful heirs of both Eden and Narnia, both Satan and Jadis prefer to corrupt and contaminate the people they envy and the kingdoms they covet.

Despite their attempts to corrupt or destroy the forces of good, Jadis and Satan are both thwarted and even, against their intended plans, bring about good. The White Witch, having killed Aslan, believes that she is victorious. As she strikes the fatal blow, she sneers, "Understand that you have given me Narnia forever, you have lost your own life and you have not saved his [Edmund's]. In that knowledge, despair and die" (*LWW* 152). However, by killing Aslan, she has invoked the "Deeper Magic from Before Time," an injunction dictating that a willing victim, giving himself up for another's fault, will be resurrected. While this echoes Christ's sacrifice, and thus *Paradise Regained* rather than *Paradise Lost*, the Witch's apparent triumph resembles Satan's determination to be busy about doing evil and his assumption that he can actually destroy God's plan. Both antagonists, however, underestimate the power of divine good to produce positive results from the most malicious of schemes. Like Satan's thwarted plans that bring about the greater good of Christ's incarnation, sacrifice, and resurrection,

Jadis's evil intentions actually bring about the good she fears. Edmund, whom she assumes will be killed without Aslan's protection, actually destroys her magic wand in combat after being reunited with his siblings. The resurrected Aslan, whom Jadis believes to be dead and no threat, releases her statue prisoners and becomes the instrument of her destruction. As Lewis wrote in one of his many letters to Catholic priest Don Giovanni Calabria, "all, either willingly or unwillingly, do the will of God: Judas and Satan as tools, or instruments, John and Peter as sons." Unlike Satan, Jadis is a flesh and blood being and not an evil, immortal spirit set upon plaguing Narnians as Satan plagues earth. She gives the illusion of immortality first in her timeless and ageless sleep in the Hall of Images. Later, after she has eaten the magical apple, she feels immortal and lives for nearly a thousand years much as Satan, in the book of Revelation, ravages the earth for a thousand years. Only Aslan is capable of killing her. Even several hundred years after the Witch's death, a hag claims that she can call up the "white lady" with the aid of occult instruments such as a magic circle and blue fire (*PC* 165). While this return is not achieved, in *The Silver Chair* one of Jadis's "same crew" attempts to achieve similar ends.[11]

Jadis is most certainly dead, and her "resurrection" never accomplished, but she is succeeded in her evil designs for Narnia by the Green Witch. Also called the Green Lady, the Lady of the Green Kirtle, or the Queen of Underland, this villainess appears in *The Silver Chair* as the seducer, enchanter, and captor of Prince Rilian. Although Jadis certainly has sexual energy, leading Digory to underestimate her malice and inspiring Uncle Andrew to put on his best clothes and cologne in a vain effort to impress her, the Queen of Underland is much more obviously sexual. It is doubtful that Lewis had changed his mind about the difficulty of including erotic love in children's books. Instead, he uses the highly structured courtly love tradition so apparent in Spenser, as well as powerful imagery from both *The Faerie Queene* and *Paradise Lost* to depict his most lively villainess. Both Milton and Spenser clearly have precedents for the Queen's snake persona; in her woman aspect, she, like Jadis, reflects the influence of Duessa and Lucifera, as well as that of the fallen Eve. Unlike Jadis, the Green Witch wields energy and vibrancy in place of sterility and coldness. Their color names emphasize this difference in approach: the White Witch is pale, frigid, solitary, and barren, capable of motherhood only by stealing a child; the Green Witch, like her color of choice, is associated with plants, which, like she, come up from the ground. While Jadis transforms others into stone and rules alone, the Green Witch turns herself into a very lively serpent and promises herself in marriage to Rilian. According to the oldest Dwarf in *The Silver Chair*, "those Northern Witches always mean the same thing, but in every age they have a different plan for getting it" (201). Their strategies may be very different, but their goals are the same; they also share precedents from Milton and Spenser.

An archetypal figure, the snake woman, or Lamia, is a being whose power largely lies in the combination of the primal forces of earth mother and serpent. The image is also a conflation of Eve and the serpent who beguiled her. Spenser and Milton both make free use of this image. Redcrosse's first dangerous encounter, in Book I, is with the embodiment of Errour, who is "halfe like a serpent" and "loathsom, filthie, foule" (I.i.14.8,9). The fact that Errour is female is a reminder of Eve's fatal "error" and places the monster in stark contrast to Una, who is female and complete truth. Errour's feminine nature also emphasizes her method of destruction. Rather than the merely brute (male) force of an Orgoglio or a Sans joy, Sans loy, or Sans foy, Errour uses both deception and physical combat with her "angry sting" (I.i.17.7) and her "endlesse traine" (I.i.18.9). Even the poisonous vomit she spews in a defensive maneuver is both a violent act and an exhibition of the deception she represents, since it includes actual poison and "poisonous" writings of heresy. The Green Witch is as violent an aggressor as the snake, although she is certainly not physically powerful in her woman guise. In her human form, she uses words and deception to lead Jill, Eustace, Puddleglum, and Rilian into the error of her supremacy and the fictitious nature of the real world from which they come: "'There never was any world but mine,' said the Witch. 'There never was any world but yours,' said they" (*SC* 154). The proliferation of lies can only be stopped by the pragmatic intervention of the earthy Puddleglum. Like Redcrosse, who defeats Errour with the tangible reality of his sword and the support of truth in the person of Una, Puddleglum uses truth — his undaunted belief in Aslan — as well as stark reality — stamping out the witch's magic fire — to defeat her evil plans of error, domination, and destruction.

The Witch most physically resembles the serpentine Errour, of course, when she becomes a "serpent green as poison" (160). Reinforcing ideas of chivalry, Lewis does not allow his male protagonists to kill the Green Witch while she is in her human form. Rilian, truly a courteous knight in action as in speech, declares, "I am glad, gentlemen, that the foul Witch took her serpent form at the last. It would not have suited well either with my heart or my honor to have slain a woman" (161). In her attempt to kill Rilian, the Green Witch attacks him in a manner almost identical to Spenser's description of Errour's attack on Redcrosse. Errour "all attonce her beastly bodie raized/ with doubled forces high aboue the ground:/ Tho wrapping up her wrethed sterne arownd ... her huge traine/ All Suddenly about his body wound,/ That hand or foot to stirr he stroue in vaine (I.i.18.3–8). Una encourages her knight to strangle the monster, and his effort to do so does cause Errour to release his body to a degree, though he must then contend with her poisonous vomit. He finally kills Errour by hacking off "her hatefull head without remorse" (I.i.24.8). The Green Witch, in her snake form, also wraps her coils around Rilian's body "intending to pinion his sword-arm to his side. But the Prince was just in time. He raised his arms and got them clear; the living knot closed ... round his chest — ready to crack his ribs like firewood when it drew tight" (*SC* 160). Rilian also attempts to strangle his attacker, "squeezing it [the snake's neck] until it choked" (*SC* 160). Finally, with the help of Eustace and Puddleglum, Rilian cuts off the snake's head. Clearly, the two scenes are remarkably similar although even in her serpent guise, the Green Witch is not nearly as repugnant as the "lothsom, filthie, foule" Errour (I.i.14.9), or even as Milton's Sin, whom she more strongly resembles.

While Errour, whose human half is deformed and ugly, has no "beautiful" aspect, Milton's Sin, even in her fallen and mutated form, is still attractive from the waist up: "The one seemed a woman to the waist, and fair,/ But ended foul in many a scaly fold" (II.651). Thus the Green Witch and Sin both have the power to seduce or to destroy. Though the Green Witch, unlike Sin, is not both a woman and a snake simultaneously, during her transformation from woman to serpent, she changes from the legs up, with her face changing last, so that she reflects Sin's appearance, however briefly, when:

Her arms appeared to be fastened to her sides. Her legs were intertwined with one another, and her feet had disappeared. The long green train of her skirt thickened and grew solid, and seemed to be all one piece with her interlocked legs…. Her head was thrown far back and while her nose grew longer and longer, every other part of her face seemed to disappear, except her eyes" [*SC* 159–60].

The Green Lady and Sin also both rule underground realms. While Sin guards the entrance to Hell, the Witch rules in Underland, biding her time until, using the enchanted Rilian, she can take over the lands above. Sin, though she is assigned to prevent anyone from leaving Hell, readily gives the "fatal key" (II.725) to her father/lover Satan for the promise that she will "reign/ At thy right hand voluptuous, as beseems/ Thy daughter and thy darling" (II.868–870). Though the Green Witch's plans are foiled, she, like Sin, plans to unloose evil upon an unsuspecting and above- ground world, in order to gain power and prestige for herself.

Although Sin's transformation is already complete when Milton introduces her, the graphic description of the serpent transformation of Satan and the other fallen angels is almost identical to Lewis's image of the Queen of Underland's metamorphosis: "His visage drawn he felt sharp and spare,/ His arms clung to his ribs, his legs entwining/ Each other, till supplanted down he fell/ A monstrous serpent on his belly prone" (X.511–514). The Witch voluntarily chooses to be a serpent when she slays Rilian's mother with a sting to her hand (*SC* 49). That shape then becomes the mode of her destruction since Rilian admits he could not have killed her in her human guise, and the transformation confirms her guilt as the Queen's murderer. It is in the snake form that she dies. Satan's voluntary serpent metamorphosis also becomes one of misery, torturing him and his followers at intervals throughout eternity, as they are forced to take on the form in which Satan seduced humanity. These transformations reflect the archetypal power and horror of the snake, but they also reflect a pattern Lewis frequently employs: people who pretend to be something long enough eventually become what they have been feigning. Prince Rabadash acts like an ass, and becomes a literal one; the Calormenes in *The Last Battle* actually meet the horrible bird-headed god Tash they have invoked; and Uncle Andrew learns that "the trouble about trying to make yourself stupider than you really are is that you very often succeed" (*MN* 126) when he convinces himself that the Narnian animals are not speaking, eventually becoming unable to understand them at all. This "be careful what you wish for; you may get it" attitude is precisely what brings Rilian into servitude in the first place.[12]

Rilian is caught by the Green Witch while seeking the worm that killed his mother. Like Redcrosse, he is on a quest, and also like Redcrosse, he becomes sidetracked by a beautiful woman. Many of the details of the Green Witch's human aspect are similar to Jadis's, and thus, to the Miltonic and Spenserian influences that shape her. Duessa, with her dual nature, is even more clearly reflected in the Queen of Underland than she is in Jadis. Jadis certainly shows Duessa's influences, but it is the Green Witch who, like Spenser's remarkable villainess, changes into a disgusting creature. In her first appearance to Jill, Eustace, and Puddleglum, the Witch looks almost identical to Duessa as Redcrosse first sees her:

> ...the two strangers were quite close. One was a knight in complete armor with his visor down. His armor and horse were black, there was no device on his shield, and no banneret on his spear. The other was a lady on a white horse, a horse so lovely that you wanted to kiss its nose and give it a lump of sugar at once. But the lady, who rode side-saddle and wore a long, fluttering dress of dazzling green, was lovelier still" [SC 75].

While Sans foy, who rides alongside Duessa at her first appearance, just as the enchanted Rilian rides with the Witch, has letters on his shield, the scene is still very much the same. Sans foy is, like Rilian, "all armed to point" (I.ii.12.5) and Duessa, like the Green Witch, is a "goodly Lady" (I.ii.13.2) with a beautiful costume and a beautiful horse "Whose bridle rung with golden bels and bosses brave" (I.ii.13.9) The Witch's ability to enchant and use Rilian for her purposes is also not unlike Duessa's use of men for protection and entertainment. She quickly attracts a new champion whenever her current one is killed or becomes aware of her true nature. The protagonists of *The Silver Chair* also have nearly as many warnings about the Lady's true identity as Redcrosse has about Duessa's. The blatant warnings of the enchanted tree, Fraudubio, about the lady in his company do not prevent Redcrosse from continuing his wanderings with her. Even after he leaves the House of Pride, he still lets himself be taken in by her charms when she "gan him fairely greet" (I.vii.3.6). In a similar failing, the children and Puddleglum all know the story of the green woman and the green snake. Upon hearing the story for the first time at the Parliament of Owls, Jill concludes, "I bet that serpent and that woman were the same person" (*SC* 52). Yet, she is just as eager as Eustace to accept the Green Lady's advice about going to the castle of Harfang, where all three adventurers are nearly eaten by Giants. Both the Witch and Duessa are able to conquer the better judgment of their victims, even when the latter have obvious warnings about the witches' untrustworthy natures. Duessa and the Green Witch have very dark sides that they generally manage to keep hidden from their victims, as they only appear in true form when they must. Interestingly, after Duessa has been exposed in Book I, and Archimago finds her "forlorne and naked" (II.1.22.1), she has used the Green Witch's emblematic color to clothe herself: "with greene mosse cou'ring her nakednes,/ To hide her shame and loathly filthiness" (II.i.224–5). Green, a color often associated with the beautiful yet dangerous and deceptive Fey of Celtic folklore, is more than appropriate for these deceptively beautiful and deadly witches.[13]

In persuasive ability, the Green Witch bears a very strong resemblance to Satan. In this respect, she is even more Satanic than Jadis. The White Witch persuades Edmund to do something he knows he probably should not do; but, unlike Jill, Eustace, and Puddleglum, he does not have a physical description of his adversary until after he has been enchanted by her magical food. He is horrified when Lucy gives a very accurate description of the White Witch and identifies her as the " perfectly terrible person" (*LWW* 37) who is tyrannizing Narnia: "When he heard that the Lady he had made friends with was a dangerous witch he felt even more uncomfortable. But he still wanted to taste that Turkish Delight again more than he wanted anything else" (*LWW* 38). The children and the Marsh-wiggle should put the description they have heard together with the woman they see and resist the Green Lady's advice. Yet, like Eve, who is also forewarned, they get themselves into trouble. In his serpent guise, Satan uses clever language and flattery to seduce Eve, calling her "Queene of this universe"

(IX.684). The Queen of Underland also uses flattery, promising to marry Rilian and referring to the children in complimentary terms of endearment: "little brother" (152) for Eustace and "pretty one" (153) for Jill. In addition, both antagonists use subtlety and coercion. Satan appears as the serpent, the most "subtil" creature in Eden, and the Green Witch uses soft music and incense to lull her victims into weakness. She even plans to use them in her plot to take over a world she has just convinced them does not exist. This is reminiscent of Satan's encouragement to Eve to break a rule that, from his perspective, does not (or should not) really exist anyway: "What can your knowledge hurt him, or this tree/ Impart against his will if all be his?/ Or is it envy, and can envy dwell/ In heav'nly breasts?" (IX.727–30). Their persuasive eloquence enables both Satan and the Green Witch to smoothly gloss over these paradoxes in their efforts to seduce and corrupt.

In a very intriguing parallel, the Green Witch and Satan both stage their initial attacks, on Narnia and Eden respectively, through a fountain:

> There was a place,
> now not, though sin, not time, first wrought the change,
> Where Tigris at the foot of Paradise
> Into a gulf shot under ground, till part
> Rose up a fountain by the Tree of Life;
> In with the river sunk, and with it rose
> Satan involved in rising mist ... [IX.69–75].

Thus a fountain, generally believed to be a source of pure water, becomes the source of corruption for Adam and Eve. The same source of corruption appears for Rilian, since he finds the Green Lady at "that same fountain where the Queen [his mother] got her death" (*SC* 51). A fountain, emerging from dark and secret places within the earth, emphasizes the primal symbolism these characters embody in their serpent forms. This motif also supports their corrupt and sinister natures, for fountains should be sources of purity. The Witch and Satan thus are essentially evil beings who come up out of the ground with a fountain and thus mix themselves in with what should be a pure substance emerging from the earth.

The Green Witch's enthrallment of the children and of Rilian also echoes Satan's female Spenserian counterpart, Lucifera. She has so beguiled Rilian that he calls her his "all but heavenly Queen" (136), and he believes himself unworthy of her "kindness." Likewise, Redcrosse, at the court of Lucifera, not only fights for the entertainment of the wicked queen and her court, but even swears fealty to her: "Falling her before on lowly knee,/ To her makes present of his service seene" (I.v.16.2–3). Both Rilian and Redcrosse have foresworn their true allegiance, and both become entangled in enchantments as a result. However, both Lucifera and the Queen of Underland are thwarted by beings whom they certainly outrank and even dismiss as unimportant. The dwarf rescues Redcrosse from the House of Pride, just as the children, with the help of Puddleglum, free Rilian. Like many prideful individuals, these vain queens fail to believe that anyone, least of all a dwarf, a child, or Marsh-wiggle, can bring about their destruction. Similar to the House of Pride and its weak foundation, they have both built their kingdoms on the assumption that they cannot be thwarted, and thus overlook those capable of freeing their victims.

One of the most interesting Spensarian characters who is echoed in the Green Witch is the sorceress Acrasia. Certainly they are both Circe figures, using enchantment and sexuality as weapons and tools. Like *The Odyssey*'s alluring enchantress, Acrasia turns her lovers into beasts, and the Queen of Underland turns Prince Rilian into a mindless pawn. Both characters also employ artifice and comfort. When Guyon first discovers Acrasia in her Bower of Bliss, she is lying on the proverbial bed of roses (II.xii.77.1). The Green Witch is initially able to distract the children from their quest by sending them to Harfang with the promise that they will find "steaming baths, soft beds, and bright hearts; and the roast and the baked and the sweet on the table four times a day" (76). This promise of comfort, after weeks of eating wild game and sleeping on the cold, hard ground, causes disagreement among the travelers and distracts them from their duty. Like Acrasia, the Green Witch is wrapped in a transparent gown. As the Lord Drinian described her after his one glimpse, she was "the most beautiful lady he had ever seen ... tall and great, shining, and wrapped in a thin garment green as poison" (*SC* 51). Lewis certainly does not detail the scanty clothing as thoroughly as Spenser does: "[Acrasia] was arayd. Or rather disarayd,/ ...in a vele of silk and silver thin,/ That hid no whit/ Her snowy brest was bare to readie spoile" (II.xii.77.3–5, 78.1).

Both enchantresses also have an army of subservient, enchanted beasts that are under their power. While Acrasia, like Circe, has transformed her lovers into animals, the Witch has placed a spell on the happy and energetic Earthmen to make them dreary and tiresome. Both groups of prisoners are removed from their natural environments, as the men are made to live like beasts and the Earthmen are taken from their fiery homeland of Bism in the depths of the earth to what they call the "shallow" lands. Both men and Earthmen are returned to their normal states and to their original lifestyles after the defeat of their enchantresses although the earthmen, whose personalities were only superficially altered, appear to suffer far less long-term damage than Acrasia's former lovers, who have a variety or responses to the their restoration: shame at what they have been and done, anger at the capture of Acrasia, and even, in the case of Gryll, regret at being changed back from a hog into a man:

> But one above the rest in speciall,
> That had a hog beene late, hight Grylle by name,
> Repyned greatly, and did him miscall,
> That had from hoggish forme him brought to naturall [II.xii.86.6–9].

Since Acrasia's victims have been morally corrupted as well as physically transformed, it is much more difficult for them to throw off the enchantment. The earthmen, who are returned to their previous state of mirth and energy, recover much more quickly than Acrasia's bestial lovers.

Acrasia, like the Green Witch, also employs music as part of her enchantments:

> Eftsoones they [Guyon and the Palmer] heard a most melodious sound,
> Of all that mote delight a daintie eare,
> Such as attonce might not on liuing ground,
> Saue in this Paradise, be heard elsewhere
> Right hard it was...
> To read what manner musicke that mote bee [II. vii.70.1–6].

When Guyon and the Palmer find Acrasia intertwined with the Verdant Knight in post-coital slumber, the strange music seems to be emanating from her, and is enhanced by the singing of nearby "faire Ladies, and lasciuous boyes" (II.xii.72.8). The Green Witch, when she realizes that Rilian has been freed from the Silver Chair and that Jill, Eustace, and Puddleglum are planning to escape with him, does not panic, but calmly tosses magic powder on the fire and "a sweet and drowsy smell came from it.... Secondly, she took out a musical instrument rather like a mandolin. She began to play with her fingers — a steady, monotonous thrumming that you didn't notice after a few minutes. But the less you noticed it, the more it got into your brain and your blood. This also made it hard to think" (*SC* 151). Throughout her attempted enchantment, the music is a crucial element that the narrative notes with each step that the children, Rilian, and the Marsh-wiggle slip further under her spell. Thanks to the practical intervention of Guyon's Palmer and the pragmatic Puddleglum, both Spenser's and Lewis's protagonists are able to resist the seductive music that is part of the witches' enchantment.

Acrasia, also like the Green Witch, is "linked with fire and water" (II.xii.78.6–8 n.) through her fiery lust and her tears and perspiration that sparkle "like pure Orient perles" (II.xii.78.5). The Green Witch is also connected to both elements. Fire is part of her tool in enchantment, especially when aided by the stupefying green powder. Only when Puddleglum stamps out the fire do the children and Rilian have a chance. She has also called up her enslaved earthmen from the fiery region of Bism, which opens to receive them once more when she is dead. She is connected with water, both from the underground sea the travelers cross to reach her kingdom, and the fountain from which she rises to kill Rilian's mother. Once she is dead, the two elements of fire and water destroy her spell-created kingdom: "That Witch has laid a train of spells so that whenever she was killed ... her whole kingdom would fall to pieces. She ... wouldn't so much mind dying herself if the chap who killed her was going to be burned, or buried, or drowned five minutes later" (*SC* 166). In fact, the water from the underground sea eventually covers the whole kingdom and "in hot summer days the Narnians go in there with ships and lanterns ... telling each other stories of the cities that lie fathoms deep below." Acrasia's bower is destroyed primarily by fire, as Guyon razes the place "with rigor pittilesse" (II.xii.83.2). Thus the enchantments of both witches are undone by the elements that the witches themselves embrace.

The greatest similarity between Acrasia and the Green Lady most likely lies in the enchantment of a knight. Acrasia's Verdant Knight has an unmarked shield "fowly ra'st, that none the signs might see" (II.xi.80.4), and when Rilian is first seen by the children he is in complete armor with the visor of his helmet lowered. His shield lacks any emblem whatsoever, and no identifying banner is attached to his lance (*SC* 75). However, Rilian, after being freed from the spell, becomes more like Guyon, captor of Acrasia and destroyer of the Bower of Bliss, than the Verdant Knight who is led away "sorrowfull and sad" (II.xii.84.2). Rilian actually kills the Witch, and her kingdom crumbles as a result. In addition, once he has been restored to his right mind and destroyed his captor, the deviceless black shield "turned bright as silver, and on it, redder than blood or cherries, was the figure of the Lion" (*SC* 168). Unlike the Verdant Knight, Rilian escapes the "horrible enchantment" (II.xii.80.9) of his captor witch.

In Book IV of *The Faerie Queene*, Spenser presents a brief but powerful image that actually encompasses both of the Green Witch's incarnations. In the Temple of Venus, Scudamour encounters a statue of the goddess that includes many of her traditional symbols, such as the winged babies fluttering around her, but his first image of the idol presents the goddess "covered with a slender veile afore/ And both her feete and legs together twyned/ Were with a snake, whose head and tail were fast combined" (IV.x.40.8–9). Another similar, more monstrous image is presented in Book VI, Canto six, in the description of the Echindna: "So hideous is her shape.... That euen the hellish fiends affrighted bee/ At sight thereof, and from her presence flee:/ Yet did her face and former parts professe/ A faire young Mayden, full of comely glee;/ but all her hinder parts did plaine expresse/ A monstrous dragon, full of fearfull vglinesse" (V.vi.10.3–9). Though the meanings and purposes of these characters are widely divergent, the images are striking in their similar depiction of the snake-woman, emphasizing the impact and power of *The Faerie Queene* on Lewis and his work.[14]

Jadis and the Green Witch, two of the most subtle and most carefully drawn villainesses in all literature, echo Spenser's and Milton's villains, both male and female, and frequently are even described in the same language used to make the model antagonists threatening to the soul as well as to the body. While Lewis, Milton, and Spenser all incorporate antagonists throughout their texts, the villains who appear first remain the most impressive and the most challenging. Milton's Satan, though accompanied by demons and accomplices, remains from his first appearance as a fallen, embittered ex-angel, the dominant force of evil — and of energy — throughout the poem. Although all of Spenser's knights face particular foes, Redcrosse's antagonists, particularly Duessa, seem far more complex than some of the later creations. Likewise, Lewis's recurring Jadis, and her protégée, the Green Lady, are far more complex and well-rounded than characters like Shift the Ape and Rishdah Tarkaan. This falling off of adversarial power does not negate the very real and threatening presence of the antagonists. Rather, it serves as a reminder that evil can lurk in flashy and complex figures like Satan, Duessa, and Jadis, or in the brute force of a Blatant Beast, or the tricks of an Ape. All are equally likely to bring good to its knees; the Christian, the knight, and the child must be wary.

# II

## The Depiction of Evil: Men, Mortals, Monsters, and Misled Protagonists

"I didn't believe in magic till to-day. I see now that it's real.... And you're simply a wicked, cruel magician like the ones in the stories."
— *The Magician's Nephew* 24

Intriguingly, both Spenser and Lewis primarily use supernatural villains who are female and mortal adversaries who are male. Perhaps this is linked to the mystical connotation that has been historically attached to women. This dichotomy could also be a subtle, even unintentional reminder, that an adversary should not be taken for granted merely because she is female; likewise, an antagonist's male gender does not always equate power: "The most convincing villains in the tales are female.... Compared to Queen Jadis, King Miraz is a paper cutout of Hamlet's wicked uncle, and Uncle Andrew a clown." In fact, the only magical male villain in the *Chronicles of Narnia* is the bungling Uncle Andrew of *The Magician's Nephew* whom Jadis calls "a little, peddling Magician who works by rules and books" (*MN* 71), and "the old gentleman probably comes closer than any other figure in the series to imitating (unwillingly, to be sure) the slapstick comedian"; truly, he is a clown. He is, however, a dangerous clown who cares little about putting others, even his own nephew, in physical danger so that he can achieve his own twisted ends: "His [Uncle Andrew's] principal fault lies neither in his curiosity nor in his interest in magic. Rather, his fault lies in the arrogance and disdain for others that allow him to isolate himself from his context and to use others for his own designs."[1]

Though Uncle Andrew does not have the magical or physical power exhibited by many of Spenser's villains, he still exhibits characteristics drawn from *The Faerie Queene*. Archimago is far more threatening and generally more successful in his plots than Uncle Andrew, but both lure the protagonists into their schemes by playing the stock role of the harmless old man. Archimago is "simple in shew" (I.i.7), while Uncle Andrew works under the pretense of being a lonely gentleman who carries on noble experiments for the good of humanity: "I am the great scholar, the magician, the adept, who is *doing* the experiment ... the idea of my going myself is ridiculous. It's like asking a general to fight as a common soldier" (23). Both, however, become so entangled in their own enchantments that they are nearly destroyed by them, placing them in situations they are physically unable to withstand. Archimago's clever scheme to disguise himself as Redcrosse backfires when he is unhorsed by Sans loy in Book I, canto three. Uncle Andrew, who prefers leaving the dangerous parts of experiments for other people to undertake, goes through a harrowing experience when he actually enters another world, Narnia. "For all his apparent desire for magical possibility, Uncle Andrew lives in a disenchanted world and is deaf to the magical qualities of what is occurring when Aslan creates the world of Narnia." So convinced is he that the Talking Beasts cannot really be talking, Uncle Andrew eventually doesn't hear their words at all. The newly created Talking Beasts, believing he is the evil that has entered their land, make a pet of him, since they cannot understand him either. After initially planting him like a tree and dowsing him with water, they try to feed him by flinging nuts and honey at him, and he is, finally, "a miserable object in muddy clothes" (168). However, despite their intrinsic failures, both magicians, in their plots, unloose greater evils upon the protagonists.[2]

When Uncle Andrew tricks Polly and Digory into using his magic rings and entering another world, he is merely thinking of saving himself from the dangers of exploration: "Suppose I got killed? What would become of my life's work?'" (23). In the process, however, he is responsible for unleashing the dangerous Jadis on the citizens of London, then upon the unsuspecting new world of Narnia, thus launching events that will mark the new world for centuries to come. Archimago attempts to besmirch the honor of his guests, which results in their separation. The deception of Redcrosse and his subsequent separation from Una is the basis of nearly all Redcrosse's troubles that ensue thereafter. Distanced from Una, the spirit of truth, he becomes the thrall of Duessa and her evil mistress Lucifera, then struggles against foes more threatening than Archimago until he is reunited with Una in canto seven of Book I. Both villains become responsible for releasing evil greater than themselves, yet both fail in their primary goals. Uncle Andrew, who briefly dreams of using the discovery of Narnia for financial gain, renounces magic altogether after his unhappy experiences in that country, and Archimago is depicted as a pathetic schemer whose ambitious plans always go awry. Though the enchanter certainly sets Redcrosse on the wrong road, Spenser's protagonist faces more danger from the Pagan knights than he does from Archimago's spells.

Lewis's villains, like Spenser's, are not always magical. At the same time, many of the merely mortal adversaries that face the Narnian protagonists do not receive the full character development of Jadis or even Uncle Andrew. For example, the Telmarines in *Prince Caspian*, particularly the usurper, Miraz, all resemble the bevy of faceless, and often nameless, wicked knights that parade through *The Faerie Queene*. The main elements that make Miraz a villain are his usurpation and his refusal to accept the spiritual, namely Aslan. Such rebellion and apostasy are both evident in Milton's Satan and his followers. Miraz refuses to acknowledge that his kingdom was once home to Talking Beasts and creatures like fauns, centaurs, and dryads; Prince Caspian's tutor, Doctor Cornelius, is the first person to even intimate that there actually was someone in Narnia for his ancestors to conquer (42). Miraz also murders his brother, Caspian's father, for the throne. In this action, Miraz certainly commits a crime against hierarchy as well as against humanity and a family member. In a sense, this connects him to the rebellion of Satan, but it is likely that Miraz's creation owes more to a tradition of scheming, murdering throne-stealers, such as Hamlet's Uncle Claudius, than to any specific influence from Milton's far more sophisticated villain. The anarchy and disorder he represents are clearly antagonistic elements incorporated in the adversaries of *Paradise Lost* and *The Faerie Queene*, and he most resembles the scheming and faithless knights who frequently oppose Spenser's protagonists, particularly the villainous uncle described by Tristam in Book VI, canto two. Upon the death of Tristam's father Meliogras, the boy's uncle "seeing mee/ An infant, weake a kingdom to sustaine,/ Upon him tooke the roiall high degree,/ And sent me, where him list, instructed for to be" (VI.ii.28.6–9). Likewise, upon his brother's death, which he had engineered, Miraz "called himself Lord Protector ... and when there was no one left who could speak a word for you [Caspian], then his flatterers (as he had instructed them) begged him to become King. And of course he did" (*PC* 56–57). While Tristam's mother, Emiline, sees to her son's safety, Caspian's mother has long since died, and is not there to protect Caspian when Miraz, upon the birth of his own child and potential heir, begins to plot Caspian's death. Instead, Doctor Cornelius, Caspian's tutor and a past recipient of the Queen's kindness, is left to act in her stead, sending the young prince into the forest for his safety. Though there are differences in each story, the usurping uncle is a clear connection between them.[3]

The villainous slavers encountered by Caspian and his companions on the island of Felimath, in the Lone Islands, also have clear sources from *The Faerie Queene*. In Book VI, the winsome Pastorella and her family, along with the other shepherds of their community, are carried off "the spoile of theeues and Brigants bad" (VI.x.40.7). These miscreants plan "soone, as they conueuient may,/ for slaues to sell them,/ for no small reward,/ To merchants, which them kept in bondage hard,/ Or sold again" (VI.x.43.3–6). In a very similar fashion, Caspian, Lucy, Edmund, Eustace, and Reepicheep are kidnapped by Pug and his gang of slavers on an island that, as Edmund says, was nearly uninhabited in his days as king, and was merely used as pasturage for sheep. Lucy also makes particular mention of the island, Felimath, as a lonely and peaceful place, much like the rural haven Sir Calidore enjoys with Pastorella and her community of shepherds before the attack of the brigands. This attack is unprovoked, like the attack on the Narnians, and, in both cases, the attackers are well-known troublemakers who live outside society and who plan to sell their captives to merchants. In *The Voyage of the "Dawn Treader,"* the marketplace at Narrowhaven draws potential slave buyers, particularly Calormenes. Spenser's "brigants" refuse to do honest work, and instead prey upon their neighbors and, like Pug and his ilk, make their home on a small island that is not heavily populated. Pug thinks of his actions as work: "I've got my living to make same as anyone else" (34); but Lord Bern calls Pug "carrion" and his practice a "filthy trade" (35) making it quite clear that he has no patience with Pug's conniving sales pitches or his feigned personal interest in his captives. Through Lord Bern's purchase of Caspian, the young King and his father's old friend are able to rendezvous with *The Dawn Treader* and free not only their own friends but all the slaves in the Narrowhaven market as well. It is indeed by great fortune that the slavers, with Caspian in tow, encounter not just a sympathetic individual, but one of the very lords whose fate Caspian seeks to learn in his eastward journey. This encounter then allows for the release of the prisoners. In *The Faerie Queene*, it is also a twist of fate that Sir Calidore is out hunting on the day of the attack against the shepherds. While he may not, as one knight, have been able to stop the enslavement of his new friends had he been there, he is free and able to stage a rescue of his beloved Pastorella, largely with the intelligence provided by the shepherd Coridon, who manages to escape. In both cases, a captive is able to ally with a powerful protector who effects a release and revenge. Certainly Calidore's destruction of the brigands is more violent than Caspian's legal actions against the slavers of the Lone Islands, just as the murder of Pastorella's family and friends, and her own mistreatment, is more extreme than the discomfort suffered by the humans and Reepicheep at the hands of the slavers. However, Calidore, as the knight of courtesy, certainly provides a strong and appropriate influence since both Caspian and Bern are remarkably courteous, even when dealing with the loathsome Governor Gumpas, who has allowed the slave trade to flourish because of the personal wealth it has brought him. Likewise, Calidore first sits down and chats with the "brigants," learning more about them and the location of the captive Pastorella, rather than immediately engaging them in combat. There also remain strong parallels between the two bands of wicked miscreants that each author places in opposition to his protagonists. In each case, these villains are powerful in their violence, though not magically powerful nor as sophisticated as other antagonists.

The most carefully developed mortal antagonists in the series are natives of Calormen, the country to the south of Narnia. Lewis has been criticized for making his villains dark-skinned: "Lewis was unconsciously unsympathetic to things and people Middle-Eastern. That Lewis opts into this cultural blindness is regrettable." Yet, not all Calormenes are evil, and they are not racial stereotypes so much as they are traditional literary antagonists for Western knights: "The Calormenes are not simply 'dark persons'—they are Moors: they are identified by their dress, weapons and manners as the traditional enemy in medieval romances." Even more than Moors the Calormenes resemble the typical "Sarazins" who oppose Crusaders. Since Lewis's characters, like Spenser's, often resemble the noblest of Crusaders, the opposition is both logical and appropriate, rather than the result of implied or intended racism. In addition, the Calormenes' allegiance to the bloodthirsty god Tash, as well as to other minor gods and goddesses, clearly marks them as pagans, the antithesis of the Narnians, who follow a positive and loving single "High King" over all high kings. So, too, Sans loy, Sans foy, and Sans joy, and other antagonistic knights of *The Faerie Queene* are all described as 'paynims" or pagans.[4]

Calormen's pantheon of deities also includes members that would probably be quite at home among the demonic inhabitants of Milton's Hell. Tash, bird-headed and with four arms, one of which usually clutches a hapless victim, demands human sacrifice, much like "Moloch, horrid king besmeared with blood" (I.392). Zardeenah, Lady of the Night, to whom Aravis is expected to sacrifice before her arranged marriage, has connotations of maidenhood and fertility that connect her to Diana and "Astarte, queen of heav'n with crescent horns" (I.439). The Calormenes as a whole also bear a resemblance to the fallen angels in *Paradise Lost*. According to the chronology Lewis created for Narnia, the Calormenes descend from bandits who were exiled from Archenland, the border country between Narnia and the Great Desert. This exile reflects the outcast nature of both Calormenes and fallen angels. The city of Tashbaan and the cruel materialism of most Calormenes follow the suggestion made by Mammon in Book II of *Paradise*

*Lost*: "This desert soil/ wants not her hidden luster, gems and gold;/ Nor want we skill or art, from whence to raise/ magnificence" (270–3). The fact that Satan is referred to as a Sultan (I.348) also links him to the fierce pagan and Sarazin elements that form the Calormenes. Since there are good Calormenes, such as Aravis in *The Horse and His Boy* and Emeth in *The Last Battle*, in a study of evil, it is appropriate to look at specific Calormenes who play antagonists in the series, as well as to examine the entire people. The most crucial of these antagonists is Prince Rabadash.[5]

Lewis, in his critical refutation of the view of Satan as a hero, emphasizes the foolishness of the chief Fallen Angel: "Milton ... believed everything detestable to be ... also ridiculous; and mere Christianity commits every Christian to believing that 'the Devil is ... an ass.'" In Lewis's view, Satan is not heroic, or even noble; he is a fool, an ass in every sense of the word. This interpretation of Satan is reflected in the villain of *The Horse and His Boy*, Prince Rabadash. Although he claims to love Queen Susan, Rabadash merely wants her as a spoil of war: "I must have her. I shall die If I do not get her — false, proud, black-hearted daughter of a dog that she is!" (106). Like Satan, Rabadash is interested in his own prestige alone. Satan clearly cares little about the well-being of his followers, who are condemned for the rebellion he has engineered, and Rabadash thinks nothing of sacrificing the men riding his "two hundred horse" (*HHB* 115) or of killing Archenlanders, whom he sees as mere obstacles to his invasion of Narnia: "Kill me every barbarian male within [Anvard's] walls, down to the child that was born yesterday" (153–4). His unfeeling pragmatism is obviously a family trait, since, in the only appearance of his father, the Tisroc, Lewis clearly presents an opportunist, like Satan, who does not care for anyone's needs but his own, and who treats his first-born son as a tool to be useful to him in life or death: "If the Prince succeeds we have Archenland, and perhaps hereafter Narnia. If he fails — I have eighteen other sons and Rabadash was beginning to be dangerous" (116). Like Satan as well, Rabadash is a violent force who festers with the desire for rebellion. Rabadash's most Satanic moment is when he, too, is seen as the ridiculous figure that he truly is. In his vicious and unprovoked attack on Anvard, Rabadash tries to create a tragically heroic moment by leaping off a ledge, waving his sword, and descending on the Narnians and Archenlanders. Instead, his mail shirt gets hung on a hook in the wall: "And there he found himself, like a piece of washing hung up to dry, with everyone laughing at him ... though he could have faced torture he couldn't bear being made ridiculous. In Tashbaan everyone had always taken him seriously" (186–7). Rabadash not only makes an ass of himself, like Satan, with his words; he actually literally becomes one: "For now what had been Rabadash was now, unmistakably, a donkey" (211). Like Satan and his followers, forced to assume the serpent guise he had used to deceive humanity, Rabadash's exterior changes to reflect his true inner nature. It is not surprising that Lewis, who asserted Milton's belief that everything detestable is also ridiculous, adds that Rabadash is recorded in Calormene textbooks as "Rabadash the Ridiculous" (213). Despite the very real threats they present, both Satan and Rabadash are ultimately as laughable as they are lethal.[6]

The other major Calormene villain of the series, Rishdah Tarkaan in *The Last Battle,* is not a highly developed character, though his denial of both Aslan and his own god, Tash, mark him as an apostate. In his scheming with the wily Cat, Ginger, he agrees that there is "no such person as either [Tash or Aslan]" (*LB* 79). He even turns his back on his original co-conspirator, Shift the Ape, for the more subtle and treacherous Ginger. In this regard his treachery and lack of spiritual submission link him both with Milton's Fallen Angels and Spenser's Pagan knights who curse God and betray their allies whenever an opportunity arises.

Rishdah Tarkaan's original accomplice, Shift the Ape, is the only major antagonist of the series who is a Talking Beast. While Rishdah is mostly a stock pagan with his eye on profit and no real belief in even Tash, Shift is a character who is intriguing both in his use of deception and in the effects his wicked choices have on him. Like Spenser's Archimago, Shift becomes overwhelmed by his own plans and soon finds himself in over his head. The two characters are also connected by the similar meanings of their names. "Archimago" defines the shifty, shape-changing aspect of his persona, while "Shift" also shifts both meanings and shapes by interpreting signs and incidents according to his own devices and creating the false "Tashlan." There are various interpretations of Shift; some focus on his representation of the negative implications of Darwinian evolutionary theory, while others concentrate on the fact that the last villain of Narnia, and the most destructive, is a native:

> Shift, the comic symbol of Lewis's evolutionary inversion ... represents some of the worst aspects of a modern life which dehumanizes man. The evil, for the first time in all the *Chronicles*, is *in* Narnia and is not the direct manifestation of external forces like Jadis or the Green Witch....

While Tumnus tells Lucy that there are animals, and even trees, working as spies for the White Witch, they are only tools and henchmen, rather than instigators of evil like Shift. The Ape's characterization is one that has a sharper edge than any other antagonist depicted in the series. Peter J. Schakel notes in *Reading with the Heart* that *The Last Battle* "is the only one of the *Chronicles* to use irony." Irony is a dominant factor in Shift and his plan; it comes into play since Shift is a Narnian, and because his destruction comes at the hands of Tash, a demon in whom he does not believe, and whom he has unwittingly called into Narnia. In addition, his lack of belief in the real Aslan leads him to create the false Aslan with Puzzle the donkey in a lionskin, not realizing or caring that his blasphemy will also call down the judgment of the Lion.[7]

One of the most crucial aspects of Shift's character, and the one that most clearly links him to the villains of both *The Faerie Queene* and *Paradise Lost*, is his predilection for twisting or "shifting" truth. Initially, Shift convinces the simple-minded Puzzle to wear a lionskin and to pose as Aslan simply to "set everything right in Narnia" (*LB* 10). However, Shift's plots grow more and more complicated and his lies more vile until he collaborates with the Calormenes to plot the seizure of Narnia by her enemies and actually blurs Aslan and Tash (32). As his plot deepens, Shift frequently combines both refutations of truth and lies as truth: "I hear some of you saying I'm an ape. Well, I'm not. I'm a Man" (29); "You think freedom means doing what you like. Well, you're wrong. That isn't true freedom. True freedom means doing what I tell you" (30–31). Shift, by overturning truth as well as order, represents a type of danger that runs as a theme throughout *The Faerie Queene* whose "many tyrants exemplify the abuse of order, and some figures represent bestial disorder." Lewis, who valued proper order, makes a powerful statement about the dangers of Shift by making him an instrument of disorder. In addition, like Archimago, who makes things seem what they are not, Shift uses Puzzle and his lionskin as tools of deception. Both Shift and Archimago use natural elements to create their surprisingly successful doppelgängers. Archimago's images, though they convince Redcrosse, are nothing more than air: "[He] made a Lady of that other Spright,/ And framed of liquid ayre her tender partes/ So liuely and so like in all mens sight,/ That weaker sense it could have rauished quight" (I.i.45.2–5); Shift's "Tashlan" is a donkey dressed up in a dead lion's hide, that, if examined closely, and in good light, would not deceive anyone. Both antagonists use the cover of darkness to prevent anyone from looking too closely at their creations. The "Tashlan" disguise also resembles the False Florimell the witch creates in Book III of *The Faerie Queene*. Like this "snowy lady," who is later declared more beautiful than the real Florimell, the false Aslan usurps the position of the true Aslan. Both beings are also traded about as playing pieces. The false Florimell is kidnaped for her beauty, and Puzzle in his lion disguise is used by Shift in the initial plot, then by Tirian in a failed attempt to convince the dwarfs of the Ape's treachery: "Tirian had never dreamed that one of the results of an Ape's setting up a false Aslan would be to stop people from believing in the real one" (*LB* 74). Puzzle himself is eager to have to lionskin removed, aware that he has been a pawn, if not entirely sure how to extricate himself from the plotting of others.[8]

Though not nearly as clever as Satan, Shift uses some of the fallen angel's techniques. Both are certainly liars, and the fact that Shift uses a donkey, not a horse or cow, to imitate Aslan, harks back to Lewis's assertion that the devil is an ass. In the history of animal lore and bestiaries, the Ape is often viewed as a Satanic character as well. Satan's name has connotations with twisting or turning from truth, just as Shift's name is a reflection of his shifting of truth. In addition, both villains are completely self-centered. Lewis noted in *A Preface to Paradise Lost* that Satan's main interest is Satan. Certainly Shift's main interest is Shift. Both characters, however, impress upon their followers the belief that they are selfless martyrs. Satan's heroic journey to Eden is really motivated by his own need to be the one to do something about the fallen angels' situation: "While I abroad/ Through all the coasts of dark destruction seek/ Deliverance for us all: this enter-prise/ None shall partake with me" (II.463–7). The operative words in his declaration are "I" and "me." He does not choose to travel alone because the journey is dangerous or because he is heroic or self-sacrificing, but because he does not wish to share the glory or antici-pated success with anyone else. Shift, under pretext of making a nice winter coat for Puzzle, is turning him to his own designs. The Ape con-vinces the Donkey that his refusal to wear the lionskin is an affront to the hard work Shift has put into it, so Puzzle reluctantly wears the "coat" while Shift gloats: "'You look wonderful, wonderful,' said the Ape. 'If anyone saw you now, they'd think you were Aslan, the Great Lion, himself'" (*LB* 9). Of course, Shift is not nearly as loquacious as Satan, or as complicated. The honest but simple Puzzle, though, is not a difficult victim to coerce.[9]

Like his sources, Lewis also peoples his fictional world with mon-sters, many of whom have symbolic power. One such type of monster is the giant. Intriguingly, the first giant introduced in the *Chronicles* is actually a good giant, Rubblebuffin:

"What a nice giant he is!" said Lucy to Mr. Tumnus.
"Oh yes," replied the Faun. "All the buffins always were. One of the most respected of all the giant families in Narnia. Not very clever, perhaps (I never knew a giant that was) but an old family. With tradi-tions, you know. If he'd been the other sort she'd [The White Witch] never have turned him into stone" [*LWW* 171].

There are other good giants in the series. Prince Caspian has Giant Wimbleweather as a loyal, if often thick-witted follower, and in the attack on Anvard in *The Horse and His Boy,* Calormen-raised Shasta is alarmed to see "six giants. For there are good giants in Narnia. But though he knew they were on the right side Shasta at first could hardly bear to look at them; there are some things that take a lot of getting used to" (170). Though Milton's angels, both good and bad, often appear gigantic, and though Spenser includes some gigantic figures who are not wicked, most of their giants are not of Rubblebuffin or Wimbleweather's ilk. Near the end of *The Lion, the Witch, and the Wardrobe*, in the list of the four Pevensies' impressive accomplishments as rulers of Narnia, Lewis takes pains to explain that the fierce giants who have been driven back over the northern border are "quite a different sort from Giant Rubblebuffin." Indeed, it is this different sort of giant that is used so effectively in an antagonistic vein by Lewis and his literary predecessors. Giants, like dwarves, are often a stock ingredient of fairy tales, along with enchanted sleeps and treacherous witches, harking back to our primal fear of things that are warped or twisted versions of humanity: "Nature has that in her which compels us to invent giants, and only giants will do." Yet Lewis also uses his antagonistic giants in a specific fashion that evokes his predecessors. In *Paradise Lost,* the fallen Satan is clearly a giant:

> With head uplift above the wave, and eyes
> That sparkling blazed, his other parts besides
> Prone on the flood, extended long and large
> Lay floating many a rood, in bulk as huge
> As whom the fables name of monstrous size,
> Titanian, or Earth-born, that warred on Jove,
> Briareos or Typhon, whom the den
> By ancient Tarsus held, or that sea-beast
> Leviathan....
> So stretched out huge in length the Arch-Fiend lay [I. 193–209].

By linking him with specifically dangerous and rebellious giants from classical mythology, Milton clearly denotes that Satan's size is monstrous, even mutated, rather than noble. Though Satan shape-shifts, becoming as small as a toad and a serpent, it is as a ruined, defeated, but defiant giant that he first appears. Despite the fact that he has lost the war in Heaven (or perhaps because of it), Satan remains a dangerous threat throughout the rest of the poem as well as throughout human history. Likewise, the dangerous Northern giants of Narnia, as King Caspian explains, were given "such a beating last summer that they pay us tribute now" (*VDT* 15), but they remain a threat which materializes in *The Silver Chair.*[10]

When Jill first sees giants on Ettinsmoor, she thinks she is seeing geographical features that look like giants, but that are really nothing of the sort: "...all the stories about giants might have come from those funny rocks. If you were coming along here when it was half dark, you could easily think those piles of rock were giants" (*SC* 68–69). When one of the giants moves, Jill is horrified to discover that they are living creatures rather than optical illusions. The giants of Ettinsmoor are stupid, crude creatures who "play cock-shies ... the only game they're clever enough to understand" (*SC* 70), get into arguments in which they "stormed and jeered at one another in long meaningless words of about twenty syllables each" (*SC* 70), beat each other over the heads with hammers, and pout when they are hurt. The crude, stupid giant is just one type Lewis uses as a villain, and, like the other types of giants he portrays, these have precedent in *The Faerie Queene*. Orgoglio, the first of many giant characters in the poem, is specifically described as "hideous" (I.vii.4) and monstrous. Like the Ettinsmoor giants, Spenser's giants are often described as being made of earthy substances rather than living flesh. Jill's giants are so much like the rocky gorge in which they stand that she assumes they are piles of rock and that their hair is birds' nests or moss, while Orgoglio is basically a sack of wind, and the his brother, the gigantic Disdayne in Books II and VI, is made entirely of iron and is as violent and deformed as the Ettinsmoor giants: "a sturdie villian.... In his right hand an yron club he held,/ And he himself was all of yron mould,/ Yet had both life and sense, and well could weld,/ That cursed weapon" (II.vii.40, 4–9); "he was sterne, and terrible by nature, and eke of person huge and hideous" (VI.vii.41.1–2). Giants in both Lewis and Spenser are sometimes just large humans and sometimes far more mutated. Jill, in her initial observations of what she believes to be giant-impersonating rocks, thinks that the ears would be too big for proportionate, anthropomorphic ears, " but then I dare-say giants have big ears, like elephants" (*SC* 69). Unfortunately for Redcrosse and his associates, Spenser's giants tend to be more intelligent, and thus more dangerous, than the crowd Jill first sees along the gorge in Ettinsmoor, and unfortunately for Jill and her companions, they soon encounter a more sophisticated brand of giant as well.

The only other humans Jill, Eustace, and Puddleglum meet in the North are the mysterious silent knight in black armor and the beautiful lady in the green dress who, as they discover later, is the Green Witch. In their short conversation, for Puddleglum will allow the children to say nothing of their quest or their identities, the charming witch tells them of Harfang "where dwell the Gentle Giants. They are as mild, civil, prudent, and courteous as those of Ettinsmoor are foolish, fierce, savage, and given to all beastliness" (*SC* 76). These giants are far more human than those Jill sees in the gorge, for they live in a fine manor, speak intelligibly, and seem to be just large humans. Of course, the witch neglects to mention that the giants eat humans and will even serve up a Marsh-wiggle if one is handy, and she specifically tells the children to report to the giants that she has sent them for the giants' Autumn Feast, implying that the children will be guests, when in fact they will be part of the feast. Spenser also employs giants that speak intelligently. One such character is the giant Artegall encounters early in his adventures in Book V. He meets the giant shortly after crossing a bridge that is "exceeding long;/ and in the same are many trap fals plight,/ Through which the rider downe doth fall through oversight./ And underneath the same a river flowes,/ That is both swift and dangerous deepe withall" (V.ii.7.7–8.2). The bridge Jill and her companions cross just before hearing of the so-called Gentle Giants is remarkably similar: "It was a huge, single arch.... In many places the great stones had dropped out, leaving horrible gaps through which you looked down on the river foaming thousands of feet below" (*SC* 73–74). The "mighty Gyant" (V.ii.30.1) Artegall finds soon after crossing the bridge is, like the giants Puddleglum and the children soon meet, much like a large human, with often persuasive human speech:

> He sayd that he would all the earth vptake,
> And all the sea, devided each from either;
> So would he of the fire one ballaunce make,
> And one of th'ayre...
> Then would he ballaunce heaven and hell together,
> And all that within them all containe; ...
> For why, he sayd they all vnequall were,
> And had encroched vpon others share, ...
> All which he vndertooke for to repaire,
> In sort as they were formed auciently;
> And all things would reduce into equality [V.ii.31.1–32.9].

The giant has convinced a large crowd of people that they will benefit from his plan to use his scales to redistribute everything in heaven, hell, and earth, including wealth and power. It is only Artegall's superior training and knowledge of Justice that allow him to stump and dismay the giant. The giants of Harfang also use persuasive speech to place Jill and her companions off their guard. The giant king and queen call them "good children" and welcome them to Harfang. They are treated like guests, never guessing, until they find a giant cookbook, the giant's true intentions.

More powerful than words however, it is the lure of comfort that truly ensnares Puddleglum and, particularly, the children, at Harfang. This attraction also has close parallels in *The Faerie Queene*, for Spenser often uses giants who are both crude and sensual, and both attributes are most clearly connected with the "gentle" giants. In Book III, Satyrane leaves off chasing the hyena-like monster that he believes has killed Florimell in order to take part in the chase of the lustful giantess Argante. Like many of Spenser's giants, she wields a "huge, great yron mace" (III.vii.40.1), a crude, blunt object with phallic connotations, emphasizing her sexual depravity and her rough nature. Born in an incestuous relationship with her twin and male counterpart, Ollyphant, Argante seeks "young men to quench her flaming thrust,/ And feed her fancy with delightfull chaunge" (III.vii.50.2–3). Yet she throws aside her would-be conquest, the Squire of Dames, and Satyrane, whom she briefly subdues, in order to lighten her load for combat. She is a crude creature, driven entirely by her sensual desires, particularly her unquenchable lust.[11]

Book I's Orgoglio is also sensual, using a club as a weapon and happily accepting Duessa as "his newfound make" (I.vii.15.5) The Harfang giants are also marked by crudity and sensuality but, more appropriately for a children's book, they are characterized by gustatory, rather than sexual, appetites. When the children and Puddleglum are first brought to the giant King and Queen, it is clear that they are crude and sensual creatures. The Queen is "dreadfully fat [with] a double chin and a fat, powdered face" (*SC* 96), and when she tries to comfort the exhausted and weeping Jill, the Queen assures her that she will be given food, wine, and a bath, appealing to her senses of taste, smell, and touch. Jill is also promised lullabies and toys, intended to attract the senses of hearing and sight. The toys, which Lewis describes specifically as "crude, badly made things, painted in very bright colours" (*SC* 99) are not of much interest to Jill, but she is delighted by a giant bath, clean clothes, a comfortable bed, and deep soft carpet on her tired feet. In fact, the entire time that the travelers are at the castle, they are tempted and swayed by sensual pleasures. Colors are particularly intense at the castle: from Jill's bright green dress, which appears to be a cast-off from the Green Witch, and her fur-edged scarlet cloak to Eustace's "scarlet stockings, blue tunic and cloak" (*SC* 116) to the Queen's green hunting costume. Though Lewis often describes meals and other experiences in great detail, it is clear that the comforts of the giants' castle are negative ones, not because there is anything wrong with baths and food and clean clothes, but because these sensual attractions have taken Jill and her companions off their quest, and she has even forgotten the Signs given her by Aslan. In fact, from the very moment that the Witch mentions the charms of Harfang, the children cannot concentrate on the quest: "whatever the Lady had intended by telling them about Harfang, the actual effect on the children was a bad one. They could think about nothing but beds and baths and hot meals and how lovely it would be to get indoors. They never talked about Aslan, or even about the lost Prince, now" (*SC* 79). Eustace and Jill become more snappish with each other and more easily aggravated with the dismal Puddleglum, for the promise of pleasure and comfort has driven everything else out of their minds. The giants are therefore, like Spenser's Argante, both slaves to their appetites as well as tempters who lure others to be ruled by their sensual desires.

The Harfang giants are also, of course, appetite-driven in another regard; they eat both humans and Marsh-wiggles, as the travelers discover when they find a giant cookbook. In a clear stroke of foreshadowing, the giant King, whom Jill initially thinks is the more pleasant half of the royal couple, startles her when he licks his lips with his very large and red tongue. While he appears to simply be wetting his lips, later events clarify that he is, in fact, licking his lips at the sight of the main course for the forthcoming feast. In Book VI of *The Faerie Queene*, the hapless Serena is also threatened with the possibility of being eaten by the "saluage nation, which did live/ Of stealth and spoile" (VI.viii. 35.2–3). The Giant Queen at Harfang calls Jill and Eustace "good children" (*SC* 96) ironically meaning how delicious they look, rather than how well-behaved they are. The savages likewise look at Serena and "praise her paps, some praise her lips and nose" (VI.viii.39.5–6), but they are not so much admiring her beauty as they are selecting the pieces of her that they think might taste the best. Just as Serena's clothes are taken away and she is decked with a sacrificial garland, Jill and

Eustace have their own clothes taken away and replaced with the gaudy ones provided by the giants. Though the Harfang giants' desire to eat the children and Puddleglum can not properly be called cannibalism, since the giants are not really human and neither is Puddleglum, it is another reminder of the dangers of sensual pleasures: those who come to eat will be eaten. Likewise, Spenser's giants, when they cannot seduce, like Argante, they destroy, like Book VI's Cormraunt or Book Five's Geryoneo. Spenser's giants often take prisoners, just as the Harfang giants imprison the unwary travelers. While Argante threatens to make her chosen lovers prisoners unless they yield to her desires, Orgoglio imprisons Redcrosse " in a Dongeon deep" (I.vii.12.9) while enjoying the blandishments of Duessa. Clearly, both in Spenser and in Lewis, those who yield to their physical desires can be imprisoned by them, a theme both authors explore in other contexts as well.

In addition to giants who interact with humans and function as characters, Lewis presents a giant that is primarily iconic: Old Father Time, whom Jill and Eustace see on their journey to Underland, and again at the end of Narnia in *The Last Battle:* "He was far bigger than any of the giants, and his face was not like a giant's, but noble and beautiful" (*SC* 126). Puddleglum, who asks his identity, is told that Time was once a King in the world above who has fallen into the world below "and lies dreaming of all the things that are done in the upper world.... They say he will wake at he end of the world" (*SC* 127). On Jill and Eustace's next trip to Narnia in *The Last Battle,* they see this prophecy come to fruition. When Aslan calls for Time, the massive giant stands and " Jill and Eustace remembered how once long ago, they had seen a great giant asleep ... and were told he would wake on the day the world ended (*LB* 150). At Aslan's command, Time blows the horn that calls home the stars, and later squeezes out the dying sun. Such an iconic giant is certainly reminiscent of Milton's massive angels, fallen and otherwise. Satan with his "Atlantean shoulders" (II.306), who is so large that his shield is like the moon and his spear "to equal which the tallest pine/ Hewn on Norwegian hills, to be the mast/ Of some great ammiral, were but a wand" (I.292–294) is a physically gigantic incarnation of the abstract idea of evil, just as the abstract idea of Time is physically manifested in the Narnian giant. Both are persons of high degree who fell, physically if not morally, to a lower place, and both are specifically geared for war, Satan with shield and spear, and Time with the horn that sounds "high and terrible, yet of a strange, deadly beauty" (*LB* 150). Yet, since Time is an instrument of Aslan's work, he is not entirely negative, and has connections with Milton's unfallen angels as well as with those who rebel. Time's first task is to blow his horn, calling all the stars, who are really people in Narnia, to come falling out of the sky and then stand behind Aslan so that their light casts into the dying world. Likewise, when God first appears, in Book III of *Paradise Lost*, "Above him all the sanctities of heaven/ stood thick as stars" (III.60). God's angels, good and bad, are clearly gigantic in the description of the War in Heaven in Book VI. Here Raphael tells Adam:

> Rage prompted them [the loyal angels] at length and
> found them arms
> Against such hellish mischief fit to oppose.
> Forthwith...
> Their arms away they threw, and to the hills
> (For earth hath this variety from heav'n
> Of pleasure situate in hill and dale) ...
> They plucked the seated hills with all their load,
> Rocks, waters, woods, and by the shaggy tops,
> Uplifting bore them in their hands [VI.635–646].

The rebel angels soon follow suit, tossing hills back at God's legions. This bizarre battle both emphasizes the size of the angels and the destructive power of their fury. Though Satan and his troops are defeated before they can cause too much more damage in heaven, it is quite clear that the angels are all terrible, beautiful giants like Lewis's Time, and they, like he, have a vital, if dire, role to fulfill; even Satan himself eventually sees his plans of destruction used by God to suit His plans and will.

Though there are a plethora of giants in folklore, Spenser's and Milton's giants can certainly be seen as precedents for the giants that Lewis employs, particularly those that function as antagonists. While there are many other monsters in Narnia, as well as in the works of Spenser and Milton, the giants clearly show the strongest connection between the three texts. Though Lewis may have also been thinking about the giant that threatens poor, simple-minded Jack, or about the giants of Norse mythology as he constructed the giants of Narnia and her surrounding lands, Ogoglio, Argante, and Milton's angels all have a powerful influence as well.

Even more realistic than Lewis's portrayal of absolute villains, forces of evil, or monstrous non-humans, is his characterization of protagonists who occasionally become the tools of evil, those who succumb to temptation, making poor choices that lead them from the true path. Like Redcrosse and the fallen Adam and Eve, positive characters in Narnia occasionally fail, but are always offered redemption. One of the most dramatic failures is certainly Edmund's alliance with the White Witch. While it would be easy to equate this betrayal to Satan's, it is, in fact, more similar to that of Adam and Eve. Though concerned somewhat with his own prestige, and wanting to "get back at Peter" for calling him a beast, Edmund is mostly interested in getting more of the magically addictive Turkish Delight. Clearly Edmund is not a very nice person even before he eats the Witch's enchanted food, as Peter declares: "You've always liked being beastly to anyone smaller than yourself; we've seen that at school before now" (*LWW* 42). However, like Eve, Edmund unwarily tries to deal with evil on his own. Even as Eve allows herself to listen to the Serpent's rhetoric about the virtues of the forbidden tree, so Edmund goes against his better judgment — fear of the Witch: he initially worries that the strange lady on the sledge will drive off with him into this strange new world, taking him away from any chance of returning home, but once the enchantment begins to work on him, he forgets his fears entirely (*LWW* 34). Although Eve tells the serpent that "we might have spared our coming hither" (IX.648) when she sees to which tree he has led her, she remains to listen to his oratory, which finally tempts her to disobedience. Neither Eve nor Edmund, at the first hint of danger, flees for reinforcements, though both know that someone more experienced is not far away: Adam could clearly help Eve resist the initial temptation, and Lucy would confirm Edmund's suspicions that the Witch might be dangerous. Instead, they both attempt to control the encounter, and become enslaved to poor choices. In the final analysis, both Edmund and the first humans are brought down by food that affects them physically as well as spiritually. Adam and Eve hide from God and are clearly fallen beings after they consume the forbidden fruit. Although the initial effect is one of elation at their courage, they soon feel overwhelming guilt and regret as they change from obedient creations into fallen mortals, "estranged in look and altered style" (IX.1132). Edmund, too, at first feels proud of himself and the deal he has made with the Witch; soon though he is "already feeling uncomfortable from having eaten too many sweets, and when he heard that the Lady he had made friends with was a dangerous witch he felt even more uncomfortable" (*LWW* 38). In addition, Mr. Beaver notes that he can tell Edmund is a traitor because of "something about ... [his] eyes" (*LWW* 81). The Witch's food has tainted him. Like Adam and Eve, Edmund has become both physically and spiritually transformed by his sin. Interestingly, both Lucy and Edmund take food from strangers: she from Tumnus, and he from Jadis. Since the results of these encounters are so radically different from one another, it is clear that what Edmund does wrong is not merely to take food from a suspicious character. Lucy, because she is a positive character, unconsciously appeals to the Faun's better nature, and though he has used his marvelous tea as bait in the trap to kidnap Lucy, he cannot go through with the plan once he knows her. Edmund, on the other hand, has already begun to go wrong before he takes his first step into the wardrobe, so he encounters the Witch and is easy prey for her ploys. The more she knows about him — his jealousy of Peter, his feeling that he is someone superior to his siblings — the more clear it becomes that he will be a useful and effective tool for her plans. This seeming paradox is also one embraced by Spenser and Milton. In *The Faerie Queene,* for example, actions such as going into a forest or engaging in a tournament are not portrayed as innately evil or good; they are colored by the characters who engage in them. Milton as well, emphasizes the fact that actions, in and of themselves, are rendered good or evil by the participant's intentions. Thus, Adam and Eve's sexual relationship before the fall is pure and positive, and their lustful romp after they taste the forbidden fruit is perverse and aggressive.

Edmund's falling away from the true path even more closely resembles that of Spenser's Redcrosse since, like Edmund, the knight is redeemed. Edmund's initial treachery does not seriously endanger anyone except himself since his brother and sisters are under Aslan's protection. While they are certainly hurt and angry, they are likewise concerned about finding him: "'All the same,' said Peter in a rather choking sort of voice, 'we'll still have to go and look for him. He is our brother after all, even if he is rather a little beast, and he's only a kid'" (81). Peter's reaction to Edmund's treachery and the relief all the children feel when Edmund is saved resemble the reaction of Una after Redcrosse's desertion. She expresses hurt, but mostly concern: "For since mine eye your joyous sight did mis,/ My cheareful day is turnd to chearelesse night" (I.iii.27.6–7). In addition, both Redcrosse and Edmund become better men through their experiences. Redcrosse becomes St. George, and Edmund becomes "a graver and quieter man than Peter, and great in council and in government ... called King Edmund the Just" (181). Intriguingly, this appellation links him with another of Spenser's knights, Artegall, the knight of Justice, and indicates that, although Edmund is redeemed, he is still scarred by the treachery that nearly destroyed both himself and his siblings, and which cost the sacrifice of Aslan himself. After all, Artegall is not a very likeable character. Lewis seems to indicate a real dislike for him in his own Spenser criticism and "the consensus is that Artegall is thoroughly disagreeable and not at all like the other glorious champions of *The Faerie Queene*." In connecting Edmund with Artegall, a knight few readers of Spenser would want to have round for dinner, Lewis emphasizes the lasting effects of Edmund's mistakes. This connection between Edmund and *The Faerie Queene* is further accentuated by the fact that Spenser's first name is bestowed on the boy who becomes both traitor and king. Fortunately, Edmund, like Redcrosse, emerges stronger from his failings, and as he develops throughout the series, the younger Pevensie brother is clearly a positive and well-rounded character who loves Aslan the more for the price paid for his life. Like the servant in Jesus' parable who has been forgiven much, Edmund develops a deep and lasting relationship both with Aslan and with Lucy, the sister he once betrayed. In *Prince Caspian, The Voyage of the "Dawn Treader,"* and *The Horse and His Boy*, Edmund defers to Lucy's judgment, respects her, and defends her. The forgiveness of Aslan makes him a far better person than he was before he met the Witch. Edmund's treachery also brings about the sacrificial death of Aslan, but even this tragedy leads to triumph with Aslan's resurrection, more powerful than ever. Because she believes Aslan dead, Jadis is taken by surprise when he joins the battle. Though it is Peter's shield that bears Aslan's image, in his gratitude and later transformation, Edmund, the victim who is replaced by Aslan, reflects his savior as clearly as Redcrosse with his emblematic shield.[12]

Redcrosse has another echo in the person of Eustace Scrubb, Edmund's tiresome cousin. "'You were only an ass, but I was a traitor'" (*VDT* 91), Edmund tells Eustace after his cousin's encounter with Aslan. While Eustace certainly is an ass, self-centered and rude, he is also in need of correction. The pattern that his correction follows is highly similar to the treatment undergone by Redcrosse at the House of Holiness. Redcrosse is certainly not turned into a dragon the way Eustace is, but he still has many of the same faults to overcome, and the baptismal-imagery scenes that embody their redemption episodes are strikingly alike. Redcrosse must give up his armor, becoming vulnerable, and he undergoes treatment so painful that "his torment was often so great,/ That like a Lyon he would cry and rore" (I.x.28.1–2). Eustace tells Edmund that Aslan led him up to a garden on a high hill where there was a large well or pool that Eustace, in his miserable dragon form, desperately wanted to enter: "The lion told me I must undress first ... dragons are snaky sort of creatures and can cast their skins" (89). After several attempts to remove his own dragon skin, Eustace is painfully "skinned" by Aslan, tossed into the pool, and made human again. The Christian idea of being made new is certainly embodied here. More important to the discussion of evil, however, is the fact that both Redcrosse and Eustace are so embedded in their attachment to the evil that has enslaved them that they must go through radical and painful transformation experiences.

Both Eustace and Redcrosse are so chagrined by their failings that they actually become self-destructive. Redcrosse, when his mistakes are conjured up before him by Despayre, "At last resolved to worke his finall smart" (I.ix.51.9) and kill himself. Until Redcrosse realizes he has been off the true path, he is not pricked by guilt. Much the same situation befalls Eustace, who believes himself always to be in the right, persecuted by his cousins and Caspian, until he becomes a dragon: "It was ... clear to everyone that Eustace's character had been rather improved by becoming a dragon" (*VDT* 83). As chances for his restoration do not immediately materialize, and he faces the possibility of being abandoned in his awful form, Eustace, like Redcrosse, suffers from despair: "For it was very dreary being a dragon" (84). Both characters can only experience true redemption and salvation from despair when they place themselves at the mercy of spiritual transformation, realizing that regret and self-destruction are not the punishments for their errors, but that true repentance can lead them to forgiveness, and it is interesting to note that Lewis chose for Eustace's form of punishment the very creature Redcrosse must fight to save Una's kingdom.

Nearly all of the major characters in the *Chronicles* experience some failing. On an island with water that turns items into gold, Caspian, like Guyon, is tempted by riches, and Eustace actually is seduced by dragon's gold, causing his unpleasant sojourn as a reptile. Jill, like Redcrosse, forgets her duties and falls prey to the power of comfort. However, the most dramatic failing, and the only one that is not repented, is Susan's rejection of Aslan and Narnia, reported in *The Last Battle*, and analyzed further in the later analysis of spiritual matters. Susan is "a self-limiting character. One with potential and freedom to develop, but whose limited vision has prevented her from enjoying the fulness of life." She has convinced herself that the Narnian adventures are "funny games we used to play when were children" (*LB* 135). She is certainly much more of an Eve character than any of the others, for she, like the mother of all mankind, is disobedient, especially when obedience is unpleasant or causes her personal discomfort. In *Prince Caspian*, Susan's inability to obey in difficult circumstances prevents her from seeing Aslan, although she knows he is present. She later tells Lucy, "'I really believed it was him — he, I mean — yesterday. When he warned us not to go down into the fir-wood. And I really believed it was him tonight, when you woke us up. I mean, deep down inside. Or I could have, if I'd let myself. But I just wanted to get out of the woods and — and — oh, I don't know" (*PC* 147). The child who used to run and throw her arms around the great lion has become ashamed to look at him and functions as an antagonist by resisting Aslan's leadership and denying Lucy's vision. In this, her last visit to Narnia, Susan's relationship with Aslan is so damaged that she gradually stops believing in Narnia at all and is not present in the eucatastrophic ending of the series that reunites all the positive characters in Aslan's kingdom. Her disobedience, like Eve's, has cost her happiness, and though redemption is possible as long as she lives on in the "old" England, the damage is still deep.[13]

While Lewis's depictions of evil often seem only natural and logical, it should be noted that he was, and sometimes still is, frequently cited for including material that was too scary or intense. Like other popular fantasy writers, such as Lewis's colleague Tolkien and literary proteges including J. K. Rowling, Madeline L'Engle, Lloyd Alexander, and Stephen Lawhead, he faced criticism despite the moral and literary value of his work: "They claim that the Narnian battles and wicked characters frighten children and give them nightmares." Lewis, who had suffered night terrors himself, was fiercely set against creating anything likely to traumatize a child, but he believed a sound killing of a wicked villain was far less damaging to a child's psyche than the popular stories which develop dangerously unlikely fantasies about the downtrodden schoolboy who wins the pretty girl, the big game, and the whole school's admiration. In the essay "On Three Ways of Writing for Children" Lewis explained the far greater danger of "realistic stories":

> It [fantasy literature] is accused of giving children a false impression of the world they live in. But I think no literature that children could read gives them less of a false impression. I think what profess to be realistic stories for children are far more likely to deceive them. I never expected the real world to be like the fairy tales. I think that I did expect school to be like the school stories. The fantasies did not deceive me: the school stories did, All stories in which children have adventures and successes which are possible, in the sense that they did not break the laws of nature, but almost infinitely improbable, are in more danger than the fairy tales of raising false expectations.

Despite his relatively scant experience with real children, or perhaps because of it, Lewis never doubted his reader's intelligence in discerning reality from his sort of fantasy. He knew that dragons and fauns were unabashedly fantastic, and therefore not misleading:

> No one can deceive you unless he makes you think he is telling the truth. The unblushingly romantic has far less power to deceive than the apparently realistic. Admitted fantasy is precisely the kind of literature which never deceives at all. Children are not deceived by fairy tales; they are often and gravely deceived by school-stories. Adults are not deceived by science-fiction; they can be deceived by the stories in the women's magazines.

One can safely imagine what his reaction would be to the violent and nihilistic entertainments to which later generations of children have been subjected: games and films that celebrate, rather than defeat evil, and which conjure far more frightening and dangerous fantasies than slaying a monster with a sword. By including a depiction of evil that is frightening, unattractive, and yet seductive even to the strongest of protagonists, he also echoes Milton and Spenser. All three authors, in the telling of their tales, must include adversaries for their protagonists. No villain will ever make anyone completely happy or completely scared enough to be satisfactory. Writers continue to walk the thin line between making an adversary frightening enough to be believable, yet safe enough to be defeated by the protagonists in the end, and evil enough not to be attractive to the reader:

> Lewis had to face the problem of creating evil characters for his
> stories without making them attractive. He does this by making them
> ludicrous like Uncle Andrew and Jadis in *The Magician's Nephew* ... or
> increasingly unhappy like ... Edmund in *The Lion, the Witch, and the
> Wardrobe*. On the other hand, by keeping evil from being attractive,
> Lewis must also avoid making it trivial, downplaying its force and
> pervasiveness. This he does by showing not only how widespread and
> damaging it is, but also how strangely natural evil can become, how
> criminal behavior gradually dulls moral sensibilities.

This dilemma is dealt with similarly by Lewis and his predecessors, all of whom drew their villains as both physically and spiritually threatening, a reminder that the protagonists of these texts do not in fact, war against enemies of merely flesh and blood. Milton and Spenser, with their embodiments of sin, deception, and the devil himself, place their protagonists in opposition to forces that at once are corporeal and threatening, as well as representational of all that is wrong and spiritually harmful in one's pursuit of completeness and goodness. In addition, Duessa, Jadis, and Satan all have a sort of seductive power about them, reminding us how easy it is to become ensnared in evil that looks beautiful. Despite this power, "Lewis makes it clear ... that the power of evil is inferior to the power of good." Evil may be appealing, but in the end, it is revealed, by all of these authors, to be the ultimate form of weakness.[14]

In addition, Spenser includes a host of knights who, as very physical combatants, provide foils for the protagonists to defeat. Lewis also creates foes like the Telmarines and the Calormenes who, in their spiritually inferior condition, are defeated by Aslan and his followers. All three authors recognize that one of the dangers of confronting spiritual foes is the possibility of being drawn into the morass of evil these foes represent. When Adam and Eve are completely turned against God, they exhibit a whole catalogue of Satanic traits: deception, selfishness, and pride. Redcrosse as well, in his succumbing to pride and despair, serves the purposes of his enemy rather than those of his queen and of his lady. Lewis's Susan, by turning away from her first love of Narnia and Aslan, gives in to selfishness and pride, while Edmund and Eustace, like Redcrosse, are able to discover better selves after straying into their most negative possibilities and undergoing painful transformation.

By drawing from his predecessors, Lewis's antagonists serve their proper purposes within the context of the novels. They also reach beyond their own stories, ringing with the power of precedent, archetype, and the reminder that evil, in Faerie Land, Paradise, Narnia, and life, can come from within or without; though it might appear as harmless as a gentle lady or an old man, evil has lasting consequences.

# III

---

## Girls Whose Heads Have Something Inside Them: The Characterization of Women

"That's the worst of girls," said Edmund to Peter and the Dwarf. "They can never carry a map in their heads."

"That's because our heads have something inside them," said Lucy.

— *Prince Caspian* 114–115

In *Studies in Medieval and Renaissance Literature*, Lewis insisted that, until the early twentieth century, *The Faerie Queene* was "everyone's poem." This accessibility, in some way, is most certainly indebted to the characters that people Faerie Land. Readers who cannot scan the first line of the first canto are still comfortably at home with the knights, ladies, monsters, and spiritual guides of Spenser's magnum opus. Milton's characters, coming directly from the sacred text of two of the world's major religions, need no qualification for their staying power. In the *Chronicles of Narnia*, as well as in *Paradise Lost* and *The Faerie Queene*, the female characters are often the most interesting. Yet Milton, Spenser, and Lewis all have been criticized for their depiction of women. A careful examination of the texts not only reveals the influence *The Faerie Queene* and *Paradise Lost* had on the *Chronicles'* females; it also becomes apparent that the female characters of Narnia are remarkable as well for their variety of roles and duties.[1]

Female characters — human, Narnian, and otherwise — are crucial to Narnia: "In each story the team always includes at least one boy and one girl. Narnia was not created for the interest of one sex alone." In the various roles Lewis assigns them, his female characters fulfill duties as diverse as catalysts, leaders, healers, rulers, and warriors. All these roles show the influence of both *Paradise Lost* and *The Faerie Queene*. In addition, these sources come into play in the depiction of females in more traditional roles. These varied and sometimes surprising roles reveal the freedom Lewis gives to his female characters and the ways in which such interesting individuals combat sexism and stereotyping in the *Chronicles* and their predecessors. For in their varied capacities throughout the *Chronicles*, Lewis's female characters, like many of those who influenced them, demonstrate that girls' heads actually have quite a bit inside them.[2]

*The Faerie Queene, Paradise Lost,* and the *Chronicles* all stem from the tradition of New Testament Christianity, so it is not surprising that they reflect the same importance the Bible gives to women. Although the biblical tradition is often interpreted as casting a woman as the instrument of humanity's destruction, the scriptures also credit a woman as the instrument of humanity's redemption. The New Testament equivalent of Eve, Mary, is the catalyst through which God redeems women as well as humanity in general. As both positive and negative figures, women, as well as non-human females, are important to the *Chronicles* as well. Certainly, the powerful enchantresses who initiate the action of *The Lion, The Witch and the Wardrobe, The Silver Chair,* and *The Magician's Nephew* are vital to the texts, even though they are negative forces. The entire series, however, began with a little girl and a large wardrobe. Of all the images in the series, perhaps none is so enduring as that of Lucy stepping into a perfectly ordinary object that magically transports her to a perfectly extraordinary other reality. Some critics are intent upon over-allegorizing and deconstructing Lucy's role in the *Chronicles*, even going so far as to equate her with the Virgin Mary: "We do not need to read far to discover that in the figure of this little girl we have an icon.... Her attitude, upon reflection, reminds us of a young girl in our own story who...said, 'Be it unto me according to your word.'" Lewis actually was strongly opposed to such algebraic, a=b, allegorizing. Lucy, rather than a carbon copy of another character, biblical or otherwise, is at once an amalgam of characteristics from a variety of sources, particularly Spenser and Milton. Rather than specifically representing the Virgin Mary, she is far more similar to the many individuals whom the Gospel writers depict in their experiences with the Savior. Like them, Lucy is fascinated by what she has discovered and longs to share it with those she loves, only to be faced with their unbelief. She remains an authentic little English girl who wants to show her discovery to her siblings and who is crushed when they don't believe her: "It's — it's a magic wardrobe. There's a wood inside it, and it's snowing, and there's a Faun and a witch and it's called Narnia; come and see" (*LWW* 21). Thus begin the adventures in the wardrobe. Though it takes a few tries to get the others to Narnia, without Lucy, the events of *The Lion, the Witch and the Wardrobe* could not transpire. Lewis's secretary, Walter Hooper, found "on the back of another manuscript of another book he was writing at this time [1939, when Lewis was hosting refugee children from London]," this passage:

> This book is about four children whose names were Ann, Martin, Rose, and Peter. But it is most about Peter who was the youngest. They all had to go away from London suddenly because of Air Raids, and because Father, who was in the Army, had gone off to the War and Mother was doing some kind of war work.

While Peter is the only one of the four names that Lewis kept, he moved Peter to a different position, both in the family order and in the story. If he was already planning to make the other brother a traitor, then "Martin" is an apt choice, indicating a slinking, untrustworthy fellow. If the second sister, Rose, was much like Lucy, her name is also an appropriate precursor to Lucy as she develops in the later manuscripts. Peter is a vital character, and becomes the High King over his siblings, yet it is Lucy through whose eyes we see Narnia. The youngest child remained the protagonist, but was recast as Lucy. This crucial decision indicates Lewis's willingness to place a female character in a central role that could just as easily have been played by a male character. She is the catalyst of the series, appearing in all seven *Chronicles,* although sometimes briefly or mentioned only in passing. In fact, "Lucy, lighthearted and golden-haired (although the illustrator always makes her hair black) is perhaps the most prominent human being in the entire series ... and is used by Lewis frequently as the central intelligence." Even in *The Magician's Nephew*, set years before her birth, she receives acknowledgment with hints of her eventual "discovery" of Narnia. Lucy's first arrival in Narnia is foreshadowed by an explanation that the lamp-post, which Jadis inadvertently plants, is the one Lucy finds hundreds of years later. Her transport through the wardrobe is also referenced by the description of the tree that grows from the core of the apple Aslan sends home with Digory: "For when Digory was quite middle aged there was a great storm all over the south of England which blew the tree down, so he had part pf the timber made into a wardrobe ... he himself did not discover the magic properties of that wardrobe[;] someone else did" (185). This catalyst quality has some resemblance to Eve's role in bringing about the action of *Paradise Lost*. However, unlike Eve, Lucy is generally a catalyst for good.[3]

Like the female characters of *The Faerie Queene*, Lucy is often the figure who sets events in motion. Numerous quests, adventures, and rescues in Spenser's epic are precipitated by a female seeking aid for herself or others: from the fleeing Florimell with pursuers hot on her horse's heels in Book III, to the mistreated messenger/ lady-in-waiting Samient in Book V. Lucy's character includes a number of traits that link her to the first and, arguably, the most appealing of these women, Book I's Una. Redcrosse's lady, the very embodiment of truth, is ignored by Redcrosse when she warns him of Errour, and she is subsequently the victim of falsehood in the second canto of Book I. Lucy, as well, is described as "a very truthful girl" (*LWW* 22). Yet her siblings seriously doubt her discovery of Narnia and even doubt her sanity: "'We were afraid it mightn't even be lying,' said Susan. 'We thought there might be something wrong with Lucy'" (*LWW* 44). Like Redcrosse, they doubt a person who is truth itself because of what their senses indicate as reality. Redcrosse, never thinking that he might be mistaken, immediately believes his eyes when the false Una attempts to seduce him "to learne Dame pleasures toy" (I.i.47.9) and when she and the sprite squire are "discovered" in a compromising position of "wanton lust and lewd embracement" (I.ii.5.5). Likewise, when Lucy's brothers and sister look in the wardrobe and see its back, with hooks on it, they believe she must have been lying because "if things are real, they're there all the time" (*LWW* 45). Despite the fact that Lucy, by her very nature, does not lie, Peter and Susan think she cannot be truthful about Narnia because their perception of reality conflicts with her words. Likewise, in spite of his knowledge of Una's purity and honesty, Redcrosse's distorted perception of reality leads him to "thinke that gentle Dame so light" (I.i.55.2). While their companions seem easily led astray by these paradoxes, both Una and Lucy seem to adjust to paradox and to accept that things are not always what they seem. Though others do not always believe them, both Una and Lucy share the truth, even when what is true and what is real appear to be at odds.[4]

For both characters, the role of truth teller is seldom an easy one, especially against the force of loved ones' disbelief. However, even when they are not believed or when they are actually abandoned, Una and Lucy are both crucial to the plots of their stories, as well as to the spiritual development of other characters. Una is the instigator of Redcrosse's adventures, by bringing him to slay the dragon; thus, she shares the hero's role in the rescue of her family. Lucy is always concerned with others, particularly in their relationships with Aslan: "'Please — Aslan,' said Lucy, 'Can anything be done to save Edmund?'" (*LWW* 124). Her brother has lied to and about her, and has gone so far as to betray her and siblings to the White Witch, who certainly plans to kill them. Though Edmund might have convinced himself that the Witch's empty promises are true, Lucy knows better. She knows that her brother's treachery has caused her devoted friend Mr. Tumnus to be caught, and perhaps killed; and that if the Witch succeeds, she and her siblings will die or be turned to stone, all stemming from Edmund's poor judgment. Yet she is the first to plead his case to Aslan, to request clemency for him before he is actually rescued. Her compassion for Tumnus, who had originally planned to hand her over to his employer, the White Witch, is similarly remarkable and leads the Pevensies to the Faun's destroyed cave and further adventures. Tumnus though, unlike Edmund, had at least asked her pardon for his planned crime against her: "Her loving nature displays itself in her kind treatment of the faun [Tumnus] after his repentant confession that he had planned to turn her over to the White Witch." She forgives Edmund even before he asks her forgiveness. When the dwarfs of *The Last Battle* are so stuck in their twisted perception of reality that they cannot enjoy the beauty of Aslan's Country, it is Lucy who feels compassion for the deluded creatures, long after everyone else has grown exasperated and given up on them: "'Aslan,' said Lucy through her tears, 'could you — will you — do something for these poor Dwarfs?'" (*LB* 146). By firmly adhering to the truth she knows, Lucy is the catalyst for Narnia's rescue, not once, but twice. In *The Lion, the Witch and the Wardrobe*, of course, Lucy's entrance through the wardrobe facilitates the freeing of Narnia, the dissolution of the Witch's spell, and the Golden Age of Narnia. In *Prince Caspian*, Lucy, the one who "sees Aslan the most," is also the one who first catches sight of the great Lion; through her determination and her unquestioning belief in Aslan, she helps the others to see him as well:

> "I can see him all the time," said Lucy. "He's looking straight at us."
> "Then why can't I see him?"
> "He said you mightn't be able to."
> "Why?"
> "I don't know. That's what he said" [*PC* 140].

Her strict adherence to her belief in Aslan causes her discomfort and a degree of unhappiness, but by following Aslan so devotedly, Lucy leads her brothers and Trumpkin the Dwarf to the aid of Prince Caspian and his army in their darkest hour, while she and Susan participate in the wild romp that frees Narnia from the restrictive and joyless rule of the Telmarines.[5]

While neither Una nor Lucy physically takes a large role in combat, both bring knights to the rescue of their countries. Peter becomes a knight and the High King over all Kings in Narnia, but he must first be led to his destiny and to his climactic battle with the White Witch by Lucy, for it is she, not he, who discovers Narnia, and he defers to her knowledge and experience, declaring: "I think Lu ought to be the leader. Where will you take us, Lu?" (*LWW* 53). Una, rather than attempting some sort of attack herself on the dragon that menaces her family, brings in reinforcements — Redcrosse. Instead of playing roles of undeveloped damsels in distress, both Lucy and Una are strong characters who, even when separated from their knightly protectors, survive quite successfully. Interestingly, both characters, while isolated from their fellow protagonists, are protected by goat-men and lions.

Certainly the urbane and civil faun Mr. Tumnus bears little resemblance to the rough and wild fauns and satyrs who gather around Una and "do kisse her feete, and fawne on her with countenence faine" (I.vi.12.9). The image, however, is still strikingly similar: a lone female, lost in the forest and being cared for by the half-goat, half-man creatures. The attitudes of these strange caretakers are also remarkably parallel. While Spenser's satyrs believe Una must be "Goddesse of the wood" (I.vi.16.9), Mr. Tumnus is deeply impressed that Lucy is a human, for humans, in the Faun's experience, are mythical creatures, as his library suggests: "On one wall was a shelf full of books.... They had titles like ... *Men, Monks and Gamekeepers; a Study in Popular Legend* or *Is Man a Myth?*" (*LWW* 12). Both Una and Lucy also face a potential threat from their goaty friends. Satyrs, throughout *The Faerie Queene*, are depicted as sexually rapacious and treacherous. Both Satyrane's mother and Hellenore become love-slaves, willing or otherwise, to their "beastly kind" (I.vi.22.9). Apparently only Una's remarkable nature protects her from the potential dark side of her rescuers, who soon become her pupils and devoted followers while she is "Teaching the Satyres, which her sat around/ Trew sacred lore" (I.iv.30.8–9). Similarly, it is Lucy's character that dissuades Tumnus from turning her over to the White Witch as he has been ordered: "Of course I can't give you up to the Witch; not now that I know you" (*LWW* 18). It is Lucy's character, not Tumnus's, that shows him he cannot fulfill the Witch's directive. Though the circumstances do differ slightly, there are clear parallels. In fact, the image of a faun carrying his packages in the snow had been with Lewis since his late teens — around the time he had read *The Faerie Queene*.[6]

The lion protector is a less closely paralleled figure. Again, the visual impression is almost identical, but Una's guardian lion and Aslan are only alike in their forms; they are quite different in their essential natures. Some of the details of each lion are concurrent. However, what really adds to the characters of Una and Lucy is the ability to develop a relationship with such powerful creatures. While Una's lion is basically a regular tooth, claw, and mane feline, he is frightening and powerful, completely mauling Kirkrapine. Her ability to subdue and earn the loyalty of this creature is a result of who she is, rather than of the beast's nature. Aslan, too, is a figure of power, though his power goes far beyond his physical ability, as Mr. Beaver explains in *The Lion, the*

*Witch and the Wardrobe:* "If there's anyone who can appear before Aslan without their knees knocking, they're either braver than most or else just silly" (*LWW* 75). Lucy, while duly awed and humbled before Aslan, is also physically close to him: "He was solid and real and warm and he let her kiss and bury herself in his shining mane. And from the low, earthquake-like sound that came from inside him, Lucy even dared to think that he was purring" (*VDT* 135). No one understands Aslan as Lucy does; she even understands his moods, sensing when he is about to roar, growl, or even laugh, and she is clearly "the one who loved Aslan the most." Like Una, it is Lucy's personality, her spirit, that connects her to a creature that makes others quake.[7]

Part of this power possessed by both women is most certainly spiritual. Both Una and Lucy are potent spiritual forces. Lucy's spirituality partially stems from the fact that she is a child, like the biblical little children of which the kingdom of Heaven is made. However, none of the other children in the *Chronicles* have the same depth and joy she possesses. In addition, she retains her innocence and closeness to Aslan all of her life. In Aslan's Country, it is the adult Lucy who is "drinking everything in more deeply than the others" (*LB* 141). Lewis also places in her mouth perhaps the most profound statement in the entire series. In *The Last Battle*, she approaches the conundrum of the stable door that leads to Aslan's Country with spiritual clarity: "In our world, too, a Stable once had something inside it that was bigger than our whole world" (*LB* 141). Una, too, knows the importance of silence as well as the value of well-selected words. In the first canto of Book I, she warns Redcrosse of the danger of Errour's cave. Rather than scolding him when he gets in trouble despite her warnings, she gives him valuable advice on how to destroy the beast: "Strangle her, else she sure will strangle thee" (I.i.19.4). Through their meaningful and often spiritually profound words, both Lucy and Una are quietly powerful forces.

Both women are also catalysts for the spiritual redemption of other characters. Their very names ring with the power of their spiritual identities. Una, Latin for "one," echoes the single truth she exemplifies and the single nature of who she is. Unlike the proverbially two-faced Duessa, Una is all she seems. Though she is veiled, she is not deceptive. There is no shadow to her. Likewise, "Lucy" — from "luce" or light — is brightness, and in her also there is illumination, not darkness. Even when Lucy struggles, or actually fails, she always returns to the truth and the light her name embodies. Spenser also features a minor character named Lucy in Book V. Although the sweetheart of Amidas is far less developed than Una, in her brief appearance, it is clear she has much in common with Lucy Pevensie. Amidas describes her as "bright" as her name would imply, and states that " To [her] but little dowre allotted was;/ Her verte was the dowre, that did delight" (V.iv.9.3–4). This maiden is also rejected by her first fiancé, Bracidas, when he meets the deceptive and over-bold Philtera, fresh from breaking her engagement with his brother Amidas whose material wealth had decreased. Like Lewis's Lucy, although abandoned and sometimes mistreated, Spenser's Lucy becomes an instrument of blessing. Even in her broken-hearted attempt to drown herself, she is blessed with the discovery of treasure, a better man to love her, and her life. Interestingly, her discovery is a wooden chest which appears perfectly ordinary on the outside, but, when opened, reveals a great treasure. Though this character only appears in a few stanzas of *The Faerie Queene,* and Lewis evidently named his Lucy after his goddaughter Lucy Barfield, there is still the distinct possibility that Book V's Lucy had a role in the creation of the little girl who steps through a seemingly plain and ordinary wardrobe and finds herself inside the remarkable treasure of Narnia.

In addition to Una, Lucy also reflects the influence of the other catalytic female character of *The Faerie Queene,* Gloriana herself. Both are queens and, like Lucy's, Gloriana's reign brings a Golden Age. Even more similar, however, is the fact that even when Gloriana and Lucy are not taking part in the action of their stories, they still influence the other characters. The knights and all their adventures stem from the Faerie Queene's court, just as the events of the *Chronicles,* both before and after Lucy's entering Narnia, revolve around the moment when she stands underneath the lamppost, realizing she is in another world:

> The lamp-post which the Witch had planted (without knowing it) shone day and night in the Narnian forest, so that the place where it grew came to be called Lantern Waste; and when, hundreds of years later, another child from our world got into Narnia, on a snowy night, she found the light still burning. And that adventure was, in a way, connected with the ones I have just been telling you [*MN* 184].

Even when Lucy and Gloriana are not present, their importance as catalysts clearly ties them to the action taking place.

While Lucy, Una, and the elusive Gloriana serve as spiritual guides, female characters in Narnia also serve as actual guides. The forest woman is a fascinating figure who makes appearances both in Narnia and in Faerie Land. In *The Faerie Queene*, Spenser's Belphoebe takes on the role of guide. As adopted daughter of Diana, Belphoebe is completely at home in the forest, hunting game and rescuing injured passers-by. In Narnia, it is Jill who is the forest guardian, leading Tirian to exclaim: "This girl is a wondrous wood-maid. If she had Dryad's blood in her she could scarce do it better" (*LB* 59). In this role, both Belphoebe and Jill reflect the almost mystical connections between femininity and nature that are more strongly echoed in mythology that casts females as protectors and spirits of the forest. Both specific classical figures, such as Diana and Demeter, as well as generic nymphs and sprites, reflect this theme. Like Belephoebe, who scorns Timias for tending to Amoret (although Belphoebe herself has no intention of returning Timias's affection for her) and often treats others with indifference, "Jill has a tendency to look down on anyone who does not possess her talents." In *The Silver Chair*, it is Jill's scorn of Eustace and his fear of heights that sets their adventure off on the wrong foot, but both Jill and Belphoebe mean well and wish to use their forest skills for good. Milton's Eve also has traces of the female forest guardian in her care of Eden's plants and her natural ease with all of creation, but Belphoebe and Jill both have stronger connections to the maidenly huntress Diana while incorporating their own unique but linked characteristics.[8]

Belphoebe, like Una, is a healer as a well as a guide. Belphoebe's rescue of Timias from the brink of death and Una's rescue of Redcrosse from death's door are both similar to the power given Lucy through her magic cordial: "He gave her a little bottle of what looked like glass (but people said afterwards that it was made of diamond).... 'If you or any of your friends are hurt, a few drops of this will restore you'" (*LWW* 104–105). Lucy's cordial bottle, in fact, is almost identical to the gift Arthur gives Una and Redcrosse: "Prince Arthur gave a box of diamond sure,/ Embowed with gold and gorgeous ornament,/ Wherein were closd few drops of liquor pure,/ Or wonderous worth, and vertue excellent,/ That any wound could heal incontinent" (I.ix.19.1–5). When Arthur finds the bedraggled and injured Amoret "Eftsoones that pretious liqour forth he drew,/ Which he in store about him kept alway,/ And with few drops thereof did softly dew/ Her wounds, that vnto strength returned her soone anew" (IV.viii.20.6–9). Belphoebe specifically uses "costly Cordialles" (III.v.50.4) to heal Timias, and Cambell, in Book IV, is given by his sister Canacee "a ring which she him sent,/ That mongst the manie vertues,/ Had power to staunch al wounds, that mortally did bleed" (IV.ii.39.7–8). Clearly the ability to heal wounds is an important characteristic that Spenser often ties to females and to royal personages, and Lewis follows suit by placing in Lucy's hands the precious cordial. The cordial is returned to her when she comes back to Narnia in *Prince Caspian*. The diamond bottle remains safe in the storehouse beneath the ruin of Cair Paravel for centuries, waiting for its former owner, and when Lucy, along with Edmund and Eustace, arrives in the middle of Narnia's eastern sea, Caspian has brought the cordial along on his adventures and returns it to Lucy since it is rightfully hers. However, once Lucy is told that she can never return to Narnia, the cordial vanishes. Although surely anyone could use it, no one else ever does. It is so linked to her character that it only appears when she does.

Although Arthur, with his own magic cordial, is most certainly male, ministering spirits in *The Faerie Queene* as well as in *Paradise Lost* and *The Chronicles of Narnia* are more frequently female characters. One of the most unconventional of these is Mrs. Beaver of *The Lion, the Witch and the Wardrobe*. Although she is an animal, Mrs. Beaver is also a ministering spirit who embodies the homey and soul-warming characteristics of the ladies of Spenser's House of Holiness and the down-to earth realism of an English farm wife. When the children and Mr. Beaver are panicking and ready to make a hasty retreat from the White Witch, it is Mrs. Beaver who remembers blankets and food for their journey. As she later reminds them, "'If you hadn't all been in such a plaugey fuss when we were starting, I'd have brought some pillows'" (99). Though she may seem to be criticizing the children and Mr. Beaver, she is genuinely concerned with their well-being and comfort and remains calm and practical even in the face of great danger. Her character is a comforter without being overbearing or patronizing.

The power to heal and to help is also linked to the power to create. In *A Preface to Paradise Lost*, Lewis emphasizes the fact that Milton's Eve is an artist: "Such impress as art had made on the beauty of paradise is largely hers." It is she who tends the "thick woven arborets and flow'rs/ embordered on each bank" (IX.436–7). Even the meal she creates for Raphael, though it consists only of fruits, is truly an artistic achievement, which she accentuates by strewing "the ground/ with rose and odors from the shrub" (V.348–9) in the performance of her divinely appointed role as hostess. Thus creativity and art are closely linked to femininity. Polly, in *The Magician's Nephew*, creates a Smuggler's Cave in her attic. The fact that an Edwardian little girl has created a hideaway generally relegated to masculine pursuits is revealing. Smuggler's Caves are, at least in most children's literature, usually created and inhabited by boys. Polly thus exhibits an imagination unlimited by restrictive gender roles. Even more interesting is the story Polly has written, which she will not let Digory see. Like a true artist, she is creating for the sake of creating, not for showing off, just as Eve's art is created effortlessly, and without emphasis on audience. Even her elaborate feast for Raphael is without pomp, springing naturally from an imagination drawn to art.[9]

One of the most delightful roles both Lewis and Spenser assign to women is the role of instigators and decision makers in their romantic relationships. While the fairy tale format implies the need for a woman to marry a man who rescues her or does some service for her kingdom, both Spenser and Lewis have knights in distress, as well as damsels requiring assistance and rescues are effected by both male and female characters. Amoret, perhaps the most pathetic literary damsel in distress ever, is actually rescued by the female knight Britomart, who goes on to rescue a variety of other female and male characters, including her own fiancé, Artegall. Likewise, the lost prince, Rilian, is rescued by Jill and Eustace. Roles of rescuer and prisoner are thus not defined by limits of male and female, knight and lady, or even adult and child. Although Caspian attempts to impress and woo Ramandu's beautiful daughter with fairy tale rhetoric, she reminds him that she is free to make a choice: "Here he cannot kiss the Princess till he has dissolved the enchantment" (*VDT* 174). One of the clear indications that Calormen's Prince Rabadash is a villain is his unsuccessful attempt to override Susan's right of marital choice by kidnapping her and invading her country. As a free Narnian, Susan has the prerogative to choose her own spouse, but Rabadash plans to take her by force if she will not willingly be his. He wants her, though he also despises her for her freedom and for being a "barbarian." He wants to acquire and subdue her rather than love and cherish her. As far as Rabadash is concerned, Susan's volition is meaningless, for only his wants and desires matter, and he is part of a culture in which women, as well as girls like Aravis, are forced to marry against their wishes: "the position of women in Calormen is ... that of property." It is in Narnia that "no maiden is forced to marry against her will" (*HHB* 36). Spenser also incorporates a woman's right to choose her heart's desire and presents negative characters who attempt to circumvent a woman's free will. Britomart literally chases Artegall until she catches her, and Amoret's refusal to give her love without her consent is the motivation for Busirane's torture. While the abuse of Amoret, both physical and psychological, is far more violent than the attempted kidnapping and imprisonment of Queen Susan, the fact that both Busirane and Rabadash are thwarted emphasizes both Spenser's and Lewis's endorsement of the right of a woman to choose her own spouse. Susan's choice is even more exemplary of her freedom because she has no other lover, such as Amoret's Scudamour, to whom she must be true. Susan is simply asserting her right to say to Rabadash's suit, "Nay... not for all the jewels in Tashbaan" (*HHB* 61). Female characters in the *Chronicles* do not have to get married simply because a male is readily available, or because he has done her some service. Aravis's desire to flee an intolerable arranged marriage leads to her friendship with Shasta, but Lewis emphasizes the fact that they get married to argue with one another more conveniently, not because Aravis is Shasta's prize or because she is grateful to him. She has gained her freedom, for which she travels to Archenland in the first place, and she is not to be traded about as chattel as she would have been in her father's house: "the balanced handling of their [Shasta's and Aravis's] stories illustrates that Lewis does not intend to say that freedom is a matter of geography and race (or sex). It is a state of mind that grows out of fortitude and expresses itself in respect for all other individuals." Shasta and Aravis become first unwilling allies, and later, friends, on their journey, an experience that denies either of them superiority. By the end of the novel Shasta exhibits no male superiority, and Aravis has lost her class snobbery toward him, even before she discovers his true identity. Although Bree and Hwin are the equine counterparts of Shasta and Aravis, they "both got married, but not to one another" (*HHB* 216), a logical plot development since the two horses seem far less compatible than their two riders. Unlike Shakespeare, whose comedy endings often force all the single characters to pair off into a mass wedding, regardless of how well-matched they are, Lewis allows his horses to have free will. Lewis also takes Spenser's idea of a woman's right to a choice one step further. Spenser's women generally choose between two men. Lewis's female characters can choose to refuse marriage even when there is no alternate spouse in the wings, and both Lucy and Susan, as queens of Narnia in their mid-twenties, do not marry, though they have numerous suitors.[10]

Surprisingly, this matter of choice is one that Milton also endorses, though less blatantly. Although Adam is, literally, the only man on earth, Eve still has a choice to accept him or not. Adam must woo her, declaring her "Part of my soul" (IV.487). Eve, of her own accord, yields to Adam's suit. Though she is meant to be Adam's mate, she has the opportunity to either accept or reject this role, and he must plead his case before he, the lord of Eden, can claim his lady. Thus their relationship begins with partnership and respect, rather than creating a situation in which Adam feels Eve is his property.

The fact that all three texts feature females who are royalty adds to the roles they must play as well. Throughout the *Chronicles*, Lewis depicts a number of female royals, and all bear the stamp of Milton's and Spenser's influence. Certainly the British monarchy, as it appeared during Lewis's lifetime, also affected his depiction of the Narnian royals. Lewis missed Elizabeth II's coronation because of foul weather and his aversion to large crowds, but his comment about the coronation is deeply indicative of his feeling toward monarchs in general: "The pressure of that heavy crown on that small young head becomes a sort of symbol of the situation of humanity itself ... humanity called by God to be his vice-gernet [sic] and high priest on earth." Although Lewis missed that coronation, it is likely that he saw, either in person or in photographs, Elizabeth's father, George VI, being crowned in 1937, since Lewis claimed he approved "of that sort of thing immensely." At that coronation, he would have seen the Princesses Elizabeth and Margaret, young girls with crowns on their heads. It would be doubtful if these moments and Lewis's immense approval of pageantry did not affect his creation of the queens and princesses in the *Chronicles*. In fact, there is almost an eerie resemblance to the way Elizabeth and Margaret appeared at their father's coronation and the way in which Lewis depicts the coronation of Lucy, Susan, and their brothers. Lucy and Susan would be about the same ages as the young princesses, and the regal formality of the Narnian coronation reflects the traditional patterns of British coronations: "Aslan solemnly crowned them and led them onto the four thrones.... So the children sat in their thrones and sceptres were put into their hands and they gave rewards and honours" (*LWW* 179). Pageantry, too, is a crucial part of *The Faerie Queene*. One of the most striking passages of such pageantry is the marriage celebration of Una and Redcrosse, led by "shaumes, and trompets, and with Clarions sweet" (I.xii.13.2) and including "meates and drinks of every kinde" (I.xii.15.1). The scene clearly finds resonance in the coronation of the Pevensies "to the sound of trumpets" followed by "a great feast and revelry and dancing" (*LWW* 179). However, although these external ceremonies are important to queenship in Lewis and in his sources, the internal characteristics of royal women are even more important.[11]

Courtly behavior, or courtesy, receives a whole book of *The Faerie Queene* and runs as a current through *Paradise Lost*. In the *Chronicles*, courtesy is both subtle and powerful in the characterizations of female royalty. It is clear from Lewis's characters that queens, such as Lucy, Susan, and Aravis, all adhere to certain standards of behavior. In *A Preface to Paradise Lost*, Lewis emphasizes the queenliness of Eve, "a great lady, doing the honours of her own house, the matriarch of the world." Since King Lune is a widower, Lucy takes on the role of "Lady of the house" as she plays hostess at Anvard. When Lucy returns to Narnia, although she is a child again, her royalty and the subsequent necessity of treating her royally are both clear: "'Little girl!' said Reepicheep. 'The lady is a queen'" (*VDT* 117). Although females in Narnia sometimes snipe and grumble, they are still queens, as Aslan declares: "Once a king or queen in Narnia, always a king or queen" (*LWW* 179*).* Their nobility becomes part of their identities.[12]

Aravis, Lucy, and Susan are all presented as young girls who grow up to be queens. One of the series's most regal characters is one of the few positive individuals who first appears as a full-grown adult. Caspian's wife, daughter of the star Ramandu, is a character almost entirely described by her roles as "great lady" and queen. She has no proper name and is referred to only as "Ramandu's daughter," "the Lady," "Caspian's Queen," "the Queen," or "Rilian's mother." While this namelessness has elicited criticism for Lewis, the Lady, by her various titles of honor, importance, and relationship, becomes even more closely associated with the nobility and royalty she embodies: "They all rose to their feet, because they felt that she was a great lady" (*VDT* 172). Similarly, Spenser's House of Holiness is home to female characters whose names, proper though they may be, are also idealized identifications of the virtues they represent. Interestingly, Speranza is the one of the three who, in appearance, most clearly resembles the Star's daughter: "Her younger sister, that Speranza hight,/ Was clad in blew, that her beseemed well" (I.x.14.1–2); Ramandu's daughter is "a tall girl, dressed in a single long garment of blue which left her arms bare" (*VDT* 171). In addition to the similar colors, Speranza, or hope, carries an anchor. This symbol would also be appropriate for the Star's Daughter, who lives on an island accessible only to sailors and gives the crew of the *Dawn Treader* hope of sailing to the world's edge and of breaking the enchantment that lies on the three sleeping Narnian lords. Ramandu's Daughter additionally fulfills characteristics of the other women of Spenser's House of Holiness, particularly Charissa, "a woman in her freshest age/ Of wondrous beauty, and of bountie rare/ With goodly grace and comely personage/ that was on earth not easy to compare" (I.x.30.1–4) who is surrounded by her many children. Like the embodiment of Charity, Ramandu's Daughter is a maternal figure who becomes a wife and "mother and grandmother of great kings" (*VDT* 216).

The character that Ramandu's Daughter most resembles, however, is Milton's unfallen Eve. Like Eve, the Lady is hostess over a fantastic feast: "And Eve within, due at her hour prepared/ For dinner savory fruits, of taste to please/ True appetite, and not disrelish thirst/ Of nectarous draughts between, from milky stream/ Berry or grape" (V.303–306). Ramandu's feast at Aslan's table, while more sophisticated than Eve's rural banquet, is more suited to the courtly palates being served:

> There were turkeys and geese and peacocks, there were boar's heads and sides of venison, there were pies shaped like ships under full sail or like dragons and elephants, there were ice puddings and bright lobsters and gleaming salmon, there were nuts and grapes, pineapples and peaches, pomegranates and melons and tomatoes" [*VDT* 166].

Aslan's table, set at his command and administered by a star and his daughter, is at least as supernatural as the feasts in Eden, hosted by the first human beings and attended by heavenly visitors. Even so, both Ramandu's Daughter and Eve are complete mistresses of their situations. Both women, though regal, are also remarkably free from pretension and keenly aware of their roles in the universe. Although Ramadu's Daughter is truly a great lady, for whom the Narnians rise in respect, she wears no elaborate crown or heavy robes, and Eve wears nothing at all, but both are described as regal and unashamed. In addition, both women recognize that, for all their greatness, they are the servants of larger forces. Both the Star's Daughter and Eve participate in similar early morning worship rituals. Eve and Adam "began/ their orisons, each morning duly paid prompt eloquence/ Flowed from their lips, in prose or numerous verse/ More tunable than needed lute or harp" (V.145–151). In much the same fashion, Ramandu and his daughter "held up their arms before them and turned to face the east. In that position they began to sing" (VDT 176). Though both women are noble, they also recognize the need to praise that which is greater than themselves.

As such great personages, it is not unusual that both Eve and the Star's Daughter are generally referred to by honorifics. Although Eve does have a first name, only after the fall does Adam use simply "Eve" to refer to her. In their unfallen condition, she is "Daughter of God and man, accomplished Eve" (IV.660); "Fair consort" (IV.610); and "Sole partner and sole part of all these joys" (IV.411). In their unfallen state, Adam treats her with the highest respect, only resorting to her unadorned name once they have both lost their glory and dignity through sin. Both Eve and the Star's Daughter are referred to as mothers of important generations. "Hail mother of mankind" (V.387) is very similar to Lewis's reference to the Lady's descendants. Both women, even after death, have a profound impact on their children. Eve, of course, brings with her the taint of original sin and passes it to her children and infinite grandchildren. When Rilian's mother is killed by the green worm, he is drawn into the web of seduction and sorcery that ensnares him for nearly ten years. Even the creature responsible for the demise of both Eve and Ramandu's Daughter is very similar. Although Eve is not killed instantly by the Satan-infested Serpent, the "bite" he gives her causes her mortality. Both serpents slink into the underbrush after completing their mission of destruction. In addition, both the fatal seduction of Eve and the death of Ramandu's Daughter take place during a floral occasion. Adam and Eve are attending to their gardening duties, while Rilian, his mother, and the courtiers are Maying. Both Rilian and Adam are brought back to stark reality by the serpent's destruction of the ones they love; Rilian and his courtiers wear leafy garlands in celebration of spring, and when they take their noisy conversations away from the sleeping Queen, she is attacked and dies "scarce ten minutes since they had heard her first cry" (*SC* 49). Adam's reaction is very similar when "From his slack hand the garland wreathed for Eve/ Down dropped, and all the faded roses shed" (IX.892–3). Both women, derived from immortal "fathers," God and a Star, are wrenched suddenly from the springtime of their lives into death, while the men who love them are left dazed, still accompanied by suddenly grotesque floral arrangements.

Perhaps the most unconventional role of women in the *Chronicles* is one that has a clear precedent in *The Faerie Queene*. The role of woman as warrior is a controversial one often depicted in literature. In many of these depictions, from Virgil to Shakespeare, female fighters are viragos or Amazons and must be killed or subdued in order to restore harmony to the plot. Spenser's virago, the Amazon Radigund, is an unsympathetic character who, angry over a man's resistance to her charms, "vow'd to doe all the ill/ Which she could do to Knights, which now she doth fulfill" (V.iv.30.8–9). Not only does she fight against men, but she also humiliates them, threatening them with death unless they will wear women's clothing and perform domestic tasks. Since she thus views female clothing and traditionally female tasks with contempt, as punishments for unworthy knights, Radigund is not actually glorifying her sex at all, but emphasizing a stereotype and denigrating both men and women. When she fights Artegall in single combat, he is taken by her beauty and spares her, though in the very act of preparing to strike off her head. Her response to his mercy is not gratitude, but violence, as she takes advantage of his hesitation, defeats him, humiliates him by dressing him in women's clothes, and forces him to "spin both flax and tow" (V.v.23.3). She is subsequently slain by Britomart, a female warrior with far more positive connotations. Spenser, setting a precedent for Lewis, incorporates many female warriors into his text who are neither destroyed nor tamed. In the *Chronicles*, Lewis's female characters often take part in the primarily male activity of waging war. In doing so, they reflect the influence of Spenser's female characters.[13]

In *The Lion, the Witch and the Wardrobe,* Father Christmas remarks that the bow he gives Susan and the dagger he gives Lucy are only for emergencies, since "battles are ugly when women fight" (105). While this comment has earned censure for Lewis as a sexist, it is important to remember that the voice in this passage is not Lewis's nor the narrator's, but Father Christmas's. As such, it is open to a variety of interpretations. Karla Faust Jones suggests that "Lewis could be likening Father Christmas to the secularization of Christianity, which, like the shopping mall culture in which it occurs, places limitations on women which are not ordained by God." In addition, Father Christmas, a figure closely linked with childhood, may be attempting to keep the girls children for just a little while longer. Clearly, the plot, as well as the narrative voice, does not support the claims of Father Christmas, since both Susan and Lucy, as well as other females, successfully take part in combat during the series. In fact, Lewis often puts women into the fray. His dryads and other female creatures are clearly engaged in battle. Lucy, in *The Horse and His Boy*, is no longer a child, but a young woman of twenty-two, "fair-haired ... with a very merry face who wore a helmet and mail shirt and carried a bow across her shoulders and a quiver of arrows at her side" (169–70). A backhanded compliment is paid Lucy by Prince Corin, who comments that she's as good in battle as a man, or at least a boy, instead of being ordinary (and, in Corin's opinion, rather boring) like her sister Susan (176). Of course, Corin is clearly depicted as an adolescent troublemaker with a sharp tongue and a penchant for picking fights and knocking people down, so his grudging accolades must be considered in light of his immaturity. Lucy is often placed in the role of leader, and her abilities exceed Corin's flippant description. She has no qualms about using her talents as a warrior and frequently employs her archery skills in battle. Even the honorific titles borne by Lucy and her sister, Susan, emphasize the difference in their priorities. Susan is "the Gentle" and Lucy, "the Valiant." Martial spirit, however, does not make Lucy masculine. Like Spenser's Belphoebe, she is capable of being tender-hearted and compassionate as well as fierce in battle. Her gifts, the cordial and the dagger, symbolize this duality in her character. She is both a healer and a fighter. Yet, rather than a paradox, the two sides of Lucy's nature reinforce Lewis's ideal of knighthood: gentle and meek in court, deadly in a fight. This well-rounded knight is also well illustrated in Spenser's Britomart, the knight ready to "steepe her dainty couch with tears" (III.ii.28.8–9) when she is upset, but in combat "him in the shield did smite/ With so fierce furie and great puissance,/ that through his three-square scuchin piercing quite" (III.iv.16.1–3). Lucy and Britomart are both set up as paragons within their texts, exemplifying important and valuable qualities that exceed the narrow roles that could have been assigned to female characters in their settings.[14]

Unlike Britomart, Lucy is never mistaken for a boy. This, in itself, is a reminder that Narnia is an equal opportunity country. Lucy has no need to mask her identity as Britomart does. She is welcomed in the army and praised for her soldiery. Britomart's disguise is not employed entirely because she will not be "allowed" to fight, but to conceal her journey from her father and for her own protection in a world that seems to be swarming with monsters, magicians, and rapacious men and satyrs. This same reasoning instigates the actions of Aravis, heroine of *The Horse and His Boy*. Like Britomart, Aravis is intentionally passing herself off for a boy when lions force her and her horse into accompanying Shasta and Bree. Once she speaks to Shasta, he realizes her true identity and, exposing his own ignorance, says she is "only" a girl (28). However, like Britomart, Aravis soon proves herself to be more than only a girl. She rides with skill that Shasta obviously envies, and she shows tremendous courage. In fact, she is so opposed to the marriage her father has arranged for her that she plans suicide as a viable option to her troubles. Her sensible mare Hwin dissuades her mistress from this course of action and encourages her to escape to Narnia where women are not forced to marry against their wills. In this action, Hwin is very similar to Britomart's nurse Glauce whose "chearefull words much cheard the feeble spright/ Of the sick virgin" (III.ii.47.1–2) and, when she fails in her attempts to cure her ward's lovesickness, advises seeing an expert, Merlin. In addition to aiding their desperate mistresses with practical advice and assistance, Glauce and Hwin accompany Britomart and Aravis, and engage in disguises to protect them; while Glauce passes herself as Britomart's squire, Hwin pretends to be a dumb horse. In their early appearances Britomart and Aravis are nearly identical. When she arrives on the scene in Book III, Britomart is mounted and so like a male knight that Spenser even uses the pronoun "him" to refer to her, delaying the surprise of her true identity. She is also using her role as more than a disguise; Britomart really knows how to be a knight, and a better one than many of the poem's men. She unhorses Guyon, much to his surprise "For never yet, sith warlike armes he bore,/ And shiuering speare in bloody field first shooke,/ He fownd himself dishonored so sore" (III.i.7.2–4). Aravis is also skilled and well suited to her role. When Shasta first encounters Aravis in *The Horse and His Boy,* Bree the Horse can tell by the sound of her riding that "That's quality.... And it's being ridden by a real horseman" (*HB* 24). He assures Shasta that the rider must be a great Tarkaan, or Calormene lord, and, when it looks as though they will be attacked by lions, Bree sees the other rider as a potential protector: "Tarkaan ... will have a sword — protect us all" (*HB* 26). Like Spenser, Lewis uses the male pronoun to refer to Aravis since, like Guyon, Shasta thinks his potential enemy is a man: "He [Shasta] saw that the other rider was a very small, slender person, mail-clad (the moon shone on the mail) and riding magnificently. He had no beard" (*HB* 27). Shasta is completely fooled by the disguise until Aravis speaks and, like Britomart, she exhibits bravery that demonstrates the armor is not just for show: "She [Aravis] also displays the sort of courage which Lewis most often holds up for our admiration — that which acts in spite of a quaking fear at the center of one's bones." Although Britomart is running to a husband and Aravis from one, the end results are actually quite similar. Both women marry and become the mothers of powerful sons. Aravis and Shasta (Cor)'s son, Ram, has a warlike career much like that of Britomart and Artegall's distinguished heirs. While Britomart sees her future in a "charmed looking glass" (III.iii.24.2), Aravis watches Shasta and his first battle in the enchanted pool of the Hermit of the Southern March: "For it was in this pool that the Hermit looked when he wanted to know what was going on in the world outside the green walls of his hermitage ... as in a mirror he could see what was going on" (*HB* 180). Though there are differences in their substance, Aravis and Britomart share a surprising number of similarities.[15]

Like Britomart, Aravis also scorns the frivolities of court and court life. Her friend, the vain and shallow Lasaraleen, serves as an effective foil to Aravis's unconventional female role: "She remembered now that Lasaraleen had always been like that, interested in clothes and parties and gossip. Aravis had always been more interested in bows and arrows and horses and dogs and swimming. You will guess that each thought the other silly" (96). In Book III of *The Faerie Queene*, Britomart is placed in contrast to the other female characters who are, like Florimell and Amoret, very nice women, but defenseless and not physically strong. Like Lasaraleen, they are effective and work within the plot of the story, but the Britomarts and the Aravises are the ones who get things accomplished.

Perhaps the only more blatantly warlike female character in the *Chronicles* is the character of Jill Pole. She attends a "mixed" school with her friend Eustace, and they call each other by last names, like men in the military. Her wood wisdom, like that of Belphoebe, is a valuable asset. However, in her role as warrior, she resembles Redcrosse as well as Britomart. Jill, like the knights of Faerie Land, fulfills the role of the questing hero with a task to accomplish. The two *Chronicles* in which she is featured, *The Silver Chair* and *The Last Battle,* are the grimmest and most violent of the series, and are frequently told from her point of view. She is thus the focal point of view of the story, the character through whose eyes and ears the reader sees and hears despite third-person narrative. Therefore it is to Jill that readers, even males, are most likely to relate and connect. *The Silver Chair,* particularly, revolves around Jill's quest to free the enchanted Prince Rilian or to die trying. No other character in the *Chronicles* is given the same kind of direct charge which Aslan gives Jill: "I lay on you this command, that you seek the lost Prince until either you have found him and brought him to his father's house or else died in the attempt, or else gone back into your own world" (*SC* 19). Like Redcrosse, Jill takes up an almost insurmountable task. Her companions, the dreary and earthy Puddleglum and her school chum Eustace, who has aided in getting her to Narnia in the first place, parallel the roles of Spenser's Dwarf and Una. Though Eustace is definitely not the paragon Una is, he does provide encouragement and impetus for Jill who, although female, parallels the role of Redcrosse. Puddleglum, like the Dwarf, offers practical advice and common sense, even when tinged with his distinctly morose outlook and his delight in discussing funerals. Although she is aided on her journey by Eustace and Puddleglum, it is Jill's perspective from which Lewis generally tells the narrative: "Jill thought that when, in books, people live on what they shoot, it never tells you what a long, smelly, messy job it is plucking and cleaning dead birds and how cold it makes your fingers" (*SC* 72). In completing the quest and rescuing Rilian, Jill goes through a number of episodes traditional in the hero's quest and in the adventures of many of Spenser's knights. One of these episodes is the descent into the Underworld when she and her companions are taken through a variety of caverns, across a dark sea, and to the underground city of the Green Witch. In completing the task and rescuing the lost Prince, Jill achieves something attempted without success by "more than thirty champions (knights, centaurs, good giants, and all sorts)" (46). She is thus a successful hero, not merely a female character, since many classic heroes, such as the lamentable Orpheus, are not able to return from their descent or do not come back with the prize they sought.[16]

Jill is generally armed in all of her appearances in the *Chronicles.* Like Britomart, who is extremely cautious about being disarmed "And her welpointed weapons did about her dresse" (III.xi.55.9), Jill seldom appears without a weapon of some kind. In *The Silver Chair,* she wears a knife on her belt and uses the riding crop Aslan provides to administer punishment to the female bullies of Experiment House while Eustace and Caspian use the flats of their swords against the boys (215). Interestingly, although Jill fights against other girls at her school, in *The Last Battle* she uses her archery to kill enemies: "Then he [Tirian] heard twang-and-zipp on his left and one Calormene fell; then twang-zipp again and the Satyr was down" (118); "One of her [Jill's] own arrows hit a man" (123). She is the only woman in the series to actually be depicted killing humans. Intriguingly, the two foes Tirian particularly notices falling under her arrows are a Calormene and a satyr. Thus, like Britomart, the epitome of virtue and chastity, she defeats the powers of paganism and lasciviousness. Part of Jill's role in mortal combat certainly has to do with the desperation and difficulties experienced by the characters in the last installment of the series, for Eustace also kills humans, but Jill's courage is frequently depicted as simply being a part of who she is: "'Jill,' said Tirian, 'you are the bravest and most woodwise of all my subjects, but also the most malapert and disobedient'" (*LB* 65). She also possesses a number of other qualities that link her to Britomart, and even Redcrosse and the other male knights of the poem. She is an excellent horsewoman and a good actress. Although Jill never passes herself as a boy, she does, like Britomart, frequently conceal her identity: "'Disguises! I love disguises'" (*LB* 53). In Harfang, she fools the giants into believing she is "a perfect little darling" (*SC* 110), thus keeping any suspicions from being cast on her multitude of questions as she and her companions seek a way to get out of the castle. These survival skills work as well for her as they would for any other knight or soldier upon a quest.[17]

With Britomart, as well as with women within the *Chronicles*, the only characters who make disparaging remarks about them or their prowess as warriors are characters who are presented in a negative light. Marinell's misogyny, which prevents him from enjoying female companionship, also causes his defeat at the hands of Britomart. He has been warned that "of a woman he should have much ill/ A virgin strange and stout should him dismay, or kill" (III.iv.25.8–9), but instead of suspecting that his mounted and armored foe might be the woman he should fear, Marinell "ever from faire Ladies love did fly" (III.iv.26.6); thus he charges a knight, and falls at the hands of a lady. One of the surest signs that there is "something wrong" about the enchanted Prince Rilian is the sexist and disparaging way in which he speaks to Jill, who is not amused by the fact that the Green Witch plans to use Rilian to invade the world above and then rule through him:

"I don't think it's funny at all," said Jill. "I think you'll be a wicked tyrant."

"What?" said the Knight, still laughing and patting her head in a most infuriating fashion. "Is our little maid a deep politician? But never fear, sweetheart. In ruling that land, I shall do all by the counsel of my Lady.... Her word shall be my law...."

"Where I come from," said Jill, who was disliking him more every minute, "they don't think much of men who are bossed about by their wives."

"Shalt think otherwise when thou hast a man of thine own, I warrant you," said the Knight, apparently thinking this very funny [*SC* 138–9].

Once he has been freed from the enchantment, Rilian treats Jill with courtesy, expressing concern for her after the gruesome death of the Queen of Underland and vowing to protect her if the Earthmen prove unfriendly; but his attitude is entirely different, and his solicitude for the lone female in the party is mixed with respect for her abilities and gratitude for her courage in rescuing him. In the actions and fates of their martial female characters, both Lewis and Spenser express approval for the courage and nobility of these women.

There are, of course, dozens of female characters within the *Chronicles*, and very frequently, the stories would not be possible without them. Certainly, the most frightening and effective villains of the series are women, as are the most effective human protagonists. Women also play traditional roles, as with the matronly Mrs. Beaver or the flighty Lasaraleen. Spenser frequently has been criticized for placing his female characters too far at one end or the other on the scale of morality: pure, beautiful virgin or depraved, deformed whore/witch. However, his male characters, because of the nature of allegory, also experience the same dichotomy: noble hero or pagan scoundrel. Subtle character shadings are not suitable for allegory, particularly when characters must represent idealized images of concepts such as chastity and temperance. Lewis himself recognized this difficulty since the "romance genre demands flat characters ... the inner self that a realistic novelist might disclose via reported thoughts must appear in the events." Although Lewis also often places characters at extremes of evil or good, they are not, in the usual sense, stereotypes. Lucy is not merely a cardboard doll going through prescribed motions. Even as she embodies archetypal elements and facets of Spenserian characters, Lucy is also a realistically drawn female who has her own reactions. One episode with Lucy is frequently pointed at as a discrepancy in her character or in Lewis's characterization. After the battle of Anvard, Aravis learns Shasta's true identity and is taken to meet his father, King Lune:

> Presently Queen Lucy came out from the castle and joined them and King Lune said to Aravis, "My dear, here is a loving friend of our house. And she has been seeing that your apartments are put to rights for you better than I could have done it."
>
> "You'd like to come and see them, wouldn't you?" said Lucy, kissing Aravis.
>
> They liked each other at once and soon went away together to talk about Aravis's bedroom and Aravis's boudoir and about getting clothes for her, and all the sort of things girls do talk about on such an occasion [*HHB* 205].

This could be seen as a glaring inaccuracy in both Lucy's and Aravis's characters. After all, both of these women have been in armor and willing to die for their respective causes. However, rather than showing inconstancy, this switch from warrior to hostess shows Lucy's flexibility and uniqueness. Just a few pages earlier, she had been wearing a mail shirt and helmet and fighting with the archers in the defense of Anvard. As an individual, she is just as likely to be interested in both fighting and decorating as knights were likely to be equally interested in poetry and hacking up enemies. By the same token, Aravis can be both delighted at planning her room in her new home and disgusted with Lasaraleen for her flightiness. Rather than being mercurial, Aravis's interest in clothes and rooms at an appropriate time shows that she knows when it is proper to be concerned about one's appearance and decor, and when it is important to place priorities elsewhere. Once she has arrived in Archenland and is safe from her father, she can abandon her disguise since she has come to a land where women are valued for who they are, and she knows that here she will be respected as a person whether she is riding along Shasta or arranging her new room in the castle. The same sense of proper timing can be seen in Una, who carefully conceals her wonderful beauty until it is appropriate, or in Britomart, who balances the feminine side of her nature with the masculine tasks she must accomplish. Like Jill, who is warned by Tirian not to weep on her bowstring, even as she is slaying enemies, Britomart can express both her emotions and her puissance when the time is right. These are not women whose characters contradict themselves but individuals who understand how to adapt and do what is appropriate in any given situation.[18]

Milton also reflects the concept of each thing in its proper time and season, just as the Bible does in Ecclesiastes chapter three. Rather than stereotypes, these female characters are actually more similar to the biblical woman of Proverbs thirty-one who does all things — business, homemaking, charity — with equal aplomb, or to the Renaissance knight, whose sprezzatura enabled him to dance, ride, fight, and discourse on the nature of the universe with apparently effortless skill. This sense of well-rounded woman (and human) kind is best summed up in the list of skills Polly Plummer acquires when she spends summers at Digory Kirke's house in the country: "That was where she learned to ride and swim and milk and bake and climb" (*MN* 184). With a combination of both traditional male and traditional female activities, Polly is allowed, like the other female characters, to be more unique and individual than if she followed a set, prescribed pattern of behavior. Though not a warrior in the same sense as Lucy or Jill, "Of the four girls whom Lewis introduces to Narnia, Polly is the most aggressive and competitive.... She simply will not allow Digory to be more daring than she is." She sees herself as Digory's partner, not his sidekick, and sees no reason why she should not leave if she wants to. When they quarrel in the Hall of Images in Charn, she exclaims, "Well you needn't be bothered by having [me] with you any longer then. I'm off. I've had enough of this place. And I've had enough of you too — you beastly, stuck-up, obstinate pig!" (*MN* 51). Yet, like Spenser's knights, she is willing to forgive and "call it Pax" (*MN* 74) when Digory apologizes, and she shows concern for his dying mother. Polly, like so many of Spenser's and Lewis's female characters, is a full and well-rounded character whose interests are uniquely her own rather than culturally required.[19]

While a general observation seems to indicate superficial or stereotypical female characters in the *Chronicles,* closer examination reveals that there is much more to these characters than a first glance may reveal: " Most of his [Lewis's] girls seems more deeply studied than his boys." In *A Preface to Paradise Lost*, Lewis emphasizes the fact that readers might take Eve's humility before Adam as general servility instead of being the proper behavior of a great lady: "We see her prostrate herself in spirit before Adam — as an Emperor might kneel to a Pope or as a Queen curtsies to a King. You must not think that if you and I could enter Milton's Eden and meet her we should not very quickly be taught what it is to speak to the 'universal Dame'.... Even for Adam, though she is 'made so adorn for his delight,' she is also made 'so *awful* that with honour he may love' [italics Lewis's]" (viii.576). Eve may be respectful to Adam, but she is not a cringing, stereotyped "weaker woman." She is a powerful yet respectful partner for Adam, a true counterpart rather than a servant or pet. Spenser's females also are more complex than initial observation may indicate. While Una and Duessa, like Britomart and Acrasia, can be seen as opposite ends of an arbitrary moral scale, they can also be seen as characters who have genuine reactions and evolved personalities. Una is both royal maid, spiritual paragon, and lonely woman abandoned by her protector. Duessa is not just a bad woman; she is a combination of elements that emphasize her moral depravity and her deceptive powers. Likewise, Narnian female characters go beyond the roles of stereotype and form to be individuals, reflecting similar attributes of Spenser's and Milton's females. Lucy can be both the innocent and loyal child follower of Aslan and the queen who rides into battle with the appellation of "the Valiant." By depicting females who are reflective of Milton's and Spenser's protagonists, Lewis incorporates the remarkably diverse elements of women in *Paradise Lost* and *The Faerie Queene* into the development of his powerful and prevalent female players.[20]

Although the *Chronicles*, like *The Faerie Queene* and *Paradise Lost*, were written by a male author, the female characters are often remarkably interesting, complex, and challenging. Obviously, portraying the opposite sex is difficult, even more so for a writer like Lewis who, though he counted many women as friends during his lifetime, had lost his mother as a child and grew up without sisters. However, by drawing upon human, rather than characteristically female traits, Lewis creates female characters who are far more well-rounded than generally believed. In addition, by working under the influence of Milton and Spenser, Lewis adds to his female characters and enhances the setting in which they live; indeed, he presents a setting in which a woman is just as likely to be the knight in shining armor as she is to be the damsel in distress. She might also be the evil wizard or the queen, as well.

# IV

## An Inside Bigger Than Its Outside: Setting and Geography

"They had seen strange things enough through that Doorway.
    But it was stranger than any of them to look round and
find themselves in warm daylight, the blue sky above them,
flowers at their feet, and laughter in Aslan's eyes."
                                        — *The Last Battle* 157

Those who are emotionally as well as academically familiar with
the *Chronicles of Narnia* are also familiar with the sensation of occasionally catching glimpses of that country. A glade of primroses, a sea
shore, a beaver's dam, all are equally likely to evoke the expectation of
a talking bird or a faun around the next bend since "what we remember and cherish about Narnia is the golden and enchanting atmosphere"; it is the place, as much as the stories themselves, that captivates
readers. Certainly part of what makes the *Chronicles* so delightful to
all age groups is the very country of Narnia:

> As we enter Narnia, we encounter an imaginary world in which
> animals can talk, in which creatures mythical in our world are real,

and in which creatures unknown in our world have an important place. And as we pass through the wardrobe into that world, we must accept it as real, we must embrace it imaginatively and yield ourselves to it as long as the story lasts.

The land of Talking Beasts is more than simply a geographical area sketched on the map of the imagination. It is also a place drawn out of the experiences, influences, and interests of the author. Lewis once stated "that he resorted to such realms because the world was so fully explored that there was no place left for wonder." While aspects of Narnia may be drawn from features of our own world, they are imbued with a greater sense of wonder and emotional power. There are certainly a few spots in our own world that resemble Narnia, but there is also much in the construction of the country beyond the wardrobe that shows the influence of Spenser and Milton. All three writers employ fantastic settings, which their readers can access only through an author's words. In these worlds, creation, geography, the balance of art and nature, the presence of human-made structures and their qualities, and the description of spiritual realms are all crucial elements that allow Narnia, like Faerie Land and Milton's Prelapsarian universe, to be as crucial to the text as a character, while remaining a place that rings with its own reality.[1]

The technique of saying something about one's own situation by transferring that situation onto other people or places is a literary strategy that goes back to the parables of Jesus and the fables of Aesop. Lewis was himself very conscious of the quality of fairy stories that allowed them to convey messages with an effectiveness unknown to other genres: "I fell in love with the Form itself: its brevity, its severe restraints on description, its flexible traditionalism, its inflexible hostility to all analysis, digression, reflections and 'gas.'" Additionally, like his predecessors, Lewis knew the importance of a fantastic location for his spiritually rich stories. He wrote Ruth Pitter that he had learned what other worlds in fiction "were really good for; for spiritual adventures. Only they can satisfy the craving which sends our imagination off the earth." In his *Preface to Paradise Lost*, Lewis analyzes the ways in which Milton's creation of his epic possibly took place. One of the most crucial steps in this creation, of course, was the choice of subject. Milton was also wrestling with the possibility of a poem featuring King Arthur's "wars 'beneath the earth.'" The decision to instead use the fall of humanity necessarily dictated to Milton the remarkable worlds in which his poem must take place. Because of its historical/mythical quality, the story of Adam and Eve requires certain settings as clearly as it requires Adam and Eve themselves. Milton's elaboration on the spiritual universe, going above, beyond, and below the words of the Bible is most intriguing in its opening in Hell, proceeding to Heaven, thence to Paradise, and back to Heaven. By taking this approach, Milton could use the grim caverns of Hades to contrast against and emphasize the beauties of Paradise and Heaven. Just as the sun seems so much brighter when one comes out of a darkened theater, so the bright worlds of Eden and Heaven are made even more spectacular for the poem's opening in lands of gloom and darkness.[2]

Spenser's choice of setting, to some degree, is also influenced by his subject matter. Lewis emphasizes the fact that Spenser unconventionally begins his poem with characters rather than with setting: "There is no *situation* in *The Faerie Queene*.... A knight and a lady ride across our field of vision. We do not know who they are, nor in what period; the poet's whole energy is devoted to telling us what they look like." This setting-free opening allows Redcrosse, Una, and the dwarf to dictate the setting, rather than presenting a setting that subsequently shapes its characters. Spenser does not lay out a stage, but only remarkably detailed, yet abstract characters. Part of what makes Spenser's setting so fantastic is the absence of the specific. Faerie Land is even more wonderful because Spenser blurs timelines and creates conflicting geography. His characters include heroic figures drawn from a variety of eras in British and classical history. Faerie Land is at once a park fit for romantic rides, a maze of confusing forests, and a country that is both a hostile wilderness and a community liberally dotted with castles, houses, and hermits' cottages. In addition, Spenser's Faerie Land allows some anonymity to his characters and events, both of which frequently reflect his society's contemporary situation through the guise of fantasy. He can allow his heroes to defeat knights that are simply "pagan dogs" rather than specifically French, Spanish, or Dutch, and his depictions of contemporary people and events are at least partially obscured by the setting, even when any astute reader of any era can ascertain to whom and to what Spenser is alluding.[3]

Lewis, having chosen a fairy story for his genre, was presented, like Milton and Spenser, with certain general parameters in terms of setting. Thus, because Lewis respected "good unoriginality," he would certainly respect the rules of fairy tales, dictating that one's characters live in castles, not ranch-style houses, and that they fight with swords and bows, not rifles and cannon. Thomas Howard reminds readers that "what we encounter in the landscape of Narnia is true — not in the sense that we will come upon the ruins of Cair Paravel somewhere (there are none), but in the sense that Cair Paravel is a castle, and the man from whose imagination castles have disappeared is disastrously deprived." Like Spenser, Lewis had chosen particular characters to take on his adventures, and those individuals dictated a certain setting. His image of the faun necessitated a faun's snug cave complete with books and a cozy hearth; the queen on a sledge required snow, wintry forests and frozen streams; the massive lion Aslan needed forests and mountains suited to his majesty and size. One of the most remarkable things about the land of Narnia is the fact that Lewis "created" Narnia even before Aslan did.[4]

The reader's perception of the creation of Narnia and its geography is largely influenced by the order in which the books are read. There is an on-going dispute over the proper order in which one should read the *Chronicles*. Walter Hooper, who served as Lewis's secretary during the last years of Lewis's life, implies in *Past Watchful Dragons* that Lewis intended for the *Chronicles* to be read in the order of Narnian history: "The right sequence, as Lewis caused me to copy it down is this: *The Magician's Nephew* (1955), *The Lion, the Witch and the Wardrobe* (1950), *The Horse and His Boy* (1954), *Prince Caspian* (1951), *The Voyage of the 'Dawn Treader'* (1952), *The Silver Chair* (1953), and *The Last Battle* (1956)." Unfortunately, this "right" sequence refers to the order of Narnian history, rather than to the order in which the books themselves should necessarily be arranged. The long accepted publication order of *The Lion, the Witch and the Wardrobe, Prince Caspian, The Voyage of the "Dawn Treader," The Silver Chair, The Horse and His Boy, The Magician's Nephew,* and *The Last Battle* makes far more sense for many readers, and in fact, the order in which the books were written is different still. Paul F. Ford, in *The Companion to Narnia*, insists that although Lewis suggested the chronological order late in his life, this order would only be better "if Lewis had been able to complete his intended revision." Although new editions now place the *Chronicles* in the order Hooper endorses, an arrangement that places *The Magician's Nephew* first removes the delightful irony when the origins of both the wardrobe and the lamppost are revealed, as well as the thrill one receives in learning that Digory becomes the beloved Professor Kirke. If one already knows that the wardrobe is made of magical wood from Narnia, there is no surprise is finding that the wardrobe has become a gateway into that world. With *The Lion, the Witch and the Wardrobe* first, the reader is more connected to Lucy, discovering along with her the wonders of the world into which she has stumbled. The chronological arrangement also hampers the remarkable and thought-provoking contrast of creation and destruction achieved by placing *The Magician's Nephew* back to back with *The Last Battle.* In addition, an order which places *The Magician's Nephew* sixth also emphasizes the striking influence of Milton's creation narrative upon the creation of Narnia. The placement of the Narnian creation narrative later in the text, rather than as the first event in a series of events, reflects Milton's placement of the creation as an event narrated by Raphael in Book VII of *Paradise Lost.* Although *The Magician's Nephew* is not framed by a narrator as Raphael frames the creation story, they both are presented as previous links in a chain that the reader has already seen. Such a presentation adds interest to the narrative, just as it is more interesting to hear the history of some person or place with which we are already acquainted than it is to read the chronology of a person or place hitherto unknown to us, and whose importance we do not recognize. This juxtaposed order also reinforces the epic idea of beginning *in medias res,* or in the middle of things. Thus, Spenser, Milton, and Lewis all begin in the middle, then, later in the narrative, fill in missing information. In both Milton and Lewis, a late placement of the creation produces a powerful sense of irony, as the creation narrative thence takes place only shortly before the narrative of the world's destruction/ corruption. Both Lewis and Milton thus dovetail creation and loss:

> Lewis was well aware of the potential emphasis in first and last things. The Genesis and Revelation of Narnia take full advantage of their chronological positions. Both contain mind-stretching elements which

are lacking in the other five books. The extinction of Charn and the birth of Narnia have an almost Miltonic quality about them, and the events which bring the days of Narnia to a close fill the mind with something of the immense scope of the book of ending which inspired it — Revelation.

In this arrangement, the creation narrative is quickly followed by a temptation scene. Although Digory's successful resistance to temptation actually takes place thousands of Narnian years before the treachery of Shift and the end of Narnia, the original order creates a pattern very close to that in *Paradise Lost*, and it is highly unlikely that Lewis, who had been so personally and professionally immersed in Milton's epic, was unaware of the similar effect. Unfortunately, the re-ordering of the books has destroyed for many younger and future readers this wonderful juxtaposition and literary connection, as well as negating the delight in making discoveries about Digory, the lamp post, and the wardrobe later in the series.[5]

Since there is an active dispute over the order of the *Chronicles*, it is perhaps more fruitful to look at the actual creation narrative itself. In this segment of *The Magician's Nephew*, Lewis presents a highly imaginative and creative rendition of Narnia's formation that is tailor-made to suit this new country. This is not a geologist's creation, replete with volcanoes and violent upheavals shaping the land over millions of years. Nor is it strictly a biblical seven day's creation; Aslan actually creates Narnia in the early hours of a single day. It is, as Wesley A. Kort notes, a creation without conflict. The creation is thus specific to Narnia and to its creator. Such a customized creation is reflective of Lewis's view that Aslan does not *equal* Christ; rather he represents how Christ might appear in a country like Narnia. Their relationship is not an equation — Aslan=Christ — but an analogy. As Christ is to Earth, so Aslan is to Narnia. In addition, since Narnia's history is far briefer than that of earth, it seems appropriate that its creation would also take less time. Yet, even in the distinctly Narnian creation of Narnia, there are several remarkable similarities to *Paradise Lost* that make this passage one of the places where Milton's influence is most felt in the *Chronicles*.[6]

One of the most poignant and striking elements of Aslan's creation of Narnia is that he literally sings the world into existence: "In the darkness something was happening at last. A voice had begun to sing.... Sometimes it seemed to come from all directions at once.... Its lower notes were deep enough to be the voice of the earth herself. There were no words. There was hardly even a tune. But it was, beyond comparison, the most beautiful noise he had ever heard. It was so beautiful he could hardly bear it" (*MN* 98–99). While this is a completely appropriate beginning for a world designed for joy and celebration, the musical element is also very similar to the creation related by Raphael: "Nor passed uncelebrated, nor unsung/ By the celestial choirs, when orient light/ Exhaling first from darkness they beheld;/ Birthday of heav'n and earth; with joy and shout/ the hollow universal orb they filled,/ And touched their golden harps, and hymning praised/ God and his works" (VII.253–259). Although in Milton's vision God's word is the actual instrument of creation, the music provided by the celebrating angels resembles both the creation song of Aslan and the accompaniment the stars provide when he creates them:

> Then two wonders happened at the same moment. One was that the voice was suddenly joined by other voices ... in harmony with it, but far higher up the scale.... The second wonder was that the blackness over head, all at once, was blazing with stars.... The new stars and the new voices began at exactly the same time. If you had seen and heard it, as Digory did, you would have felt quite certain that it was the stars themselves who were singing and that it was the First Voice, the deep one, which had made them appear and ... sing [99].

The stars, like Milton's angels, provide harmony for the creation sequence.[7]

The actual results of Aslan's song and of God's word are remarkably similar. While Lewis changes the traditional order of creation to a distinctly Narnian order, the same quality of God's powerful word calling the world into existence in *Paradise Lost* is reflected in the way Aslan creates Narnia. In both cases, the creator makes things "out of [his] head" (*MN* 107). Even the language used in the creation sequences is similar. This is most clearly apparent from the description of the creation of plant life on earth and on Narnia. In both cases, the land is bare and empty, "til then/ Desert and bare, unsightly, unadorned" (VII.312–13). Then, the germination of the plants is rapid and complete:

> ...the bare earth...
> Brought forth the tender grass, whose verdure clad
> Her universal face with pleasant green,
> Then herbs of every leaf, that sudden flow'red
> Opening their various colors, and made gay
> Her bosom smelling sweet: and these scarce blown,
> Forth flourished thick the clust'ring vine, forth crept
> The swelling gourd, up stood the corny reed
> Embattled in her field: add the humble shrub,
> And bush with frizzled hair implicit: last
> Rose as in dance the stately trees, and spread
> Their branches hung with copious fruit; or gemmed
> Their blossoms: with high woods the hills were crowned ...
> [VII. 313–324].

Aslan even creates the plants of Narnia in the exact same order as Milton's God chooses for earth: grass first, then flowers, and then trees. As Aslan walks along, singing the powerful creation song, the grass spreads out from around him and races up the hillsides and then the lower mountains. Other plants spring up, including heather growing on the higher slopes of the new world. Then, just as in Milton's order, "Patches of rougher and more bristling green appeared in the valley" (*MN* 104). Digory is puzzled by these objects until one appears next to him: "It was a little, spiky thing that grew out dozens of arms and covered these arms with green and grew larger at a rate of about an inch every two seconds. There were dozens of these things all around him now. When they were nearly as tall as himself he saw what they were. "Trees!" (104–5). The two accounts resemble each other more than either one resembles the biblical description. Aslan's newly created plants, like those God creates, are in full bloom. Their rate of growth is equaled only by their rate of maturity. In both narratives, the world progresses rapidly and completely from emptiness and sterility to maturity and ripeness.

The most remarkable demonstration of Milton's influence on the Narnian creation is the creation of the animals. Like the plants, the animals appear full-grown in both accounts. Both Milton and Lewis use the same visually stunning motif: the animals burst out of humps of earth and appear, head first, from the soil: "The earth obeyed, and straight/ Op'ning her fertile womb teemed at a birth/Innumerous living creatures, perfect forms,/ Limbed and full grown: out of the ground up rose/ As from his lair the wild beast where he wons/ In forest wild, in thicket, brake or den; Among the trees in pairs they rose" (VII. 453–7). Lewis takes the image further by giving his readers a homey English analogy to the appearance of the animals coming from the earth. He describes the earth resembling boiling water as it forms humps of many different sizes. Some are tiny, some are massive, but all are moving and growing until they finally erupt to reveal an animal emerging from each. "The moles came out just as you might see a mole come out in England. The dogs came out, barking the moment their heads were free, and struggling as you've seen them do when they are getting through a narrow hole in a hedge" (113–14). Both Milton and Lewis, in the general creation of all animals, focus on a number of specific creatures. They each pay particular attention to stags, large felines such as leopards and tigers, and elephants. When Digory sees the stags coming up, he at first thinks they are more trees, because the antlers appear first, looking like tree branches. Milton uses the exact same illustration of antlers resembling the branches of a tree: "The swift stag from under ground/ bore up his branching head" (VII. 469–70). Milton's cats also include lions among their numbers, and they shake the dirt off themselves just as Lewis's cats do: "The panthers, leopards and things of that sort, sat down at once to wash the loose earth off their hind quarters" (*MN* 114). The pièce de résistance to both creations is the mighty bulk of the elephant, whom Milton calls "leviathan." Lewis's elephants obviously emerge from two mounds of earth that he describes as being as large as cottages. Both authors also describe amphibians and butterflies, although Milton's format necessitates a more cryptic diction than Lewis's straightforward fairy tale telling. While Lewis simply explains that the butterflies appear, Milton avers that:

> At once came forth whatever creeps the ground,
> Insect or worm; those waved their limber fans
> For wings, and smallest lineaments exact
> In all the liveries decked of summer's pride
> With spots of gold and purple, azure and green [VII.475–9].

Both of these narratives stem from the biblical command, "Let the land produce living creatures according to their kinds." The idea of instantaneous generation is interpreted identically by both authors. Milton's descriptions of the animals bursting up out of the earth, particularly with a focus on certain animals, undoubtedly had an impact on the Narnian creation Lewis devised, though "it is much more detailed in Lewis's narrative and written in the lighter tone suitable to his genre." Just as Milton's humans are stately, more grand than the children Digory and Polly, the incorrigible Uncle Andrew, and the earthy cabby Frank, so too his creation is more dignified, while Lewis's, though clearly a reflection of Milton's work, resembles a rather noisy day at a joyful and exuberant zoo more than a sophisticated procession of new creations.[8]

*The Magician's Nephew* also focuses on geographical details of Narnia that clearly reflect the influence of Milton. When Digory is sent to fetch the Apple of Protection, Aslan describes his destination thus, "You will journey through those mountains till you find a green valley with a blue lake in it, walled round by mountains of ice. At the end of the lake there is a steep green hill. On the top of that hill there is a garden. In the centre of that garden is a tree" (143). When Digory reaches the garden, he finds the fruit-laden trees peeping over a wall of green turf around the perimeter. Although the garden, like all of Narnia, is only a day old, the trees are already fully mature, with fruit at the peak of ripeness. Like Lewis's and Milton's animals, the garden has come into being fully formed. Once inside the golden gates of the garden, Digory finds the tree he seeks and a softly flowing fountain, as well as a phoenix who seems to be observing all the proceedings. Above all, it is a very private place. This is a tamer, more parklike setting than Paradise, but Milton's depiction of the Garden of Eden is very similar:

> Where delicious Paradise,
> now nearer crowns with her enclosure green,
> As with a rural mound the champaign head
> Of a steep wilderness, whose hairy sides
> With thicket overgrown, grotesque and wild,
> ...a woody theater
> Of stateliest view. Yet higher than their tops
> The verduous wall of Paradise up sprung
> ...And higher than that wall a circling row
> Of goodliest tress loaden with fairest fruit [IV. 132–47].

Both gardens are located in remote areas, on hills, and walled, though apparently no other walls, barriers, or other artificial constructions exist in either new creation. In both cases, the fruit trees are visible above the wall, tantalizing those who are outside, and the wall and the hill both enforce a similar sense of privacy, or actual holiness. Satan is clearly an intruder, if not because of his true nature, then because of his means of arrival. Both he and Jadis are intruders because they leap the walls of private, holy Gardens that are not intended for them. The gardens are also both home to remarkable trees. Though Eve eats first of the tree which gives her the knowledge of good and evil, the tree from which Digory takes the silver apple resembles the second crucial tree in Eden: the tree whose fruit gives immortal life. It is partly to prevent Adam and Eve from consuming this fruit, thus escaping God's punishment, that the angelic guard is set up outside Eden. Because Digory and Jadis are visitors from other, fallen worlds, they do not require knowledge of good and evil; immortality is a far greater temptation, particularly to Jadis, who has already cheated death once by placing herself in the Hall of Images among her ancestors as she destroyed every other living thing in her world of Charn.[9]

The location of the garden is also reminiscent of Eden, which, as the angel Michael tells Adam, will be moved by the great flood to come in the days of Noah:

> then shall this mount
> Of Paradise by might of waves be moved
> Out of his place, pushed by the horned flood,
> With all his verdue spoiled, and trees adrift
> Down the great river to the opening gulf,
> And there take root an island salt and bare [XI. 829–834].

The walled garden of Narnia also seems to move out to sea, though by less violent means than Noah's great deluge. Eustace, miserable and transformed into a dragon during the *Dawn Treader*'s stay on the appropriately named Dragon Island, has a remarkable spiritual encounter with Aslan who "led me a long way into the mountains ... at last we came to the top of a mountain I'd never seen before and on the top of this mountain was a garden—trees and fruit and everything" (*VDT* 88). Though Eustace, in his dragon form, had flown all over the island, he had never seen this garden on any of those flights. He is inclined to think that the whole episode was a dream except for the change that has come over him, and for the fact that Edmund thinks the encounter to be a very real experience with Aslan. Clearly, the garden is one that is located where Aslan wants it to be, rather than in a fixed location in Narnia or anywhere else, and, like Eden, it is closely linked with heaven, or, in Narnian terms, Aslan's Country.

The Eden imagery of this same garden is intensified in *The Last Battle* when Tirian is presented to Frank and Helen, the first king and queen of Narnia, as they sit in thrones under the tree in the center of the Garden: "And Tirian felt as you would feel if you were brought before Adam and Eve in all their glory" (179). In this final incarnation, the Garden actually becomes more like both Eden and Heaven, as it grows to encompass all of the new Narnia. In this setting, the garden becomes the eternal destination for the faithful, or heaven, and actually includes all the good places of both Narnia and our world, from Cair Paravel to Professor Kirke's marvelous old house that he believed had been torn down. In *The Magician's Nephew*, however, the external Narnia resembles Eden, and the animals hunting the "Neevil" or "new evil" on the loose, are not unlike Milton's angels seeking out the escaped Satan: "if within the circuit of these walks/ ...by morrow dawning I shall know" (IV.585, 588). Both locations are infiltrated by the forces of evil despite the best efforts of their protectors.

The other garden that is clearly a source for Aslan's walled orchard is found in *The Faerie Queene*'s description of the Garden of Adonis in Book III, canto six. This garden also is walled and one of its two sets of gates is "bright gold" (31.3). These gates, like those of Aslan's Garden, prohibit "overstriding" or leaping the wall, though the gatekeeper, Genius, is in charge of keeping out gate crashers and wall jumpers. The phoenix in the Narnian garden keeps watch, but does not appear to confront any visitors. It simply observes, even when it pretends to be sleeping. In addition, the Garden of Adonis has a round mountain in its center that resembles the location of the Narnian garden: "There stood a stately Mount, on whose round top/ A gloomy grove of mirtle trees did rise" (43.2–3). Both gardens also give off an enticing, seductive smell. The Garden of Adonis "threw forth most dainty odours, and most sweet delight" (43.9). The smell of Aslan's Garden is so beautiful that the children and Fledge the winged horse actually notice the scent before they catch sight of the mountain and garden: "a heavenly smell, warm and golden, as if from all the most delicious fruits and flowers of the world, was coming up to them" (*MN* 156). Both gardens also represent a life and vitality that their powerful smells emphasize; they are so imbued with life that immortality is possible there. The goddess Venus here honors and restores to life her beloved Adonis, and the Narnian garden is the home of the fruit that can make those who eat it live forever. Certainly Lewis, in his much criticized interpretation of the Garden of Adonis in *The Allegory of Love*, paid particular attention to the positive associations of the Garden, especially in contrast to the corrupt Bower of Bliss, so it is not surprising that his positive but powerful Garden should reflect Spenser's.[10]

*Paradise Lost*, with its focus on Heaven, Hell, and Eden, does not include the ocean as an important aspect of its setting, but it is a geographical detail central to both *The Faerie Queene* and the *Chronicles*. In *Spenser's Images of Life*, Lewis pays particular attention to the role the sea plays as the "world's end," providing a serious and terrifying obstacle for Florimell in her endless flight from danger as she is nearly raped in a boat, only to be saved from her attacker and taken captive beneath the waves. For Britomart, however, Lewis notes, the sea is simply a beautiful location for her reverie: "Britomart addressed the sea in lyrical meditation, encountered Marinell, and rode on." Likewise, the seashore that laps around Cair Paravel is at one point a beautiful and poignant place for refreshment; at another time, it is an almost insurmountable obstacle. In *The Lion, the Witch, and the Wardrobe*, the children have a delightful visit to the shore before their formal coronation:

> The castle of Cair Paravel on its little hill towered up above them; before them were the sands, with rocks and little pools of salt water, and sea weed, and the smell of the sea, and ... the waves breaking for ever and ever.... And oh, the cry of the sea gulls! Have you heard it? Can you remember? [178].

This scene represents one of the last times the children appear to still be children before they mature into the remarkable monarchs of Narnia's Golden Age, and the narrator's plea to the reader to remember the sea seems to reflect the fact that the Pevensies soon forget their life in this world, and, once they do return to England, it is only by remembering their experiences in Narnia that they continue to live as Narnians. The memories of their years as beloved monarchs in a fantastic kingdom must be haunting and poignant, much like the cry of the gulls. When the Pevensies, children once again, return to Narnia in *Prince Caspian*, a year of their time has equaled a thousand Narnian years and the once-friendly sea has now made the Cair an island, separated from the coast which they desperately want to reach. Though they walk all around the island, thinking that it is a peninsula and they will be able to reach the mainland, they are disheartened to realize that "the channel between them and the opposite coast was only about thirty or forty yards wide; but they could now see that this was its narrowest place" (7). Like Spenser, Lewis shows that the same seashore can present either touching beauty or heartbreaking difficulties. Both authors present a sea that can make characters think or weep. This duality reflects the biblical attitude toward the sea. Large bodies of water are frequently obstacles for God to overcome on behalf of His people, as with the Red Sea in the Exodus. The Israelites, trapped between the Egyptian army and the sea, experience God's power with the sea's parting. In His relations with His disciples, Jesus often uses the sea as an object lesson and a form of transport. It is an appropriate setting for teaching, fishing miracles, and the calming of terrific storms, and can be both beautiful and terrible, depending on the situation. The character of the sea is as changing as its surface.[11]

The *Chronicle* most concerned with the sea is, of course, *The Voyage of the "Dawn Treader,"* in which the sea is both a goal in itself and a means of travel to new and wonderful lands. One of the islands the crew discovers holds a remarkable secret: the waters of one of its streams turn objects into gold. This island, later named Deathwater, evinces only greed and envy that must be settled by Aslan's intervention. In fact, Caspian's and Edmund's attempts to exert authority over one another very nearly end in a fight, as each tries to pull rank over the other in order to lay claim to the island's remarkable waters. Likewise the Rich Strond in Book III of *The Faerie Queene* provokes Marinell's suspicious aggression and nearly costs him his life at Britomart's hands when she in fact "them despised all; for all was in her powre" (III.iv. 18.9). Britomart cares nothing for the wealth scattered along the seashore, but Marinell, blinded by his greed, assumes she is there to steal it. In both cases, greed is deadly, and the water's gifts are ones best left unaccepted, for they bring out the worst in human beings. Like a Siren's song, these gifts promise much, but deliver only death and disharmony. Both Britomart and the protagonists of *The Voyage of the "Dawn Treader"* are protected from the destructive possibilities of the valuable bodies of water. Britomart's goodness and Aslan's intervention both prevent disaster. The untrustworthiness of water thus mirrors the dangerous ambiguity of wealth. Both are beautiful and treacherous, and both challenge the spiritual power of protagonists.

Other sources for *The Voyage of the "Dawn Treader,"* which takes place almost entirely at sea, include the nautical motifs of the narrative in the first two books of *The Faerie Queene*: "Now strike your sailes ye jolly Mariners" (I.xii.42.1). The sea continues to be important throughout Spenser's epic, providing many crucial images and motifs incorporated by Lewis. For instance, Lewis perceived the third book of the poem to be the beginning of its "most watery part." A similar wateriness is apparent in the *Chronicles*, four of which (*The Lion, the Witch, and the Wardrobe, Prince Caspian, The Voyage of the "Dawn Treader,"* and *The Horse and His Boy*) have at least some connection or plot element that depends upon the ocean. The island journeys of *The Dawn Treader* also resemble the sea travels of Guyon. In his journey to Acrasia's Bower of Bliss, Guyon's voyage includes a number of brief nautical adventures, some of which find their way into *The Voyage of the "Dawn Treader"* as more complex and elaborate adventures. Guyon encounters both sea monsters and a dark island. He is challenged by "an hideous host arrayd,/ Of huge Sea monsters, such as living sence dismayd.... Spring-headed Hydraes, and sea-shouldring Whales... Bright Scolopendraes, armed with silver scales... All these and thousand thousands many more" (II.xii.228–25.1). A few stanzas later "they [Guyon and his Palmer] greatly were dismayd, ne wist/ How to direct their way in darknesse wide,/ But feard to wander in that wastful mist" (II.xii.35.1–3). These are both important kinds of experiences in Lewis's text. Shortly after Eustace is restored to human form and the eastward voyage has continued, the crew sees a bizarre sight: "It came up on what they first took to be a huge neck, but as more and more of it emerged everyone knew that this was not its neck but its body and that at last

they were seeing what so many people have foolishly wanted to see —
the great Sea Serpent" (96). The monster, with sea creatures and encrus-
tations growing on its body, is a formidable obstacle that costs the
grand ship her carved dragon's tail stern in the close escape. The Dark
Island is not even an island proper, "nor even, in an ordinary sense, a
mist. It was a Darkness" (151). While Guyon sails unscathed through
his adventures, the journeys of Caspian's ship are somewhat more dangerous and taxing. The battle with the Sea Serpent, which essentially
involves pushing the ship through the creature's looped body so that
it cannot tighten itself and crush *The Dawn Treader*, is an exhausting
ordeal for everyone from Caspian to the common sailors. The Dark
Island is a psychologically harrowing experience, conjuring up every
dream the adventurers have ever had, and bringing their night terrors
to life. However, nothing physically happens there. Characters each
describe what they are hearing, from claws climbing onto the ship to
ominous gongs being sounded, but each crew member only encounters his own night terror made real. The island's terrible power exists
primarily in the minds of those foolish enough to travel there. Since
Lewis's protagonists are more like ordinary people than the often-
allegorical figures of *The Faerie Queene*, it is logical that their ordeals
should be more physical and painful than those of Guyon, who discovers that all the horrors of his journey are illusions conjured by Acrasia, defeated by the spiritual power wielded by the Palmer, Guyon's
advisor and companion.[12]

Although the sea is not an important motif in *Paradise Lost*, one
geographical feature that runs through both *The Faerie Queene* and
*Paradise Lost*, and consequently the *Chronicles*, is that of an underground world. Not only does Lewis's Underland resemble Spenser's
cave of Mammon and Milton's Hell, but the gloomy kingdom of the
Green Witch receives the same negative connotation as Milton's and
Spenser's underground lands. All three authors present these underground places as negative counterparts to "sunlit lands."

One of the most interesting characteristics shared by all three lands
is their populousness. While many caves, both literary and actual, are
distinctive for their emptiness, Spenser's underground cave of Mammon is stocked with allegorical figures such as "Cruell Revenge, and
rancorous Despight" (II.vii.22.2), as well as deformed fiends enslaved

in goldsmithing. Milton's Hell is also populated by symbolic figures such as Sin and Death and by hordes of maimed fallen angels. While *The Silver Chair*'s Underland is not so clearly a spiritual realm for the punishment of evil doers, its population certainly resembles those of both Hell and Mammon's cavern.[13]

On their long underground journey into Underland proper, Jill, Eustace, and Puddleglum see an enormous bearded man sleeping gently and bathed in a clear, silvery light. This figure, though gigantic, is beautiful, and he is identified as Father Time, a representational figure much like Spenser's underground dwellers, who appears again at the end of the Narnian world. In addition, the Queen of Underland has enslaved masses of Earthmen who have distinctive appearances, ranging from horns to feathers to fur; but "in one respect they were all alike: Every face in the whole hundred was as sad as a face could be" (123). These downcast creatures reflect the overall gloom that pervades Underland through the Green Witch's enchantments. One of the first indications that the Witch's spell has been broken is the sudden restoration of the silent and melancholy Earthmen to their true, joyful natures. Jill, realizing this transformation, exclaims, "'I'm so glad they aren't really horrid and gloomy...'" (178). While many of the details of Lewis's Underland share characteristics with traditional depictions of underground worlds, this large, stagnated population is an element consistent with both *The Faerie Queene* and *Paradise Lost*.

The terrain of Underland is also reflective of Spenserian and Miltonic influence. In each text, the underground world is reached through a crevice in the earth, then through a gradual descent with separate stages. Since Milton's Hell is described from the bottom up, so to speak, its gradations are presented in reverse. Rather than a descent into the depths, Satan's journey in Book II is an ascent from the depths through the traditional Hades, "a universe of death" (II.622), through the gates of Hell and their gruesome guardians Sin and Death, to the dark sea of Night and Chaos in the "nethermost abyss" (II.969) before Satan can actually leave his dungeon. Guyon's descent in Book II of *The Faerie Queene* is more reminiscent of the classical heroic journey to the underworld, complete with the shadowy fiend waiting to destroy him if he touches any of the treasures he sees: "The which with monstrous stalke behind him stept/ And ever as he went, dew watch upon him kept" (II.vii.26.8–9). These two depictions are both mirrored in the terrain of Underland. Jill, Puddleglum and Eustace slide down a seemingly endless defile, only to be confronted by the Earthmen who take them prisoner and lead them through gradual levels of descent that include huge cathedral caverns, underground mushroom forests, cramped tunnels, and an underground sea.

Most importantly, in all these texts, the underground environment is a negative one. Hell, Mammon's cave, and Underland are all dangerous and pervaded with negative emotions. A twist to this negative emphasis is the Land of Bism, far deeper in the earth than Underland. The fiery native land of the Earthmen is not a land of gloom or condemnation, but one of vibrance and excitement:

> They thought they could make out a river of fire and, on the banks of that river, what seemed to be fields and groves of an unbearable, hot brilliance — though they were dim compared with the river. There were blues, reds, greens, and whites all jumbled together: a very good stained-glass window with the tropical sun staring straight through it at mid-day might have something the same effect [180].

Although it is not a negative environment, Bism is still a dangerous alien setting in which human beings probably could not survive. Rilian must be dissuaded from exploring this fascinating and dangerous world, from which he could not possibly have returned. Since the fissure to Bism closes before the very eyes of the travelers, and the whole of Underland is subsequently flooded, it is also safe to say that no other humans or other Narnians have the opportunity to travel there. With the exception of Bism, all underground places in Narnia are presented negatively. Though Narnians often use caves, the only good caves are those that are least cave-like. Mr. Tumnus's cave is really a house, both in form and in function, with doors, books, furniture, and lamps; even this abode has negative connotations since Tumnus is originally supposed to kidnap Lucy. Though it seems warm and comfortable, the cave is a trap and, if Tumnus had not freed Lucy, she would doubtless have been killed or turned to stone by the White Witch. The fauns' cave where Jill and Eustace are taken to rest after their escape from Underland is also more like a house, complete with a fireplace and grandfather clock. Even the cave in which the Beavers hide the Pevensies is "just a hole in the ground" (99) rather than a real cave. The popular interpretation for the negative presentation of caves generally refers to a misogynist fear of the maternal earth. However, this anti-feminine possibility for underground places in Narnia is lessened by the fact that the character whose aversion to caves sets the negative mood for Underland is, in fact, female: "Now it happened that Jill had the same feeling about twisty passages and dark places underground, or even nearly underground, that Scrubb had about the edges of cliffs" (*SC* 86). Since it is Jill, rather than Eustace or Rilian, who is terrified of caves, the cave phobia becomes a fear that relates to all humans, rather than exclusively belonging to men who fear being consumed by the feminine. Although the female Green Witch is the creator and ruler of Underland, all its other inhabitants, including the gnomes, appear male. Likewise, Milton's underground Hell does contain Sin and other female figures, but is largely populated by male fallen angels. Guyon also views male figures in his underground journey. For Lewis the negative connotation of the underground is dictated by the sort of people who generally inhabit caves, regardless of their gender, and by the fact that it is not Narnia, but a sub-world. More importantly, the negative nature of Underland is also influenced by the negative natures of Hell and Mammon's cavern.[14]

The Narnian terrain above ground also reflects the influence of both Spenser and Milton. In a sense, all three are England. Milton's paradise blooms with flowers that would be at home in any English garden: "Laurel and myrtle," "Iris all hues, roses," "Crocus, and hyacinth" (IV.694, 698, 701). Spenser's forests are distinctly British tangled woods and parks prone to sudden rainshowers. In Narnia, spring comes as it does in England: "Coming suddenly round a corner into a glade of silver birch trees Edmund saw the ground covered in all directions with little yellow flowers — celandines. The noise of water grew louder. Presently they actually crossed a stream. Beyond it, they found snowdrops growing" (*LWW* 117). Like his predecessors, Lewis creates his fictional world to include elements of his own familiar environment. In fact, this blending is part of what makes these fictional worlds so appealing: they are at once both comfortable and novel. Peter J. Schakel attests that "the distinctive atmosphere of Narnia is shaped by the blending of familiar things with unfamiliar." In a more general sense, all three settings represent an idealized, European-flavored environment of unspoiled nature.[15]

In all these texts, there is a strong dichotomy of nature versus artifice. Lewis analyzes the Bower of Bliss and the Garden of Adonis as illustrations in the issue of art contrasting to nature in *The Allegory of Love*: "The one is artifice, sterility, death: the other, nature, fecundity, life." Rather than rejecting all art as completely opposed to all nature, Lewis emphasizes Spenser's opposition as one placing artifice, rather than art, on the opposite side from the best aspects of nature. Lewis stresses the fact that this Nature is not primal, primitive, or earthy as it is often defined: "But most commonly he [Spenser] understands Nature as Aristotle did — the 'nature' of anything being its unimpeded growth from within to perfection, neither checked by accident nor sophisticated by art." What Spenser would view as "natural" would then have some measure of art, to prevent its going wild or dying, but no trace of artifice, artificiality, or excessive intrusion. Milton endorses an artful treatment of nature without descent into artifice in his descriptions of Adam and Eve's work in the garden. Eve's summation of their various duties includes gardening skills that bring out the best in nature without resorting to artifice:

> Let us divide our labors, thou where choice
> Leads thee, or where most needs, whether to wind
> The woodbine round this arbor, or direct
> The clasping ivy where to climb, while I
> In yonder spring of roses intermixed
> With myrtle, find what to redress till noon [IX.214–219].

Adam and Eve are artistic in their approaches to their work, but artifice is far from the Garden of Eden. They seek to help the plants reach their greatest potential, rather than trying to make them fit prescribed molds.[16]

The same balance of art and nature is clear in Narnia. Artisans are in no shortage, and they are nearly always presented positively when their work is art and not artifice. Narnia is only a few days old when the Dwarfs begin exhibiting their positive artistry. Strange gold and silver trees spring up from Uncle Andrew's pocket change dropped onto the fertile Narnian soil, and the Dwarves are equipped, seemingly from nowhere, with "a little anvil, hammers, tongs, and bellows…. Next moment (how those Dwarfs loved their work) the fire was blazing, the bellows were roaring, the gold was melting, the hammers were clinking…. Under the clever fingers of the little smiths two crowns took shape" (*MN* 171–2). The crowns are delicate, beautiful circlets rather than the cumbersome crowns worn by modern monarchs, and their beauty and simplicity reflect the Dwarves skill. Art is thus depicted as the magnification, or praise of nature, and artifice as the corruption or deception of nature: "In the land of Narnia, beauty — even the beauty of music and poetry — can be used against God…. But Lewis has no Puritan fear of art as deception and frivolity." Lewis, like his predecessors, makes it clear that art created with the intention of celebrating beauty and caring for the natural world is positive, while art created to deceive others or to pervert, replace, or strictly control the natural world was hardly distinguishable from artifice. The negative view of artifice is clearly demonstrated in the characters of the Calormenes and Jadis and in their architecture.[17]

Tashbaan, the capital of Calormen, is beautiful but hard, a city of stone, in which the only gardens are the private retreats of the wealthy. In Calormen, nature is tamed, controlled, and enclosed. Like its citizens, who are forced into rigid social constructs, Calormen's plants and tress are forced into forms that suit the culture. Jadis's castle is also clearly an artificial construction, with its pointy towers, all the more unpleasant because of the contrast with the natural environment. Unlike Cair Paravel, which shines like a star and opens onto the sea, the Witch's castle is out of place in its setting. Perhaps the most obvious example of artifice as an enemy of nature is in the White Witch's statue collection. Although the assortment of stone creatures is beautiful, it is cold, lifeless, and devoid of activity: "There were stone satyrs, and stone wolves, and bears and foxes and cat-a-mountains of stone. There were lovely stone shapes that … were really the spirits of trees … a centaur and a winged horse and a … dragon. They all looked so strange … in the bright cold moonlight" (*LWW* 92). Aslan and his followers, including the restored statues, stand in contrast as a lively, colorful, and "natural" romp. Rather than the deathly white and silence of the moonlit courtyard of statues, the group around Aslan is "a blaze of colours; glossy chestnut sides of centaurs, indigo horns of unicorns, dazzling plumage of birds, reddy-brown of foxes, dogs, and satyrs... the whole place rang with the sound of happy roarings, brayings, yelpings, barkings, squealings, cooings, neighings, stamping, shouts, hurrahs, songs and laughter" (*LWW* 166). This happy liveliness pulses in the very landscape of Narnia, which is commanded by Aslan on the first day of its creation: "'Narnia, Narnia, Narnia, awake. Love. Think. Speak. Be walking trees. Be talking beasts. Be divine waters'" (*MN* 116). As a living country, Narnia is meant to be artful, but never artificial, for artifice is in direct opposition to life.

The generally negative attitude toward artifice is presented in the representation of dwelling places and other buildings in *The Faerie Queene, Paradise Lost,* and the *Chronicles.* In *The Faerie Queene,* houses are never merely structures. They are at once shelters from the elements and representations of vices like Pride or virtues like Holiness. In *Paradise Lost,* the most "sophisticated" structure is Pandemonium, the castle created by the fallen angels. Adam and Eve's bower reflects their innocence and lack of artifice in its natural beauty. So, too, in Narnia, dwellings reflect the characters of their occupants. Miraz's castle, like Miraz himself, lacks character and is "a thing of yesterday" (*PC* 50); the castle of the White Witch, with its towers like sorcerer's caps (*LWW* 88) is as cold, magical, and hostile as she is; the Beavers' damtop house is practical and welcoming just as they are themselves. For the most part, structures that welcome and incorporate nature are positive, and those that restrict or forbid nature are negative. Positive homes are welcoming, warm, and usually involve large quantities of food: "Houses in Lewis often take on maternal qualities." Generally, the negative, artificial dwellings and structures are destroyed by natural forces. One of the clearest examples of this conflict is the freeing of the river (and the river god) at the Bridge of Beruna. As Aslan and his followers, including Bacchus and his Maenads, approach ivy appears and immediately begins entwining the bridge's supports "wrapping the stones round, splitting, breaking, separating them. The walls of the bridge turned into hedges gay with hawthorn for a moment, then disappeared as the whole thing with a rush and a rumble collapsed into the swirling water" (*PC* 193). The Telmarines have built the town and its bridge to contain and control nature, for they are terrified of the natural. They fear the forest which has grown up around the ruins of Cair Paravel, both because they have created legends of ghosts in the ancient castle and because they fear the trees themselves: trees whose spirits they have attempted to stifle even as they have silenced the beasts and other fantastic creatures of Narnia. Like all invaders, they seek to silence and confine that which they fear and do not understand in order to maintain their sense of control.[18]

The contrast between the proper and improper balance of nature is abundantly clear in the contrast between Tashbaan and Cair Paravel. Tashbaan is an urban maze of walls, stones, and trash heaps. Only the palaces of the wealthy are beautiful and cool, with splashing fountains, but even they demonstrate only artifice in their strict control of nature. Symmetry and artifice are clear as Shasta goes through "a wide doorway in a white wall with two tall, dark cypress trees, one on each side of it" (*HHB* 57). On the other side of the archway, Shasta enters a garden courtyard: "A marble basin of clear water in the centre was kept continually rippling.... Orange trees grew round it out of smooth grass, and the four white walls which surrounded the lawn were covered with climbing roses" (57–8). This garden is clearly work of artifice. Cair Paravel, by contrast, is a true castle and the home of all true kings of Narnia.: "modeled after the Turkish and Persian Empires of the Near East, it [Calormen] stands out in sharp contrast to the free state where justice is administered by King Peter and his compeers." The Cair's relationship to nature is clear from its actual location. Rather than isolated in the desert, like Tashbaan, Cair Paravel is located on the very border between the land and the ocean, and its eastern door opens "right onto the sea" (*LWW* 178). In *Prince Caspian,* nature has almost entirely taken over Cair Paravel, leaving it a ruin with apple trees growing in its front gate and isolated from the mainland on an island, emphasizing the country's degraded relationship with nature. Caspian restores the castle to its former glory, even as he restores the Narnians' relationship with the trees and the ocean by welcoming the tree spirits into his court and becoming a seafarer.[19]

Perhaps the most creative settings used by Spenser, Milton, and Lewis are those that have heavenly or paradisal characteristics. Spenser, while never depicting heaven per se, employs the motif of climbing to heights in order to gain spiritual insight. This "higher up" method of seeking spiritual truth is a concept Milton uses in the visions Michael gives Adam in Books XI and XII. In Lewis's Aslan's Country, this "higher up" image is a powerful one that is further accented by Lewis's remarkable idea of "further in."

Mountains, in biblical tradition, are frequently places to commune with God. Spenser describes the mountain Redcrosse climbs with Contemplation as "Such one as that same mighty man of God... Dwelt fortie dayes upon" (I.x.53.2, 7). By invoking the image of Mount Sinai, where the Israelites believed Yaweh dwelled and communed with Moses, Spenser is emphasizing the fact that the view from this mountain is not merely an uninterrupted vista; it allows Redcrosse to see spiritually as well as physically. His vision of the "new Hierusalem" (I.x.57.2) harks back to the vision of Saint John in the Revelation. In addition, this vision indicates that Redcrosse is both seeing into the future and gaining a "sneak preview" of the spiritual future home of the believers: "that God has built/ for those to dwell in, that are chosen his" (I.x.57.2–3). It is also here that Redcrosse sees the truth of both his past — that he is a Briton, not an elf— and of his future role as Saint George.

Milton incorporates a sense of height and of blurred time definition into his depiction of Heaven and the vision of Adam. In God's first appearance in Book III of *Paradise Lost*, he is "High throned above all highth" and must bend "down his eye" (58) in order to view his works. He is clearly placed on a level above Heaven proper. This position both exalts the Paternal Deity and gives him a good view. The need to see, both spiritually and physically, is also why Adam must ascend the highest hill in Paradise to see "all earth's kingdoms and their glory" (XI.384) and to see with his "mental sight" (XI.418). Here too, time is blurred, as Adam sees into the future to witness both the horrors his sin will produce and the glorious redemption God has planned. The literal height of the mountain emphasizes the spiritually uplifting experience of seeing God's plans for humanity.

The "more real" Narnia of Aslan's Country also employs the idea of going "higher up." Prior to *The Last Battle*, Aslan's followers are allowed glimpses of his country. What they see is always mountainous: "And the mountains must really have been outside the world. For any mountains even a quarter of a twentieth of that height ought to have had ice and snow on them. But these were warm and green and full of forests and waterfalls however high you looked" (*VDT* 212). When Jill looks down from the cliff in Aslan's Country, she sees a chasm so deep that after looking down for several thousand feet, she sees "little white things that might, at first glance, be mistaken for sheep" but are actually clouds (*SC* 11). As Aslan brings his followers into the Narnian equivalent of Heaven, they are continually urged to go "higher up" until they reach the "more real" version of the mountaintop garden Digory and Polly visited when they were children. This garden is spiritually more impressive than the corporeal world's imitation of the "real Narnia, which has always been here and always will be here: just as our own world, England and all, is only a shadow or a copy of something in Aslan's real world" (*LB* 169). Therefore, the mountain's size is increased with its value. Lucy looks down from the wall and finds "this hill was much higher than [she] had thought: it sank down with shining cliffs, thousands of feet below them and trees in that lower world looked no bigger than grains of green salt" (*LB* 180). Time constraints are removed from Aslan's spiritual mountaintop as they are from the mountains depicted by Spenser and Milton. Within the garden, Lewis reunites all the heroes of the *Chronicles,* from King Frank and Queen Helen to Tirian's own father. None of the restored protagonists, however, looks a day out of his or her prime. Time, like space, is under the control of a higher law in Aslan's Country. While the removal of physical laws is not surprising in the work of a twentieth-century author who also wrote science fiction, the time and space transformations in Narnia are clearly connected to equivalent motifs in Milton and Spenser.

One aspect of Lewis's spiritual realm in which he departs from his sources is the concept of "further in" that accompanies the cry of "higher up" throughout the last few chapters of *The Last Battle.* Milton, in a world uncomplicated by space exploration, could place his Heaven in the literal heavens, without concerns of conflicting stellar cartographies. Lewis's paradise, however, appears to exist in another dimension, one which does not have spatial limits: "The further up and further in you go, the bigger everything gets. The inside is larger than the outside" (180). Inside the limits of the hilltop garden, Aslan's Country encompasses all good things that were ever part of the corporeal world. Mr. Tumnus uses the analogy of an onion in reverse. Each layer one pulls away reveals a bigger layer underneath. This remarkably paradoxical concept is sometimes lumped under Digory Kirke's oft-repeated blanket statement that everything is "in Plato." However, the concept of something with a bigger inside than its outside is one that Lewis does not draw from his sources, even Milton or Spenser. Rather, it is the physical manifestation of the paradox of spirituality, an even more dramatic paradox than the space and time manipulations both previous authors used. Lucy's reminder that a Stable on earth once contained something that was larger than all the world (*LB* 141) connects the seeming paradox of going "higher up and further in" to the seeming paradox of a spiritual kingdom in which the last are first and the king dies like a slave for those who do not deserve his mercy. As with many spiritual matters, sensory logic must be superceded by faith, even in the face of apparent paradox. From the very first adventures into the wardrobe, in which the Pevensies ponder whether or not the entire country of Narnia is, in fact, within the wardrobe in the spare room, the concept of small things encompassing larger ones is woven into the very fabric of the *Chronicles*. Since Lucy is described as going "further in" (*LWW* 5) during her very first excursion into the wardrobe, it is only fitting that it is she who notes the same reversed layering quality in Aslan's Country and converses with Mr. Tumnus about the hilltop garden's peculiar spatial characteristics.[20]

At a very basic level, the element that makes Aslan's Paradise so similar to Milton's Heaven is the fact that both present a Christian heaven permeated by the character of God in the Miltonic universe, by Aslan in the Narnian universe. Christian doctrine teaches that what defines heaven is the presence of God. Both Milton and Lewis, in the presence of divine glory, must shirk away as narrators. "May I express thee unblamed?" (III.3), asks Milton, unable to truly put God down on paper. Lewis simply explains the presence of Aslan in his true form thus, "And as He spoke He no longer looked to them like a lion; but the things that began to happen after that were so great and beautiful that I cannot write them" (*LB* 183–4). The images of light, beauty, and goodness upon which both authors rely are perhaps the only ways in which Milton and Lewis can depict this setting; unlike the other settings of their texts, heaven is a place both Lewis and Milton believed to be an actual place that their readers could reach through Christ. This, perhaps, is the real conundrum in describing heaven. Most readers have little chance of comparing Narnia, Underland, Faerie Land, or Eden with the "real thing." Heaven, for Christians, is a real place, not a place conjured up in an author's imagination, and a place they actually will experience after death.

In creating the geography of Narnia and its surrounding countries, Lewis looses his creative power, flavored with the fragrances and scenes of Faerie Land and Eden. Perhaps the most remarkable resemblance between Narnia and the fabulous lands of Milton and Spenser is in the creation narrative, which follows the Miltonic sequence and includes the images of God's creation of the earth related by Raphael to Adam and Eve. Milton and Spenser, like Lewis, also incorporate their own land into the worlds of their texts. All three authors draw upon the beauties of their England to embellish the beauties of the lands they create for the reader to explore. Other features, such as the enchanted garden and the sea, all hold prominent positions in these texts. The underground terrain that all three authors present is also crucial to the overall geography of their texts. While the caves and caverns are all varied in purpose, origin, and associations, they all carry a negative connotation that relates directly to their rulers and residents. All three realms are populated but dreary and contain allegorical as well as physical denizens. The wonders and beauties of the natural realm are contrasted with the artificiality and sterility of structures that fight or pervert nature. Reflecting the Spenserian and Miltonic balance of art and nature, Narnian buildings and people that are in harmony with nature are positive figures, while those who fear or fight nature are negative. The natural world in these texts is highlighted by the presence of a spiritual realm. While Spenser does not take his readers directly to heavenly lands, both Milton and Lewis take on the daunting challenge of presenting a place they believe to be truly existent, but as yet unmapped. The spiritual realms of Heaven and Aslan's Country thus ring with hope as well as imagination and symbolism.

Narnia, despite all its resemblance to, and perhaps its reliance upon, the worlds of Milton and Spenser, is still very much its own place. The beauties of the land that lies north of Archenland and between the Great Waterfall and the sea are much more than its details of creation, geography, and even architecture. Although *Paradise Lost* and *The Faerie Queene* both contribute to Narnia, the land still has its own character and its own ambiance. The sources that contribute to the Land of Narnia deepen its reality as much as the "real" Narnia beyond the stable deepens the reality and meaning of the Narnia readers of the *Chronicles* have grown to love as they travel there with each book.

# V

# Knowing Him Better There: Spirituality and Belief

> "Oh yes! Tell us about Aslan!" said several voices at once;
> for once again that strange feeling — like the first signs of
> spring, like good news, had come over them.
> —*The Lion, the Witch and the Wardrobe* 74

There is little doubt that *Paradise Lost, The Faerie Queene,* and the *Chronicles of Narnia* are all separate and distinct texts. Despite the clear patterns of influence that have been demonstrated thus far, Lewis, Spenser, and Milton are all still the authors of their own stories. Perhaps the most important aspect of these texts, the one that illuminates all the other similarities, is the fact that all three were essentially written with the same goal: creating a vivid, beautiful, and powerful narrative that rings with a common spiritual truth. Such a goal would fulfill the once-revered belief that poetry was intended to both entertain and instruct. Each writer is driven by the impetus to create something both beautiful and edifying, using his own means to do so: Milton, by drawing upon actual biblical events and characters and augmenting them with literary traditions to create his poem; Spenser by featuring a number of virtues in chivalric episodes filled with spiritual, biblical, and epic overtones; and Lewis by telling fairy tales that exhibit

Christian beliefs by translating them into Narnian terms. Despite their apparent differences, *Paradise Lost, The Faerie Queene,* and the *Chronicles* all three include elements of a variety of mythologies while still clearly demonstrating the Christian principles of a theocentric universe ruled by a majestic and loving God; the need for obedience and the free will to either obey or disobey; sin and its consequences; repentance and salvation; the discipline needed to maintain a correct spiritual attitude; and the empowerment and completeness given to those who persevere to complete their spiritual journeys.

There is little doubt that all three authors believed their texts to be inherently Christian; while Milton is re-telling a biblical account and Spenser creating an obvious allegory, "we must remind ourselves to resist the temptation to see allegory where Lewis meant only examples and illustrations. These are adventures in another world which convey truth in their own terms."

Lewis's *Chronicles,* though seemingly simple children's stories, are far less obvious than the works of his predecessors. Lewis "is of course too accomplished an artist ever to engage in pedestrian moralizing. Yet his stories, poems, and essays have deeply moral implications which the reader can hardly avoid." As a twentieth-century author, Lewis knew well the cynicism and doubt that even the youngest readers might exhibit toward Christianity, so his stories convey their message in much subtler tones than those used by either Spenser or Milton. There is seldom any mention of anything overtly Christian: churches are mentioned only as architectural features, the Bible only as a very large book. In addition, unlike both Spenser and Milton, Lewis does not condemn any particular religious group or practice, even depicting a Calormene, Emeth, as "an anima naturaliter Christiana, a naturally Christian soul"; although Emeth has spent his life in devotion to Tash because he perceived Tash as loving and good (qualities truly ascribed to Aslan), rather than the vicious monster he truly is, Aslan accepts the young man's commitment as to him rather than to Tash. While Milton and Spenser often include both subtle and overt indictments against other religious practices, Lewis does not. Though he borrows heavily from Spenser's Duessa, gone is the imagery that links her with Catholicism. Considering that Lewis's good friend, J.R.R. Tolkien, was both a Catholic and one of the people most responsible for guiding Lewis into an acceptance of Christ, it is not surprising that Lewis chose not to transmit Spenser's anti–Catholic references. Milton clearly condemns the corrupt religious leaders of his era in the "predictions" of the future given to Adam:

> Wolves shall succeed for teachers, grievous wolves,
> Who all the sacred mysteries of heav'n
> To their own vile advantages shall turn
> Of lucre and ambition, and the truth
> With superstitions and traditions taint [XII.507–512].

Lewis, however, has no clear criticism for church leaders of any faith. The practices he condemns are those that can appear in any faith or political system: selfishness, refusal to accept the spiritual, pride, bureaucracy, interfering in the affairs of others. In short, these are the very features that stand at the opposite pole from the short summation of the acts that make Peter, Susan, Edmund, and Lucy such excellent monarchs and their reign Narnia's Golden Age: "they made good laws ... kept the peace ... saved good trees from being unnecessarily cut down ... and generally stopped busybodies and interferers and encouraged ordinary people who wanted to live and let live" (*LW* 180). In a work originally intended for younger readers, such features are easier to understand than complex theological issues, but they also represent the potential of any system to become corrupt while avoiding any outright reference to a particular faith or practice.[1]

Despite the negative portrayal of particular religious persuasions that is to be found in *The Faerie Queene* and *Paradise Lost* they, like the *Chronicles* after them, interweave a variety of pagan mythological elements alongside overtly Christian ones. Spenser's Faerie Land includes Amazons, satyrs, Greco-Roman figures such as Venus and Adonis, the Egyptian goddess Isis, and a host of other non-Christian features along with allegorical representations of Christian virtues and ideals. Milton uses material from Judeo-Christian writings and traditions, but also from pagan origins. His fallen angels come from a variety of cultures. While this may merely indicate that the false gods of these cultures are essentially demonic, these fallen angels were once heavenly angels, God's followers. The Hell to which they are consigned draws much of its imagery from the Greek Hades, just as Heaven contains elements of Mount Olympus. Milton frequently uses figures from non–Christian mythology, both in positive and negative connotations. Lewis, in turn, while writing books that clearly reflect his own Christian experiences and beliefs, also includes in them elements from a variety of non–Christian belief systems. Beginning in his childhood, Lewis was fascinated with stories from Norse and classical mythology. When night falls on Narnia in *The Last Battle,* there is certainly reference to the Book of Revelation and the Gospels: the stars fall, the sun and moon are extinguished, the faithful are separated from the unbelievers. Yet, there are also powerful echoes from the Norse Ragnarok, or Twilight of the Gods, echoes enhanced by the fact that in the American editions of *The Lion, the Witch, and the Wardrobe,* the White Witch's Secret Police is headed by the wolf Fenris Ulf. The Fenris Wolf, according to Norse myths, is the creature that will swallow the sun and initiate Ragnarok. Other Norse elements, from dwarfs to magic rings, occur throughout the books. Father Christmas, an originally pagan figure from several cultures who has been merged with the Christian saint, Nicolas, appears in Narnia, and we are told that we sometimes hear of his sort of people in our world, but in Narnia they are real. Also real in Narnia are a variety of creatures from classical mythology. From the first Narnian Lucy meets, the delightful Mr. Tumnus the Faun, to the winged horse Fledge, to the dryads and naiads who inhabit Narnia's forests and streams, to Bacchus and Silenus themselves, figures from the Greco-Roman pantheon abound in Narnia and, most importantly, are completely subservient to Aslan. When Bacchus appears, it is because Aslan's return is a time for jubilation, and, as Lucy and Susan observe, they would not be safe around Bacchus and his Maenads were not his wild nature tamed in service to Aslan: " Lewis did not need to do much cleaning up to bring the god of wine [Bacchus] into the land ... he was really the god of animals and vegetation, and the vine was simply the symbol of his domain. His wildness and the breathtaking dances of his "wild girls" illustrate the very characteristic Lewis wants to emphasize.... Without a ruler, nature will be nothing but a bonfire of energy. Its antics will be unpredictable and frightening." Thus, instead of becoming dangerous, Bacchus is joyful, exuberant, and capable of creating great feasts. At Beruna, Aslan frees the river god from the burden of the great bridge built by the Telmarines, and is addressed as "Lord" by the strange spirit. Though a variety of mythologies supply figures to Narnia, there is no question who is their true ruler. No matter their origin, these figures are under the law of Aslan and in Narnia by his invitation and his pleasure. Lewis includes these various mythological elements, but there is never any doubt who the true King is, nor that the *Chronicles*, like *The Faerie Queene* and *Paradise Lost* before them, are inherently Christian texts that ring with spiritual truth.[2]

Those who seek to investigate the spiritual truths in both Lewis's life and work often turn to his autobiography, *Surprised by Joy*. Within his narrative, he equates his fleeing from and gradual conversion to Christianity to the actions of a hunted animal or of a chess player whose opponent is relentlessly closing in on him: the chapter in which Lewis relates his conversion to Theism is entitled "Checkmate." For him, a universe in which God is supreme is not always gentle and easy. He describes himself as "the most dejected and reluctant convert in all England.... The Prodigal Son at least walked home on his feet. But who can duly adore that Love which will open the high gates to a prodigal who is brought in kicking, struggling, resentful, and darting his eyes in every direction for a chance of escape?" In explaining some of this same feeling to readers of the *Chronicles*, Lewis has Mr. Beaver explain that Aslan "'isn't safe. But he's good. He's the King, I tell you'" (*LWW* 76). It is doubtful that many people who would describe themselves as having a real and active relationship with Christ believe Him to be safe. Christ, like Aslan, has an inconvenient way of making one love the unlovable, touch the untouchable, and do the impossible. In the New Testament, Christ's commands to his disciples convey faith, power, and love, but not conventional safety. In Matthew chapter 10, for example, He assures the disciples that they needn't be afraid, for God has numbered the hairs on their heads, and He values them over the sparrows, not one of which "will fall to the ground apart from the will of your Father"; yet, in the same chapter, Christ also warns that He is sending the disciples out "like sheep among wolves," and that His message brings not "peace, but a sword" that will alienate even family members from one another. He sends His disciples out without supplies, trusting that God will provide. Such leaps of faith certainly cannot be called "safe." At the same time, however, this lack of safety does not preclude the goodness of either Christ or Aslan. Although the wildness of Aslan is used as ammunition against his followers in *The Last Battle*, Lewis is firm in endorsing the idea that Aslan is not a genie in a bottle to be brought up at an individual's whim. Rather, he has the power to call others when he needs them, not vice versa. As Lucy explains, "'I mean, when a magician in *The Arabian Nights* calls up a Jinn, it has to come. We had to come, just like that'" (*PC* 96). This power would be truly terrible if it were not wielded by someone inherently good. Aslan also causes discomfort. In *The Lion, Witch, and the Wardrobe*, Edmund's resistance to Aslan, to whom his siblings immediately connect, accentuates the rift in the Pevensie family. This rift is echoed in *Prince Caspian* when Lucy's unswerving trust in Aslan, and Edmund's in her, isolate them from Peter and Susan, who want to take what seems to be an easier path to reach Caspian's army. "Like Christ, he [Aslan] is a divider of houses." Aslan repeatedly lets his followers face dangers rather than insulating them from all unpleasantness: he sends Peter to fight the Wolf, Fenris Ulf/Maugrim, in order to "win his spurs" (*LWW* 125) rather than destroying the beast himself or allowing others more experienced in combat to do it; he sets Lucy the unpleasant task of convincing her siblings and the Dwarf Trumpkin to follow her on what will seem a wild goose chase since they cannot see Aslan; he allows Prince Cor of Archenland to grow up miserably in Calormen with an abusive "father" so that he will be able to save his country from her greatest danger. Aslan, who can see the bigger picture, never shirks from making his followers temporarily uncomfortable or unhappy in order to secure a greater good for them and for others. Despite the dangers he presents, Aslan's "righteousness can always be counted upon," and it always clear that Lewis's protagonists are "safer," at least in a larger sense, with Aslan than without him.[4]

The same unsafe goodness can be seen in Milton's Son, when "into terror changed/ His countenance too severe to be beheld/ And full of wrath bent on his enemies ... in his right hand/ Grasping ten thousand thunders" (VI.824–6, 834–5). When the Son rides into the battle against the rebel angels, his victory is so swift and so sure as to make the previous fighting seem inconsequential. Much the same result is achieved by the arrival of the resurrected Aslan at the battle Peter is leading against the forces of the White Witch: "The battle was over a few minutes after their arrival" (*LWW* 175). Both Messiah and Aslan achieve almost instantaneous victory, obliterating their foes. The Son and Aslan are unsafe but loving to their followers, so that Lucy realizes Aslan has "[t]errible paws...if he didn't know how to velvet them!" (*LWW* 125) and the Son declares " I can put on/ thy [God's] terror, as I put thy mildness on" (VI.734–5). To those who oppose the powers of good, their lack of safety is terrifying, causing Satan and his followers to fling themselves "Down from the verge of heav'n, eternal wrath/ Burnt after them to the bottomless pit" (VI.865–866) and inspiring the White Witch to pick "up her skirts and fairly run for her life" (*LWW* 141) when Aslan gives a small sample of his power.

As both military victors and kings, Messiah and Aslan are each described in conventionally royal terms. In Aslan's first appearance in *The Lion, the Witch and the Wardrobe,* he is set into a heraldic tableau of royalty, accompanied by "two leopards of whom one carried his crown and the other his standard" (123). When the Father declares the sovereignty of the Son, he refers to two of the primary indications of royalty: the anointing and his placement at the Father's right hand (V.605–6). In addition, both Milton and Lewis use gems as accents to the glory of the Son and Aslan and to add to their images of royalty and wealth. The son's chariot is virtually a huge piece of jewelry, with "the wheels of beryl ... a sapphire throne, inlaid with pure/ Amber" (VI.756, 758–9). Overhead, "the great ensign of Messiah blazed" (774). This dazzling image is strikingly similar to that of Aslan's pavilion "with sides of what looked like yellow silk and cords of crimson and tent pegs of ivory; high above it on a pole a banner, which bore a red rampant lion" (*LWW* 122). In the Miltonic hierarchy that Lewis commends in *A Preface to Paradise Lost,* the Son is entirely justified in appearing in such regality; he is a naturally superior being, a born king. Aslan's royalty, vivid and lively, is clearly more powerful and more genuine than the cold and false veneer of queenship the White Witch takes upon herself: "It was the oddest thing to see those two faces — the golden face and the dead white face — so close together" (*LWW* 138). Both Aslan and the Son are Kings who have every right to bear the title and to reflect this majesty in their courts.

Aslan also shares one of the most complex characteristics of Milton's God: both are omnipotent, but both also allow events to unfold rather than always interfering to prevent seeming disaster. As High King over all High Kings in Narnia, Aslan not only rules and guides the land, but he also permeates it. As Shasta says, "he seems to be at the back of all the stories" (*HHB* 199). Yet there are times when he seems to be completely absent, allowing others to take advantage of his absence. Shift uses the Lion's infrequent intervention to justify his Tashlan plot, rationalizing that "he [Aslan] never turns up, you know. Not now-a days" (*LB* 10). Some of the same paradoxical qualities are apparent in Milton's God. The Father is presented as a powerful figure whose presence inundates Heaven and Paradise. In his first appearance, he scans "His own works and their works at once to view" (III.59), shifting his sight in a matter of seconds from the glories of Heaven, to the happy amusements of Adam and Eve in Paradise, to the lurking figure of Satan skulking "on this side Night" (71). When God the Father speaks, "ambrosial fragrance filled/ All heav'n" (III.135–6). Even this power and omniscience does not prevent what seems to be a massive blind spot in God's knowledge. Although he banishes the rebel angels to Hell, there seems to be nothing to really prevent Satan from infiltrating Paradise. The key to Hell, which Satan needs to escape his prison, is given to Sin, his daughter and paramour, who certainly has no qualms about releasing her father/lover or defying God's order to keep "These gates for ever shut, which none can pass" (II.776). Giving the key to Sin seems like an invitation for Satan to escape, even more unwise than putting the fox in charge of the henhouse. These are the sorts of problems that have befuddled believers throughout history. It seems beyond comprehension that a good God should allow bad things to happen, particularly things that even mere mortals think they could see coming. However, both in *Paradise Lost* and the *Chronicles*, these apparent oversights are actually opportunities for God and Aslan to show their love and mercy, and to transform tragedy into greater redemption.

Both Milton and Lewis include in their theocracies a ruler whose justice is tempered by his sacrificial love for his creation. This portrayal is an obvious one from the biblical depiction of Christ, because of the "Biblical cosmology which forms the basis of both Milton's and Lewis's work" (Christensen 69). In addition, there are some specific areas in which Lewis's Aslan behaves very much like Milton's Son. In the Scriptures, there is no detailed account of the pre-incarnate Christ's initial volunteering to die for humanity. Although Jesus' pre–Calvary wrestlings with the decision are carefully chronicled in the Gospels, Milton goes back even further than Gethsemane to narrate the Son's initial decision to give his life for humanity, rise again, and "with the multitude of my redeemed/ ... enter heaven long absent, and return,/ Father, to see thy face, wherein no cloud/ Of anger shall remain, but peace assured/ And reconcilement" (III.260–3). Although the actual events of the Son's incarnation and sacrifice are implied but not related in *Paradise Lost*, his commitment to save humanity is reflected in Aslan's exchange of his life for Edmund's. Both Milton and Lewis emphasize the fact that disobedience is punishable by death and that the tempter responsible for the disobedience becomes the object of torment. Thus Satan, in causing Eve's downfall, believes he will drag down both the first humans and their "numerous offspring" to the roomy land of Hell. Jadis, having tempted Edmund to become a traitor, then claims his life as forfeit because "for every treachery I have a right to kill" (*LWW* 139). Aslan does not refute Jadis's claim, but instead draws upon a superior claim by offering himself as the replacement sacrifice. Likewise, the Son does not contest Satan's right to sinners; he provides a way for all humans to be forgiven of their sins and released from the threat of Hell. Rather than breaking the laws of the Emperor Over Sea or of God the Father, Aslan and the Son volunteer to fulfill the punishment and thus revoke it, providing an alternative that neither Jadis nor Satan, who lack divine love, compassion, and foresight, can fathom or predict.

Perhaps it still seems as though it might be easier for all concerned if God had never placed the tempting tree in the garden to begin with or if the tree were somehow so repugnant that Adam and Eve would find the prohibition against its fruit reasonable. Instead, the tree's very smell adds to the tempting words of the serpent, and it is described as "delicious fare" (IX.1028). Obedience, by its very nature, is not easy. After all, Lewis states in *Surprised by Joy*, "God was to be obeyed simply because he was God." If obedience always made sense, one would obey because the obedient action was common sense, not because he or she was consciously obeying God. In fact,

> In his own analysis of *Paradise Lost*, Lewis takes pains to emphasize his understanding that for Milton (as for Augustine before him), the Prohibition was arbitrary; the point of the forbidding was to give

Adam and Eve the opportunity to obey God in a meaningful way — not to keep anything of particular importance from them.

This brand of obedience is also demonstrated in the *Chronicles of Narnia*. In *Prince Caspian*, there is no logical reason why the Pevensies and Trumpkin should not travel to meet Caspian's army using the route they have mapped out, rather than in the direction indicated by Lucy's vision of Aslan. Only after Lucy unconditionally obeys Aslan's commands can the rest of the group see him and see that the way he has indicated is better than the one they had been traveling.[5]

Obedience becomes even more difficult for the followers of Aslan when, like Eve, they encounter an enemy who tries to turn their obedience against them. In his seduction of Eve, Satan indicates that God will not indeed punish her for eating the fruit but will "praise/ Rather your dauntless virtue, whom the pain/ Of death denounced" (IX. 693–5). He thus tries to convince Eve that the test presented by the tree is not an obedience test, but an intelligence or initiation test, that God does not want her to display obedience, but courage. Shift uses the same tactics in coercing first Puzzle and then the Narnians of *The Last Battle*. When Puzzle has misgivings about the lionskin ruse Shift has planned, there is a thunderclap and earthquake that the donkey immediately knows is an indication of Aslan's displeasure:

> "There!" gasped Puzzle... "It's a sign, a warning. I knew we were doing something dreadfully wicked. Take this wretched skin off me at once."
>
> "No, no," said the Ape (whose mind worked very quickly). "It's a sign the other way. I was just going to say that if the real Aslan, as you call him, meant us to go on with this, he would send us a thunderclap and an earth-tremor.... You know you don't understand these things. What could a donkey know about signs?" [*LB* 11].

When Shift is brainwashing the Narnians at his midnight meetings, their very obedience is used to keep them in submission to the Ape's twisted leadership. Believing that "Tashlan" will be angry with them for doing good, they thus do nothing (*LB* 11). In *A Preface to Paradise Lost*, Lewis emphasizes the fact that "order can be destroyed in two ways: (1) By ruling or obeying natural equals, that is by Tyranny or Servility. (2) By failing to obey a natural superior or to rule a natural inferior — that is, by Rebellion or Remissness." Both paths to the destruction of order are presented in Paradise and also in Narnia.[6]

Although the person of Christ is not a character in *The Faerie Queene*, the poem is still very decidedly Christian, featuring characters like Una, Arthur, and the inhabitants of the House of Holiness who embody aspects of Christ. Rather than focusing on Christ's interactions with individuals, Spenser, particularly with Redcrosse, focuses more closely on the experiences of a Christian in a hostile and tempting world that often makes obedience difficult. This Christian experience is one that requires unflagging devotion even when the person of Christ is not physically present. Bearing the Cross of Christ, Redcrosse continuously carries a reminder of his devotion to his "dying Lord,/ For whose sweet sake that glorious badge he wore,/ And dead as living ever him adored/ ... Right faithful true he was in deede and word" (I.i.2.2–4,7). By carrying the symbol of his obedience, Redcrosse declares his loyalty, much as Peter does with a similar shield "the colour of silver ... across it there ramped a red lion, as bright as a ripe strawberry at the moment when you pick it" (*LWW* 104). The enchanted Prince Rilian's shield has no device until he is restored in obedience to Aslan, then it is "bright as silver, and on it, redder than blood or cherries, was the figure of the Lion" (*SC* 168). All three knights exhibit their obedience by a device that indicates their allegiance.

Although Lucy does not wear a badge of her obedience, she is the most loyal of all Aslan's followers, often withstanding the temptation to disobey. In *The Voyage of the "Dawn Treader,"* Lucy goes through a temptation episode much like that experienced by Guyon in the second book of *The Faerie Queene*. While Guyon is presented with material objects in Mammon's cave that look beautiful but would prove his destruction, Lucy is presented with the opportunity to say "an infallible spell to make beautiful her that uttereth it beyond the lot of mortals" (129). The spell is accompanied by pictures, clearly depicting future events that the spell will produce. Lucy is sorely tempted to say the spell, but Aslan's picture, "such a bright gold that it seemed to be coming towards her out of the page" (131), prevents her and reminds her to be obedient. Likewise, Guyon's roving eye at the Bower of Bliss falls upon the bathing maidens who cause him to "somewhat gan relent his earnest pace,/ His stubborne brest gan secret pleasaunce to embrace"

(II.xii.65.8–9). The Palmer's stern rebuke is not unlike the growl Lucy sees on Aslan's face. Although obedience is sometimes difficult, help is often given to prevent disobedience. This assistance may appear to be criticism or punishment, but it is intended to lead characters back onto the path of obedience.

The reward for obedience, strangely enough, is often another task. Both Lewis and Spenser demonstrate the unending demand upon obedience. Redcrosse, having defeated the dragon and rescued Una's family, cannot merely enjoy his success with his beloved: "He naught forgot, how he whilhome had sworne,/ ... Unto his Faire Queene backe to returne:/ The which he shortly did, and Una left to mourne" (I.xii.41.6, 8–9). Instead of resting upon his laurels and living happily ever after, Redcrosse returns to his sovereign for further orders. In *The Horse and His Boy*, Shasta experiences a similar "reward" for bringing news of Rabadash's invasion. Scarcely has he arrived at the compound of the Hermit of the Southern March, than he is instructed to immediately run, on foot rather than on Bree's back, to warn King Lune in person: "Shasta's heart fainted at these words for he felt he had no strength left... he writhed inside at what seemed the cruelty and unfairness of the demand. He had not yet learned that if you do one good deed your reward is usually to be set to do another and harder and better one" (*HHB* 140). For both Spenser and Lewis, obedience is not a single event, but a continuous way of viewing life. Sometimes, obedience does not even seem to make sense.

One of the most humorous passages in *The Voyage of the "Dawn Treader"* involves the Duffers, a tribe of monopod dwarfs ruled by the retired star Coriakin. They question his every command, particularly commands that would make their lives easier or that would be otherwise beneficial to them: "A few months ago they were all for washing up the plates and forks before dinner: they said it saved time afterwards.... One day the cat got into the dairy and twenty of them were at work moving all the milk out; no one thought of moving the cat" (141). Yet, to the Duffers (or the Dufflepuds as they finally decide to call themselves) their way of thinking is much more important than following the very sensible orders of the magician. They are so set on not obeying him that they do not even obey logical commands meant for their good. Although the Dufflepuds may seem foolish, their stubborn disobedience is no more ridiculous than Redcrosse's inability to comprehend Duessa's intentions, even after Fraudubio's warning, or his blindness to the true nature of the House of Pride. Perhaps both Spenser and Lewis are each reminding their readers that all of humanity, in the childish refusal to obey, does itself harm as surely as the Dufflepuds and Redcrosse do.

Redcrosse, fortunately, does not remain as blind and stubborn as the Dufflepuds. He has a choice to either remain in disobedience or to return to Una and to truth. The allegorical nature of the characters in *The Faerie Queene* may seem to preclude their ability to make choices. However, they are at once representational figures of virtues and of Christians: As H.S.V. Jones notes, "Redcrosse is, of course, not simply Holiness, but, like Everyman and Bunyan's hero, a universalized type of Christian man advancing through sin and repentance to realization of his difficult ideal." Redcrosse, like any Christian, has a choice of disobedience or obedience. He can be simply a knight, blindly fighting and following his own will, or he can fulfill his potential and become Saint George. It is his choice, though. Regardless of his symbolic elements, Redcrosse is still a human being, imbued with free will.[7]

The most powerful reference to choice and free will is found in *Paradise Lost*. Adam and Eve choose their disobedience; it is not chosen for them. Although God knows in advance what their choice will be, he still does not wrench their autonomy away from them. Rather, he insists, "I formed them free, and free they must remain" (III.124), even when this freedom comes at such a dear cost. The freedom to choose good or evil is even more dramatic in Satan, who has no more or less potential for evil than any other angel: "Ingrate, he had of me/ All he could have; I made him just and right,/ Sufficient to have stood, though free to fall" (III.96–8). God prefers to let both angels and humans choose their own happiness or failure, rather than merely making them into obedient sheep or robots. The same value placed on free will is apparent in Aslan: "For Lewis, the primal stance of human beings before God is to be obedient: not to be slavishly devoted, but to be freely attentive." Some of the clearest examples of the use of free will in the *Chronicles* are in *The Magician's Nephew*. Uncle Andrew, in his trick to use Digory and Polly in his experiment, assures Digory that he does not have to rescue Polly: "Go down and have your dinner. Leave the little girl to be eaten by wild animals or drowned or starved in Other World or lost there for good, if that's what you prefer" (26). This manipulation is actually an attempt to circumvent Digory's free will, for Uncle Andrew does not want Digory to go after Polly to protect her from harm; he wants to reclaim Digory and Polly, his human guinea pigs, along with his Rings, in order to collect data and complete his experiment. Though going after Polly is the moral choice for Digory to make, Uncle Andrew, whose intentions are distinctly immoral, uses unethical methods to motivate his nephew. In sharp contrast to this episode is Digory's decision to be obedient to Aslan's command to fetch the Apple of Protection. The entire time that Digory is on his quest, he has a Ring in his pocket that could take him home and eliminate all the troubles of his time in Narnia. However, he resists this temptation, as well as the urge to take a magical apple for himself or for his terminally ill mother. By making the right choice, Digory thus validates the use of his free will. No one has to trick him; he knows the right choice and makes it freely. Other characters do not always make the right choice.[8]

Perhaps the most troubling use of free will in the *Chronicles* is Susan's choice to abandon Aslan and Narnia for the shallow and fleeting symbols of worldly maturity: "nylons and lipstick and invitations" (*LB* 135). Lewis has been criticized for implying that growing up is undesirable, that adulthood is inferior to childhood, and thus, that maturity is inferior to immaturity. However, "Lewis believed that fortitude is a virtue fundamental to all others. Only the soldier or martyr who stands firm in the face of danger or death can claim the virtues of loyalty or faith." Susan is not being punished for growing up, but for abandoning her post: the childlike faith she once possessed. It fact, it is not even true maturity that Susan has embraced at the cost of Narnia and her happiness. Rather, she has sacrificed her belief in Narnia, and in Aslan, for a cheap imitation of maturity, what Polly, a truly mature individual, calls, "the silliest time of one's life" (*LB* 135). Susan has "succumbed to the lure of teenage pleasures and fashions." She has not chosen to pursue a meaningful course in life by continuing her education, marrying, having children, or, like Polly, by mentoring those younger than herself. In fact, Susan not only wants to rush to the idealized age of young adulthood; she wants to stay there, avoiding any further growth or development. Clearly, this is not maturity, which seeks to better a person, turning age to wisdom. What Susan wants is stagnation, not maturity. Instead of aging and reaching her full potential, Susan, like Jadis and her Hall of Images, seeks to freeze herself in time, to stay just as she is. Ironically, because she forsakes her belief in Aslan and Narnia, Susan will presumably continue to age until her eventual death. Her siblings, however, are transported to the new Narnia, where everyone appears at the peak of vigor, neither elderly nor childish. Tirian has difficulty deciding whether Jill looks older or younger, and both Polly and Digory, though well advanced in years, are without gray hair or wrinkles. Susan's self-absorbed, superficial focus has cost her a true youthful eternity, and is anything but mature. In fact, Susan's desire to remain as she is also resembles part of the temptation of Milton's Eve. While some critics have viewed Eve as childish, and her fall as an important, if painful, step on the path to maturity, Lewis certainly did not concur. Though in his *Preface to Paradise Lost*, Lewis admits that he had, before reading *Paradise Lost*, anticipated a childish and immature Adam and Eve, in fact, they were created "fullgrown and perfect," not as semi-developed beings. Milton's Adam and Eve are physically and intellectually complete and mature. The unfallen Eve is inexperienced, but she is not immature. Like the fruit in the garden and the animals that burst from the soil, she is fully adult. Clearly, she and Adam have a mature physical relationship: "nor turned I ween/ Adam from his fair spouse, nor Eve the rites/ Mysterious of connubial love refused" (IV.741–3). Eve's maturity is internal as well as external, as evidenced by her sophisticated speech and reasoning techniques:

> small store will serve, where store,
> All seasons, ripe for use hangs on the stalk
> Save what by frugal storing firmness gains
> To nourish, and superfluous moist consumes:
> But I will haste and from each bough and brake,
> Each plant and gourd will pluck such choice
> To entertain our angel guest, as he
> Beholding, shall confess that here on earth
> God hath dispensed his bounties as in heav'n [V.322–330].

Eve does experience a new kind of maturity after the fall, but it is a painful maturity born of loss, not the maturity God intended, for indeed, there is no indication that Milton's God plans to arrest Adam and Eve's development in any way. In fact, as Lewis noted in the *Preface,* Raphael tells Adam that the "time may come when men/ With angels may participate ... and winged ascend/ Ethereal..." (V.493–5, 498–9). If the Fall had never occurred, humans would presumably still continue to grow and advance until they would be converted to an angelic state. But this intended development is one based on obedience, not failure. Even as a failure, however, Eve is not left unredeemed. Though she has cost herself and her descendants the blissful relationship with God that she once enjoyed, she is still offered reconciliation, albeit a painful and costly one. Her pain in bearing children will eventually produce a second Adam, Christ, to defeat Satan and bring salvation to humanity. Susan, too, is not eternally excluded from Narnia. Perhaps she will become "old enough to start reading fairy stories again" (*LWW* dedication) and will achieve a maturity that is genuine, not superficial. She, like Eve, still has choices. She can exercise her free will to remain focused on herself and fleeting trappings of beauty, or she can choose to return to the genuine faith of her childhood and, as Lewis indicated on a number of occasions, join her family in Aslan's Country after her natural death at a later time. Her denial of Narnia does not cost her eternal salvation, but it does revoke her joy and her connection with those who truly love her.[9]

Obviously, the antagonists of all three texts are those who have used their free will to make the wrong choices and do not look back, as readers hope that Susan eventually will. Positive characters, however, are able to see their decisions as wrong and to make the choice for repentance. One of the most important choices made by a character in the *Chronicles* is Edmund's "to let Lucy down" (*LWW* 41). Lewis describes this as the "meanest and most spiteful thing he [Edmund] could think of" and indicates that Edmund's decision is a split second one. Instead of exercising his free will to support Lucy, Edmund makes a snap decision that will cause Lucy grief and will create the rift between himself and Peter that augments Edmund's betrayal. Adam and Eve also use their free will to make the wrong decision, setting off a chain reaction of pain and separation from God. Though Edmund's action is on a much smaller scale, his wrong choice, like that of Adam and Eve, is his choice, and not imposed on him or denied him. Freedom also entails the freedom to do the wrong thing. Like Adam and Eve, Edmund takes food offered by an unknown individual, although there are clear signals that this individual is up to no good. Both Edmund and Eve attempt to take on the forces of temptation singlehandedly, and both fail. Fortunately for these characters, there is still the opportunity for salvation and redemption.

The cycle of sin, repentance, and reconciliation is one that runs through all three texts. Redcrosse's experiences in the first book of *The Faerie Queene* are clear illustrations of the believer's failing, followed by his forgiveness and return to the truth. The return is not an easy one. For Redcrosse, the road to repentance includes a despair that borders on the suicidal and treatments that include sackcloth, ashes, fasting, and physical punishment. Part of his repentance includes a stinging saltwater bath that cleanses him as he continues in his journey toward holiness:

> In ashes and sackcloth he did array
> His dainte corse, proud humors to abate,
> And dieted with fasting every day...
> And ever as superfluous flesh did rot
> Amendment readie still at hand did wayt,
> To pluck it out with pinchers firie whot...
> And bitter Penance with an yron whip,
> Was wont him once to disple every day...
> And sad Repentance used to embay
> His bodie in salt water smarting sore [I.x.26.1–27.6].

This episode's baptismal imagery, as well as its painfulness, is reflected in the redemption of Eustace after he has become a dragon. Although Eustace is a perfectly unpleasant person long before he is turned into a dragon, "we know from the outcome ... his case is not hopeless. Lewis believed in the depravity of boys but not their total depravity." Like Redcrosse, Eustace must undergo the painful ripping away of his corrupted self, represented by the dragonskin. Then Aslan places him into a pool of water, and "it smarted like anything but only for a moment" (*VDT* 90). Like Redcrosse, Eustace is separated from his companions during his restoration. Though Una tears her clothes and hair at the sound of Redcrosse's roars of pain and frustration, and Eustace's friends desperately hope for a cure so that they will not have to abandon the huge creature he has become, both individuals must face their trials alone in taking the difficult path to redemption.[10]

The most noticeable example of redemption and restoration in the *Chronicles* is in the sacrificial salvation of Edmund: "The theme is that most basic of all themes, redemption through Christ." Edmund, like Redcrosse and Eustace, is taken away from those he loves to be restored by Aslan who walks with him "in the dewy grass, apart from the court. There is no need to tell you (and no one ever heard) what Aslan was saying, but it was a conversation which Edmund never forgot" (*LWW* 135). Just as Redcrosse is returned to Una, "who him joyd to see" (I.x.68.9), a better man for his ordeals, so Aslan brings Edmund back to his siblings, reminding them "there is no need to talk to him about what is past" (*LWW* 135). Both Edmund and Redcrosse are nearly stabbed shortly before their spiritual and physical rescue. Redcrosse is almost convinced by Despayre to commit suicide with a dagger "sharpe and keene" (I.ix.51.2) before Una's timely intervention, and the White Witch, determined to prevent at least one throne in Cair Paravel from being filled, binds Edmund and prepares to cut his throat with her stone knife before the intervention of Aslan's rescue party. Redcrosse and Edmund both emerge from their sin and repentance as better men: "Edmund's story parallels that of Red Crosse. He too, is figuratively 'resurrected from the dead' through heavenly intervention...." Redcrosse goes on to become England's Saint George, and Edmund becomes King Edmund the Just, a noble soldier who destroys the White Witch's wand at great personal risk, a loyal brother who never again lets Lucy down, and a wise king who helps lead Narnia's Golden Age. Like Redcrosse, Edmund becomes an emblematic and inspirational figure to future generations.[11]

Lewis, like his predecessors, also presents hope even in the midst of failure. Although Adam and Eve are irreversibly removed from Eden, unable to return despite their contrition, God comforts them and allows them to see his plans for their descendants when the angel Michael gives Adam his vision of the redemption of humanity. The first humans cannot be restored to their previous relationship with God, but they can repent, and, through their failing, God can produce "Light out of darkness" (XII.472). In Narnia, this restoration is equated with Aslan's explaining "that no one is ever told what *would have happened*" (*VDT*

136). Aslan can refresh spirits and extend forgiveness, but he does not make things as they might have been. When Lucy regrets having magically eavesdropped on her friends back in England, hearing hurtful comments about herself, she realizes that the friendship is severed and that whatever possibility of future relationship she might have with her friend is now tainted. Although they may still be friends, things are not as they might have been. On a larger scale, Adam and Eve, having broken their pristine relationship with God, can have a restored communion with him, but it will never have the intimacy of their previous relationship, and they cannot know what their lives might have been like had they remained unfallen. Since Aslan tells Lucy both in *Prince Caspian* and *The Voyage of the "Dawn Treader"* that we can never know what might have happened if we had made different choices, we can only guess how those alternate paths might have affected our lives.

One of the most interesting aspects of Christian development that frequently appears in the *Chronicles* is the element of discipline. Like the knights of *The Faerie Queene*, characters in the *Chronicles* must often exercise discipline over themselves in order to achieve their goals. The quest is an illustration of this discipline. In all the quests of the *Chronicles*, characters are required to demonstrate control over themselves in order to prevail. This is most apparent in *The Silver Chair*. Jill's experiences in her quest to rescue Prince Rilian are strikingly similar to those of the knights in *The Faerie Queene*. Interestingly, one of the most disciplined characters in Spenser's epic is also a woman, Britomart. Unlike Britomart, Jill must struggle to keep her discipline and does not always resist the urge to give in to the lures of comfort and ease. Britomart's vigil in the House of Busirane demonstrates her determination not to be sidetracked by comfort or sleep; instead she "drew her selfe aside in sickernesse,/ And her welpointed weapons did about her dresse" (III.xi.55.8–9). Although Jill succumbs to the desire for comfort when she lets down her guard at Harfang, she is chastised by Aslan in a dream and becomes a vigilant, and eventually successful, seeker of the lost Prince. Both Britomart and Jill, while imprisoned in an enemy's castle, encounter cryptic messages. Britomart, in Busirane's house, sees "*Be bold, be bold*, and every where *Be bold*" (III.xi.54.3). Jill, having briefly lost sight of her goal and her practice of reciting the Signs given by Aslan, finds her course again when she looks out her window at the giants' castle and sees "in large, dark lettering across the center of the pavement, ... the words UNDER ME" (*SC* 102). Both Jill and Britomart must rely on their training and make decisions about how to proceed. Because they remain true to their callings, Jill and Britomart are both able to rescue a captive and defeat an evil enchanter.

Both Jill and Britomart, because of their determination and discipline, succeed where others have failed. A recurring element of spirituality in the *Chronicles* and their predecessors is the theme of reward for faithful service. Those who persevere and remain obedient receive physical as well as spiritual empowerment. There is every indication that Redcrosse would not last one round against the dragon without the chastisement and spiritual growth he experiences at the House of Holiness. Having gained spiritual strength, he is thus physically able to challenge and defeat the monster. Likewise, the rejuvenating well and tree that aid him in the battle are not merely physical helps but spiritual aids as well. He is restored by The Well of Life that "unto life the dead it could restore,/ And guilt of sinfull crimes cleane wash away" (I.xi.30.1–2). Thus Redcrosse is absolved as well as healed. The same kind of restoration occurs when Edmund, mortally wounded from fighting the Witch, is healed by Lucy's cordial. She finds him after he has recovered "standing on his feet and not only healed of his wounds but looking better than she had seen him look — oh, for ages; in fact ever since his first term at that horrid school where he first began to go wrong. He had become his real old self again and could look you in the face" (*LWW* 177). Because he has been restored both in body and soul, Edmund's healing, like Redcrosse's, is a complete one, restoring him to a degree of spiritual rightness much higher than he knew even before his failures. Physical and spiritual rightness are so closely linked that spiritual healing leads to a restored physical state as well.

When Aslan sends Lucy to wake her siblings and Trumpkin for a midnight journey, Aslan's mane gives her strength, and he tells her, "Now you are a lioness" (*PC* 138). She becomes physically stronger by being spiritually strong. This powerful spirituality is also clear in Britomart, whose chastity makes her invulnerable to the wicked Busirane's fire and allows her to rescue Amoret. In Narnia, the children who are following Aslan's orders frequently change physically to reflect their inner growth. Tirian notices that Jill and Eustace "both seemed to be already much stronger and bigger and more grown-up than they had been when he first met them a few hours ago" (*LB* 57). This concept incorporates the biblical idea of being strengthened by God's approval and the chivalric ideal that the soldier, army, or cause that God favors will be blessed with victory.

The reverse of this spiritual and physical connection is, of course, that the spiritually weak will be physically weak as well. Uncle Andrew is perhaps the best example of this concept in the *Chronicles*. Although he should be rejuvenated by the air of Narnia, he is so crippled by fear of Aslan and of the spiritual power of the Lion that he has a nervous breakdown and becomes the plaything of curious animals. In *Paradise Lost*, Adam and Eve are physically made mortal, and therefore weaker, as a result of their spiritual weakness. Their physical bodies become a shame to them that reflects their inner spiritual shame making them "unlike/ To that first naked glory" (IX.1114–5). Their demeanors change as irrevocably as their souls, for when God finds them skulking in the shadows: "Love was not in their looks, either to God/ Or to each other,/ but apparent guilt,/ And shame, and perturbation, and despair,/ Anger,/ and obstinacy, and hate, and guile" (X.112–114). A very similar fate befalls Ginger the Cat in *The Last Battle*. Believing that there is no Aslan and conspiring with Shift and the Calormenes to enslave the Narnians, Ginger plans to "act scared" of the "Tashlan" in the Stable. Instead, he is so terrified by the real Tash that he is no longer a Talking Beast: "...the Cat was trying to say something: but nothing came out of its mouth except the ordinary ugly, cat-noises you might hear from any angry or frightened old Tom in a backyard in England. And the longer he caterwauled the less like a Talking Beast he looked" (109). His transformation back into a dumb beast is a physical manifestation of his spiritual beastliness, just as Adam and Eve, after their disobedience appear less "God-like erect, with native honor clad/In naked majesty ... lords of all" (IV.88–89) and more like dumb animals cringing from a displeased master. In *The Horse and His Boy*, Rabadash's transformation into a donkey, although temporary and far more comical than the changes undergone by Ginger or Adam and Eve, reflects the same principle: since he insists on making an ass of himself, he literally becomes one. Although he is transformed into a physically more powerful form, Eustace's "dragoning" also reflects the Spenserian and Miltonian ideas

155

of inner, spiritual characteristics affecting outer, physical features: "Sleeping on a dragon's hoard with greedy, dragonish thoughts in his heart, he had become a dragon himself" (*VDT* 75). The heart thus manifests itself in the outer appearance, turning characters into what, at least internally, they already are. Fortunately for both Rabadash and Eustace, their transformations are not permanent, and both become better individuals for their experiences. Eustace becomes a courageous friend who throws himself into combat against the Sea Serpent, a loyal subject of Caspian who devotes himself to finding the King's lost son, and a noble follower of Aslan who eventually gives his life for the true King of Narnia in *The Last Battle*. Though Rabadash is not a model citizen, he does, at least, behave himself, and, since Aslan forbids him to travel abroad from Tashbaan, he is unable to make war upon his neighbors and acquires a reputation as a peaceful leader.

Transformation of both spiritual and physical attributes in the *Chronicles* is often positive as well. The change that comes over those who enter Aslan's Country clearly illustrates that spiritual and physical states are linked. In *The Silver Chair*, Aslan reverses the signs of aging in Caspian until he is "a young man, or a boy. (But Jill couldn't say which, because of people having no particular ages in Aslan's country)" (212). This ageless transformation is dramatically illustrated in the great reunion of *The Last Battle*. Tirian does not even recognize the restored Jill for she is "not Jill as he had last seen her with her face all dirt and tears.... Now she looked cool and fresh, as if she had just come from bathing. And at first he thought she looked older, but then he didn't, and he could never make up his mind" (133). Polly and Digory, who were older people in England, realize that they have been "unstiffened" and there are no wrinkles or gray hairs on either of them. The most drastic physical restoration to occur in Aslan's Country is, of course, the restoration from death to life. In their own world, the Pevensies, Digory, Polly, Jill, and Eustace have all been killed in a horrific railway accident, but in Aslan's Country they are alive and restored to that unparticular age of people in that land, along with Narnians who have been dead, in the old Narnia, for centuries.

Although the influence of Spenser and Milton can be seen in many aspects of the *Chronicles*, the most unifying element of these texts is their consistently Christian outlook. Lewis, while attempting to get around the "watchful dragons" that so often prevent acceptance of Christian principles, has drawn upon the presentation of spiritual issues in both Spenser and Milton. No matter how fantastic their created worlds, how thrilling the adventures portrayed there, all three authors realized, as Lewis himself wrote, that "to construct plausible and moving 'other worlds' you must draw on the only real 'other world' we know, that of the spirit." In addition, all three authors brought in a variety of elements from non–Christian belief systems, yet looked to the Bible as the ultimate source for the texts they were creating. Milton's God the Father and God the Son both set clear precedents for Aslan. Though the great lion still remains a unique representation of a possible Christ, he also incorporates many elements from *Paradise Lost*. In creating their deities, Milton and Lewis wrestle with a number of issues common in Christian thought: the permeating power of the divine, the problems of a good God and bad events, and the joys of mercy and love. The spiritual issues of obedience and free will are powerful components of the *Chronicles, Paradise Lost,* and *The Faerie Queene.* In exploring these issues, all three authors emphasize the importance of choice and the possibility of redemption that exists even for those who make incorrect choices. In the process of redemption, characters from all three texts exhibit the painful transformation that the disobedient must often undergo in order to atone for their straying from the true path. Discipline, by keeping the loyal individuals close to their source of power, also provides empowerment and strength. By the same token, the recalcitrant are both spiritually and physically deformed. While many of these similarities are clearly the result of Lewis's conscious use of work he respected and admired, others are far more subtle, demonstrating all three authors' desire to use fantastic fiction to illuminate spiritual fact.[12]

# Conclusion

With each passing year, the *Chronicles of Narnia*, along with many of Lewis's other creations, become more and more popular. Christian bookstores and publishing houses continue to reprint and re-issue everything from the cryptic and remarkable *Till We Have Faces* to previously unavailable essays on a variety of subjects. The highly successful film *The Chronicles of Narnia: The Lion, the Witch, and the Wardrobe* brought children and adults alike into a fully realized Narnia. New approaches to the series have allowed the series to be enjoyed in a variety of media from radio theater to calendars, from richly illustrated storybooks to action figures, from school curricula to jewelry. As Lewis's works experience this revival, there is the chance that perhaps, someday, all of his copious and delightful borrowings, influences, and nuances, will be tracked to their sources in art, literature, life, and faith. However, for the present, we can hope that the Miltonic and Spenserian sources for Narnia's antagonists, females, geography, and spirituality will lead readers to a deeper understanding of the *Chronicles* and their sources.

These areas are obviously not the only aspects in which Spenser and Milton make their presence known in the *Chronicles of Narnia*. Other hints and glimpses of their influence can be detected throughout the series, as well as in Lewis's other writing. *Paradise Lost* has left its imprint most noticeably on the Space Trilogy, but touches of Milton's influence can be seen throughout both Lewis's fiction and nonfiction. *The Faerie Queene*'s influence runs throughout the Lewis canon as well, from the allegorical figures of *Pilgrim's Regress* and *That Hideous Strength* to his use of both Christianity and classical mythology in *Till We Have Faces*.

Though one can certainly spot patterns of influence in the depiction of evil, the roles of women, and the creation of fantastic worlds, it is within the spiritual realm that Lewis most connects to his predecessors. Yet it is here that specific patterns become more amorphous and elusive. Perhaps it is because Milton and Spenser overlap in Lewis's work so much on spiritual issues that specifics are not always readily available. For although these authors are all telling different stories, they are still telling the same story. This is the story Lucy reads in Coriakin's magic book, the spell for refreshment of the spirit. The story is so beautiful that Lucy wants to go on reading it, but she cannot turn back the pages or even clearly remember the story's details: "And she never could remember; and ever since that day what Lucy means by a good story is a story which reminds her of the forgotten story in the Magician's Book" (*VDT* 133). Milton, Spenser, and Lewis are all telling the story of what it means to try to follow Christ, what it means to be obedient, to fail, and to be restored. At the same time, they are telling rousing good stories of battles, love, heroes, monsters, and incredible adventures. Both Milton and Spenser like "Lewis knew that the first business was to tell a story that would live in the mind of the reader. The 'messages' if the story is to be effective, must be subordinate to the action." If a story is stilted, preachy, or not engaging, all the moral messages in the world will not save it from the groans of miserable readers. By using the fairy tale, Lewis tapped into the special ability such stories possess: "Fairy tales can be Christian without being parochial, moral without being rationalistic or hortatory, shining with goodness, wonder, and love without being in the least sentimental." All three authors tell wonderful stories that can be enjoyed for the stories' sake, and their messages, whether subtle or overt, all spring from the same origins. Thus, although Lewis was undoubtedly influenced by *The Faerie Queene* and *Paradise Lost*, one important reason why his *Chronicles* so resemble these texts is that they are all drawing from the same source. All three texts are, in some way or another, the authors' rendition of the biblical and Christian traditions. They all also draw upon other important Western traditions and texts, such as *The Iliad* and *The Odyssey*, leading to some of their similarities. In a sense, Milton, Spenser, and Lewis are all three painting the same landscape. Side by side, the paintings may resemble each other only slightly, but they will still undoubtedly resemble each other. Lewis, however, has gone beyond merely using the same inspiration as his sources. At times, even his brush strokes are the same.[1]

Although Lewis draws on many of the other great texts of Western Literature as well as less weighty tomes, these two epic poems seem to have had some of the most profound influence on the *Chronicles*. They were early and frequent personal reading and lifelong scholarly interests, but Lewis also found great delight and food for thought and criticism in other texts. Why then do Spenser and Milton seem to have such a presence in Lewis's best-loved books? Lewis often saw himself as a poet rather than a prose writer, and his first published works were his early poems, so these writers, great poets as well as great storytellers would have held for him an irresistible dual power. It is even likely that much of the *Chronicles'* connections to Milton and Spenser were subconscious, with Lewis referencing the texts without even realizing he was doing so. However, it is unlikely that he never noticed the way in which his own creations resembled those of his favorite authors. Perhaps in referencing these authors, Lewis was seeking to continue his lifelong quest to slow the decline of intellectual thought and the rise of mediocrity by passing along hints of these vital Western authors, like breadcrumbs in the dark forest of ignorance, leading readers to the texts that Lewis himself regarded as both enjoyable reading and vital pillars of Western thought and literary tradition.

It would be tempting to attest that the *Chronicles'* dependence on outside sources is a flaw in their literary value. However, the predominance of influence, rather than demonstrating the weakness of Lewis's literary skill, exhibits the extraordinary power of the *Chronicles*. Lewis has not merely copied from the authors he respected and enjoyed. Rather, the currents of influence from Milton and Spenser add to the overall depth of the *Chronicles*. *The Faerie Queene* and *Paradise Lost*, as important parts of Lewis's personal and professional life, are woven as smoothly into his writing as his delight in good food, his enjoyment of a pipe, and his compassion for animals. While Lewis may have consciously included many elements that resonate with the tones of his respected predecessors, other references are no doubt far more natural in their inclusion, as much an unconscious part of Lewis's writing style as the vision he had of Tumnus and his packages under the snowy lamp-post, or of Aslan himself, who bounded unexpectedly into the stories. Rather than detracting in any way from the value of the *Chronicles*, the discovery of their connections to other texts adds to their richness and deepens both the readers' interest in the stories themselves and in their remarkable author, who brings his readers to a greater understanding of the Christ he loved, but also to an appreciation of the things he loved, from "northerness" and large breakfasts to two of the authors who influenced him most profoundly. Like the Stable in *The Last Battle,* the *Chronicles* have more inside them than the exterior belies. While they may appear as small and simple as that humble wooden structure, the *Chronicles,* like the Stable, encompass a world that grows ever more wonderful, "the higher up and further in" one goes. The influences of Milton and Spenser, as well as those from the Bible and other innumerable sources, certainly add to the beauty and depth of the *Chronicles.* However, children all over the world continue to read and enjoy them without any knowledge of the obvious or hidden sources woven into the fabric of Narnia. Perhaps by loving and appreciating the *Chronicles,* these readers will escape the "watchful dragons" that often thwart literary interest, as well as those that guard against Christian virtues. These readers, as well those to come, may know Milton and Spenser, as well as Aslan, all the better for having known them for a little while in Narnia.[2]

# Chapter Notes

## Introduction

1. C.S. Lewis, *Of Other Worlds: Essays and* Stories (Ed. Walter Hooper. New York: Harcourt, Brace and World, Inc., 1966) 24; C. N. Manlove, *Christian Fantasy: From 1200 to the Present* (Notre Dame: University of Notre Dame Press, 1992) 232; Walter Hooper and Roger Lancelyn Green, *C. S. Lewis: A Biography* (New York, Harcourt, Brace Jovanovich, 1974) 251; in the opening sentences of *The Magician's Nephew*, Lewis references the Bastables, Nesbit's protagonists in many of Lewis's favorite stories, by listing them alongside Sherlock Holmes to set the time period of the story. Not only do these references place the time period, but they also define the Bastables, Holmes, and, consequently, Lewis's characters, as real entities as well as one another's contemporaries. Shakespeare also receives a similar homage in *The Voyage of the "Dawn Treader"* when Lucy, searching through Coriakin's magic book, finds the spell to put an ass's head on a man, " as they did to poor Bottom" (129); Hooper and Green 62.

2. C.S. Lewis, *On Stories and Other Essays on Literature* (Ed. Walter Hooper. San Diego: Harcourt Brace Jovanovich, 1966, 1982) 42; *Ibid.* 31; C.S. Lewis, *The Abolition of Man* (New York: Touchstone, 1996) 31.

3. C.S. Lewis, *Surprised by Joy* (New York: Harcourt, Brace, and Company, 1955) 228; *Ibid.* 237; Lewis's conversion, so connected with a trip to the zoo, reflects the inextricable connection between Christianity and animals that finds its form so beautifully in Narnia; Lewis, *Surprised by Joy,* 214; Peter J. Schakel and Charles A. Huttar, eds., *Word and Story in C.S. Lewis* (Columbia: University of Missouri Press, 1991) 190; George Sayer, *Jack: A Life of C.S. Lewis* (Wheaton, Illinois: Crossway Books, 1994) 108; in *Jack: A Life of C. S. Lewis*, George Sayer writes that Lewis read the enormous text of *The Faerie Queene* in a single sitting. In actuality, Lewis took several weeks to read *The Faerie Queene,* according to his letters to Arthur Greeves. In a letter dated October 5, 1915, he writes that he has been reading the poem both at home and on his holidays at Great Bookham, where he was being tutored; and "and [I] am now half way thro' Book II. Of course it has dull and even childish passages, but on the whole I am charmed" *They Stand Together: The Letters of C.S. Lewis to Arthur Greeves (1914–1963)* (New York: Macmillan Publishing Co., 1979) 83. In his letter written on March 7, 1916, Lewis proclaims that he has at last finished the poem, though he wishes Spenser had finished the six additional books. Although it took him five months to completely read the poem, he was only reading it on weekends, for pleasure, when he had a respite from his "serious" school reading assignments; Hooper and Greene 292; In *Studies in Medieval and Renaissance Literature* Lewis's secretary Walter Hooper collected a variety of essays from Lewis's popular lectures. Most of his lecture notes were lost

since Lewis quickly discarded notes and manuscripts, either using them for scrap paper or immediately tossing them into the wastebin. This is why so few of his original manuscripts are in existence today. Most of the essays in the collection are those that Hooper found or salvaged, sometimes literally out of the wastepaper basket. However, one of the essays collected in the section on Edmund Spenser is also contained in another collection. The essay entitled "On Reading *the Faerie Queene*" originally appeared as the entry "Edmund Spenser" in Lewis's *Fifteen Poets* which is quoted below. In the preface to *Studies in Medieval and Renaissance Literature* Hooper acknowledges the permission of Oxford University Press for the reprint (ix); Katharine Gardiner, "C.S. Lewis As A Reader of Edmund Spenser" (*Bulletin of the New York C.S. Lewis Society* 16.11 [September 1985]: 1–10) 3; Paul Piehler, "Visions and Revisions: C.S. Lewis's Contributions to the Theory of Allegory" (*The Taste of the Pineapple: Essays on C.S. Lewis as Reader, Critic, and Imaginative Writer*. Ed. Bruce L. Edwards. Bowling Green, OH: Bowling Green State University Popular Press, 1988. 79–91) 79; Margaret Patterson Hannay, "Provocative Generalizations: The *Allegory of Love* in Retrospect" (*The Taste of the Pineapple: Essays on C.S. Lewis as Reader, Critic, and Imaginative Writer*. Ed. Bruce L. Edwards. Bowling Green, OH: Bowling Green State University Popular Press, 1988. 58–78) 74; Paul L. Holner *C.S. Lewis: The Shape of his Faith and Thought* (New York: Harper and Row, 1976) 11; N.S. Brooks, "C.S. Lewis and Spenser: Nature, Art, and the Bower of Bliss" (*Essential Articles: Edmund Spenser*. Ed. A. C. Hamilton, Hanover, CT: Archon Books, 1972) 13; C.S. Lewis, "Edmund Spenser" (*Fifteen Poets*. London: Oxford University Press, 1951) 40; C.S. Lewis, *Spenser's Images of Life* (Ed. Alastair Fowler. Cambridge: Cambridge University Press, 1967) 1; by this token, *The Faerie Queene* would undoubtedly qualify as "good literature" by the standards Lewis himself set forth in *An Experiment in Criticism*. In characterizing readers, rather than literature itself, one quality that sets good literature apart from bad is the reader's desire to re-read: "The majority [readers of "bad" literature] never read anything twice" (2). In the essay "On Stories," he also avers that "no book is really worth reading at the age of ten which is not equally (and often far more) worth reading at the age of fifty, except of course, books of information" (14).

4. C.S. Lewis, *The Collected Letters of C. S. Lewis: Family Letters 1905–1931*, vol. 1 (Ed. Walter Hooper. San Francisco: HarperCollins, 2004) 476. Letter tentatively dated Feb. 14, 1920; for more on Milton's influences, including Spenser, see Harold Bloom's essay "Milton and his Precursors" which can be found in the Norton Critical Edition of *Paradise Lost* as well as in its original context in *A Map of Misreadings* (Oxford: Oxford University Press, 1975); George Sayer, *Jack*, 51. Hooper and Green in *C.S. Lewis: A Biography*, emphasize the way in which the diary entry about reading *Paradise Lost* contrasts with the other activities young Jack included in his diary for that day: the weather, his school lessons, meals, and a sword he was constructing (24). Clearly, he was a "real boy" in many of his pursuits, but the academician was already developing; Hooper and Green, *C.S. Lewis* 160; Charles A. Huttar "Milton" (*Reading the Classics with C. S. Lewis*. Grand Rapids, MI: Baker Academic, 2000. 161–186) 170; C. S. Lewis, *An Experiment in Criticism* (Cambridge: Cambridge University Press, 1965) 105; Hooper and Green, *C.S. Lewis* 223; Lewis, *An Experiment in Criticism* 140–141.

5. Lewis initially began *The Lion, the Witch, and the Wardrobe* in the fall of 1939 but did not actually complete a final draft until the spring of 1949. He then began what is often referred to as "the LeFay Fragment," a piece that was later partially woven into the fabric of *The Magician's*

*Nephew,* which he actually completed last of the series, in the winter of 1954. For an excellent timetable on the composition and the publication of the *Chronicles* and other important texts, see Appendix One of Paul F. Ford's *Companion to Narnia* (New York: Macmillan Publishing Company, 1986); even Lewis's close friend and literary associate J. R. R. Tolkien found the *Chronicles* simplistic and not fully realized. Considering Tolkien's own devotion to detail and history within his fantastical creations, it is understandable that he thought that "Jack's children's story [*The Lion, the Witch, and the Wardrobe*] ... really won't do" (Humphrey Carpenter, *The Inklings: C. S. Lewis, J.R.R. Tolkien, Charles Williams, and their Friends.* [Boston: Houghton Mifflin, 1979] 223). While Tolkien labored for years over his *Lord of the Rings* saga, creating elaborate histories, languages, geographies, and cultures to imitate a real history of a real place, Lewis dashed the Chronicles off in rapid order, often leaving loose ends that he had no intention of tying up to Tolkien's satisfaction. One may imagine that were Tolkien writing *The Lion the Witch, and the Wardrobe* that he would have to give his readers the entire history of the knight who once wore Professor Kirke's suit of armor which Peter and Edmund consider dismantling; the exact contents of each of Mr. Tumnus's wrapped packages; and the full story of how each statue in the White Witch's collection came to be there, along with epic poems describing their adventures. Lewis, however, leaves these details up to the readers' imagination, intent on delivering the story. In addition, Tolkien was alarmed by Lewis's style of putting anything into the stories if it suited his fancy. Lewis used figures from Norse and classical mythology, as well as details straight from modern Europe, seemingly at random, so that Mr. Tumnus, a classical Greco-Roman faun, works for a Norse snow witch, eats a very British tea with sardines and cake, and uses a modern umbrella to defend himself from the snow. While most readers of all ages delight in the whimsy and variety that result, "for Tolkien, the suspension of disbelief, the entering into a secondary world, was simply impossible ... and he turned his back on it" (Carpenter 224). For, unlike Lewis, "Tollers" was not inclined to treat a piece of writing mercifully simply because it was created by a friend. Ironically, Tolkien's own most beloved creations, the Hobbits, particularly Bilbo Baggins, are surrounded by anachronisms as jarring as Tumnus's umbrella and packages. These anachronisms, including tobacco, mantel clocks, and pocket handkerchiefs, are far more noticeable in *The Hobbit* than in *The Lord of the Rings*. In fact, in the Prologue of *The Fellowship of the Ring*, Tolkien takes great pains "to make the whole history of the Shire correspond point for point with the history of early England" (Tom A. Shippey, *J.R.R. Tolkien: Author of the Century* [New York: Houghton Mifflin, 2000] 9) and goes to great lengths to explain the presence of tobacco. Lewis, of course, would have made no such effort, leaving the inconsistencies as part of the peculiar quirks of the Hobbits and their world; Lewis, *An Experiment in Criticism* 60; Kathryn Lindskoog, *The Lion of Judah in Never-never Land* (Grand Rapids, MI: Eerdmans, 1973) 128; In the *Proceedings of the Thirteenth Annual Conference of the Children's Literature Association,* Jackie Eastman analyzes the opening events of both *The Lion, the Witch and the Wardrobe* and Book I of *The Faerie Queene* in light of their similar labyrinth plots (Ed. Susan R. Gannon and Ruth R. Thompson. Kansas City: University of Missouri, 1988. 140–143). Nancy-Lou Patterson traces some of the connections between Errour and the Green Witch in her article "'Halfe Like a Serpent,'" published in *Mythlore* 40 (Autumn 1984).

6. Lewis, *A Preface to Paradise Lost* 100; Lewis, always fond of the novels of George MacDonald, may have been thinking of

characters such as Diamond in *At the Back of the North Wind* when he pondered the difficulties of creating convincing "good" characters. Although he wrote to Arthur Greeves that the very title of the book was "alluring" (*They Stand Together* 96), Lewis likely found the protagonist to be one of those less successful characters, since, unlike Lewis's own fictional children, the angelic Diamond never loses his temper, misbehaves, or otherwise acts like most real live children.

7. Paul L. Holner, *C.S. Lewis: The Shape of His Faith and Thought* (New York: Harper and Row, 1976) 12.

# Chapter I

1. Tom Shippey, *J.R.R. Tolkien: Author of the Century* (New York: Houghton Mifflin, 2000) 141; In his masterful *J.R.R. Tolkien: Author of the Century*, Tom Shippey contends that Tolkien's view of evil, particularly the evil of the One Ring, is both unusual and orthodox because the Lord's Prayer actually mirrors the two kinds of evil manifested in *The Lord of the Rings*: the evil that individuals cause by their choices or negligence ("Shadow"), and the evil that is clearly external and beyond individual control ("Darkness"). Shippey argues that Lewis, Tolkien's friend and colleague, took a more rational, or Boethian view, that evil is not a force itself, but merely the absence of good. However, these two types of evil are reflected in the *Chronicles*, albeit less dramatically than in *The Lord of the Rings*, and they can certainly be seen in *Paradise Lost* and *The Faerie Queene*, both of which feature seemingly irredeemable (and often supernatural) evil characters as well as mortals who perpetuate evil by their disobedience or weakness.

2. C.S. Lewis, *A Preface to Paradise Lost* (London: Oxford University Press, 1979), 58; *Ibid*; Until 1994, the "Adventures of Snow White" ride in Walt Disney World's Magic Kingdom was a scary trip through a variety of scenarios featuring the Wicked Queen/Witch. Warning signs were posted to alert parents to the Witch's presence in the attraction. The ride was closed down for renovation, and re-opened with a friendlier atmosphere and adventures in which Snow White played a more dominant role; the Witch's part was reduced significantly.

3. C. S. Lewis, *Of Other Worlds: Essays and Stories* (Ed. Walter Hooper. New York: Harcourt, Brace and World, Inc., 1966) 42; This character is referred to as "the White Witch" in *The Lion, the Witch, and the Wardrobe*, and as "Jadis" in *The Magician's Nephew*. For the sake of clarity, the two names are here used interchangeably; Lewis, *Of Other Worlds* 36.

4. Lewis, *Of Other Worlds* 36; Katherine Lindskoog, *The Lion of Judah in Never-never Land* (Grand Rapids, MI: Eerdmans, 1973) 96.

5. C. S. Lewis, *The Allegory of Love: A Study in Medieval Tradition* (Oxford: Oxford University Press, 1958) 332; Wesley A. Kort, *C.S. Lewis Then and Now* (Oxford: Oxford UP, 2001) 153–154.

6. Meredith Price, "'All Shall Love Me and Despair.' The Figure of Lilith in Tolkien, Lewis, Williams, and Sayers" (*Mythlore: A Journal of J.R.R. Tolkien, C.S. Lewis, Charles Williams, and the Genres of Myth and Fantasy* 31 [Spring 1982]: 3–7) 3; see Paul F. Ford, *Companion to Narnia* (New York: Macmillan Publishing Company, 1986) for further information on the Lilith demon and her connection with Jadis, 269; Lionel Adey, *C. S. Lewis: Writer, Dreamer, and Mentor* (Grand Rapids, Michigan: William B Eerdmans, 1998) 167; It is interesting to note that in Book II of *The Faerie Queene*, Spenser specifically mentions the Caspian Sea. He mentions the "Adrian gulf" as well (II.vii.14.4) but no other bodies of water; see Walter Hooper and Roger Lancelyn Greene, *C. S. Lewis: A Biography* (New York, Harcourt, Brace Jovanovich, 1974)

250, 262–263 for more about the attempted Psyche poem.

7. C.S. Lewis, *Mere Christianity* (New York, HarperSanFrancisco, 1952, 2001) 124; Peter J. Shakel, *Imagination and the Arts in C.S. Lewis: Journeying to Narnia and other Worlds* (Columbia: University of Missouri Press, 2002) 96; C.S. Lewis, *A Preface to Paradise Lost* 100; Wesley A. Kort, *C.S. Lewis Then and Now* (Oxford: Oxford UP, 2001) 41.

8. C.S. Lewis, *A Preface to Paradise Lost* 95; Satan, not the narrative John Milton, makes this judgment against Eve's character. Clearly, though Eve is somewhat younger and less experienced than Adam, she is not a fool, and Milton does not paint her as one — see Lewis's analysis of Eve in *A Preface to Paradise Lost* 121; C.S. Lewis, *A Preface to Paradise Lost* 99; Evan K. Gibson, *C. S. Lewis, Spinner of Tales: A Guide to his Fiction* (Grand Rapids, MI: Christian University Press, 1980) 12.

9. Joe Christopher also explores the connection between Milton's garden of Eden and the Narnian garden and the similar temptation scenes in his *C. S. Lewis* (Boston: Twayne Publishers, 1987) 119; In *Perelandra*, his most obvious homage to *Paradise Lost,* Lewis, intriguingly, dispenses with fruit as a temptation tool, using instead the temptation to stay overnight on the solid, or unmoving, land; Charles A. Huttar, "Milton" (*Reading the Classics with C. S. Lewis.* Grand Rapids, MI: Baker Academic, 2000. 161–186), 177; Evan K. Gibson, 199–200.

10. C.S. Lewis, *A Preface to Paradise Lost* 96.

11. C.S. Lewis and Don Giovanni Calabria, *The Latin Letters of C.S. Lewis* (Trans., ed. Martin Moynihan. South Bend, Indiana: St. Augustine Press, 1998) 32. Fr. Calabria began corresponding with Lewis in 1947, shortly after he read an Italian translation of *The Screwtape Letters.* Since Fr. Calabria spoke no English, and Lewis no Italian, they corresponded in Latin. The collection of letters includes the letters both in Latin and translated into English. Unfortunately, few of the letters to Lewis survive since Lewis burned many of his letters and private papers, usually hoping to protect the privacy of his friends and colleagues. The original passage reads: "Omnes enim aut volentes aut nolents voluntatem Dei faciunt: Judas et Satanas ut organa aut instrumenta, Johannes et Petres ut fillii."36.

12. Intriguingly, when the Green Witch begins her horrific transformation, Jill, Eustace, and Puddleglum are momentarily distracted. "When they did look, their hair nearly stood on end" (*SC* 159). In *The Faerie Queene,* Book III, Britomart has an identical reaction when she encounters dark sorcery. While Busirane reads from his book of evil spells, "horrour gan the virgins hart to perse,/ And her faire locks vp stared stiffe on end" (III.xii.36.5–6). Since Spenser states quite clearly earlier in the book that Britomart's hair, when released, hangs to her feet, standing it on end is no mean feat. Though Britomart and Lewis's protagonists are experiencing different types of evil spells, it is interesting to note that having one's hair stand on end is the natural reaction in both cases.

13. With his work in Ireland, Spenser was undoubtedly aware of Celtic legends about the Fey, who also figure so prominently in many of the W. B. Yeats poems that so enchanted Lewis from his early teens. In her delightful illustrated version of the Scottish folktale *Tam Lin* (New York: Harcourt Brace Jovanovich,1990), Jane Yolen emphasizes the fact that green is the Fey's particular color, and she dresses her beautiful, but malevolent, "Faery Queene" in a dress that is "all the greens of the forest" (18). The particular use of green, as Yolen indicates in her notes, is in one of the original versions of the ballad, which she researched for the book. The ballad is documented from at least 1549, but is likely far older.

14. The statue of Venus, entwined with the tail-eating serpent, includes associations of eternity and the cyclical nature of

life that love and reproduction certainly include. The combination also echoes the fact that, as Scudamour says, she "hath both kinds in one" (III.x.41.6), incorporating both symbols, and representing the ultimate incarnation of fertility.

## Chapter II

1. Lionel Adey, *C. S. Lewis: Writer, Dreamer, and Mentor* (Grand Rapids, Michigan: William B Eerdmans, 1998) 166; Evan K. Gibson, *C. S. Lewis, Spinner of Tales: A Guide to His Fiction* (Grand Rapids, MI: Christian University Press, 1980) 199; Wesley A. Kort, *C.S. Lewis Then and Now* (Oxford: Oxford UP, 2001) 43.

2. Kort, *C.S. Lewis Then and Now* 43.

3. As noted in the textual notes of the Hamilton edition of the poem, Spenser relied heavily upon the work of Sir Thomas Malory for some elements, including Tristam's years spent in the forest, like Caspian, hiding from his uncle and learning the ways of the animals in the forest. However, Spenser made a number of changes in the story, including the fact that in Malory's version, it is "his mother Elizabeth [who] dies, not his father Melyodas; and his step-mother, not his uncle, threatens him" (VI.ii.27 n.). Clearly, though Lewis was also quite familiar with Malory, it was Spenser's version of the tale that influenced the creation of Miraz.

4. Paul F. Ford (*Companion to Narnia*. New York: Macmillan Publishing Company, 1986) 95n; Considering Lewis's background and experience, it seems unlikely that the Calormenes grew out of some personal, anti-Arab sentiment. Such a charge would, it seems, be more believable if levied against a post–2001 American or British author. Since Lewis was a World War I veteran and a strong British voice during World War II, the people group he could logically have been seen as

feeling antagonistic toward would be Germans, or even Italians or Japanese. Yet, German cultural elements, with the exception of the occasional bad Dwarf, are not portrayed negatively in the *Chronicles* at all; Peter J. Schakel, *Reading with the Heart: The Way into Narnia* (Grand Rapids: William B. Eerdmans Publishing Company, 1979) 13–14.

5. Walter Hooper, *Past Watchful Dragons* (New York: Collier Books, 1971) 44.

6. C.S. Lewis, *A Preface to Paradise Lost* (London: Oxford University Press, 1979) 95.

7. Donald E. Glover, *C.S. Lewis: The Art of Enchantment* (Athens, Ohio: Ohio University Press, 1981) 181; Peter J. Shakel, *Reading with the Heart* 118.

8. Adey, *C. S. Lewis: Writer, Dreamer, and Mentor* 73.

9. The connection of Satan's name with being twisted or bent was certainly not lost on Lewis. In his Space Trilogy, unfallen creatures with no experience of evil use the word "bent" to describe sin; Lewis, *A Preface to Paradise Lost* 102.

10. C. S Lewis, *On Stories and Other Essays on Literature* (Ed. Walter Hooper. San Diego: Harcourt Brace Jovanovich, 1966, 1982) 8.

11. Though Spenser specifically describes Argante riding "a Courser dapled grey" (III.vii.37.3), Lewis explains that the members of the giant hunting party at Harfang are not on horses "for there are no giant horses in that part of the world, and the giant's hunting is done on foot; like beagling in England" (*SC* 107). Perhaps Lewis was concerned by the strange visual image conjured by the giantess Argante whose horse is not described as any larger than a normal horse, and he thus decided not to deal with the horse issue at all. This paradox is also an issue when considering that so many of the giants in the poem take human lovers who must be considerably smaller than themselves. It is probably best not to examine

the issue and its crude connotations much more closely.

12. T. K. Dunseath, *Spenser's Allegory of Justice in Book Five of the Faerie Queene* (Princeton, NJ: Princeton University Press, 1968) 12.

13. Karla Faust Jones, "Girls in Narnia: Hindered or Human?" (*Mythlore: A Journal of J.R.R. Tolkien, C.S. Lewis, Charles Williams, and the Genres of Myth and Fantasy* 49 [Spring 1987]:15–19) 16; In his *Companion to Narnia*, Paul F. Ford asserts the possibility that Susan, having lost her entire family in the railway accident, may truly "grow up," and return to the faith of her childhood (402). Clearly, this is speculation, but based on the redemptive experiences of other disobedient characters in the series, it is likely that a repentant Susan would join her family in Aslan's Country after her natural death in England.

14. Walter Hooper, *Past Watchful Dragons* (New York: Collier Books, 1971) 25; C.S. Lewis, *Of Other Worlds: Essays and Stories* (Ed. Walter Hooper. New York: Harcourt, Brace and World, Inc., 1966) 30–31. Many critics have pondered what Lewis's reaction might be to the enormously popular *Harry Potter* books. It is likely that if Lewis could present his opinions on the books, he would be more troubled by Harry's fame, along with his remarkable ability to win at sports and earn the House Cup, than by the monsters and other obstacles Harry and his friends must overcome. A particularly insightful speculation on Lewis's hypothetical reaction to Rowling's work is provided by Peter J. Schakel in the chapter entitled "'Let the Pictures Tell Their Own Moral': Lewis and the Moral Imagination" in *Imagination and the Arts in C.S. Lewis: Journeying to Narnia and other Worlds* (Columbia: University of Missouri Press, 2002); Lewis, *On Stories* 37; Lewis, *An Experiment in Criticism* 67; Kort, *C,S, Lewis Then and Now* 114; Lindskoog, *The Lion of Judah in Never Never Land* 40–41.

# Chapter III

1. C. S. Lewis, *Studies in Medieval and Renaissance Literature* (Collected by Walter Hooper. Cambridge: Cambridge University Press, 1966) 132; in his essay "The Taste of the Pineapple: A Basis for Literary Criticism," Jerry L. Daniel avers that the reason Lewis advocated curling up with a large, illustrated edition of *The Faerie Queene* was not because of the poem's literary theory, but because of its "beauties and horrors," including, in particular, the knights themselves (*The Taste of the Pineapple: Essays on C.S. Lewis as Reader, Critic, and Imaginative Writer.* Ed. Bruce L. Edwards. Bowling Green, OH: Bowling Green State University Popular Press, 1988. 9–27) 22; because Milton, Spenser, and Lewis are all male, they have each experienced some censure for their depiction of women. The attitudes of Spenser's and Milton's cultures regarding women are often regarded by critics as troublesome because of their tendency to either draw women as completely pure and holy or as completely depraved and evil. These same criticisms are often (unfairly) placed upon the Bible and upon Judeo-Christian attitudes toward women despite the remarkable value Jesus and the early church placed upon women and their contributions. In a culture that treated women as sub-human property, Jesus and his followers taught both men and women. The Apostle Paul, often excoriated for his statements regarding women, actually made the radical first-century statement that in Christ men and women were equal (Galatians 3:28). Lewis, although a twentieth century writer, comes under criticism for placing women in stereotypical roles of weakness or domesticity. While these issues come into play in the characterizations of Lewis's female characters and their sources in Milton and Spenser, one goal of this text is to demonstrate how unfounded and misdirected such criticism often is, particularly when it ignores historical atti-

tudes and projects modern ideas onto the past.

2. Evan K. Gibson, *C. S. Lewis, Spinner of Tales: A Guide to his Fiction* (Grand Rapids, MI: Christian University Press, 1980) 175.

3. Thomas Howard, *The Achievement of C.S. Lewis* (Wheaton, Illinois: Harold Shaw, 1980) 40; Katherine Lindskoog, *The Lion of Judah in Never-never Land* (Grand Rapids, MI: Eerdmans, 1973) 12; according to Green and Hooper's *C. S. Lewis: A Biography* (London: Collins, 1974, third edition, 2002) 303, the manuscript was actually the notes for "Broadcast Talks" stuck in between pages of *The Dark Tower*; Evan K. Gibson, *C. S. Lewis, Spinner of Tales: A Guide to his Fiction*, 137.

4. Intriguingly, the villains of the *Chronicles*, as well as those who menace the protagonists of *The Faerie Queene* and *Paradise Lost*, often succeed in leading their victims to believe a distorted version of the truth, even when it conflicts with reality. Though Lucy is not believed for telling her siblings that there is another world on the other side of the wardrobe, the Green Witch of *The Silver Chair* nearly succeeds in convincing the children and Rilian that there is not a world above, even as she is contriving to use them in her conquest of that world. See Chapter I, above.

5. Evan K. Gibson, *C. S. Lewis, Spinner of Tales: A Guide to his Fiction* 137.

6. In his insightful *C. S. Lewis* (Boston: Twayne Publishers, 1987), Joe Christopher points out that J. R. R. Tolkien took issue with Lewis's transforming the nature of the mythical creatures he included in his narrative (although the same charge might be levied against Tolkien for his original touches with his elves). In particular, Tumnus presented a problem, for, if he acted according to his "true" nature, Lucy would be raped, not entertained with cakes and toast (111). Lewis seems to have acknowledged this problem by distinguishing between fauns and satyrs in Narnia (see Paul F. Ford's useful definitions of

each race in his *Companion to Narnia*) although in classical mythology they are often indistinguishable. In Narnia, satyrs are wilder, more goatlike, and fairly dangerous; a satyr is among the Narnians who turn against King Tirian in *The Last Battle*. Lewis's fauns, by contrast, are more gentle, civilized, and less goat-like. Thus Mr. Tumnus is less threatening than a satyr, and more likely to prove an ally; however, he still presents a very real danger to Lucy, as he does initially plan to give her to the White Witch, who will undoubtedly kill her outright or kill her metaphorically by turning her to stone. This is a far more intellectual danger than the physical threat presented by classical satyrs and fauns and a threat more appropriate to a children's text.

7. Katherine Lindskoog, *The Lion of Judah in Never-never Land* 90.

8. Evan K. Gibson, *C. S. Lewis, Spinner of Tales: A Guide to His Fiction* 183.

9. C.S. Lewis, *A Preface to Paradise Lost* (London: Oxford University Press, 1979) 121.

10. Evan K. Gibson, *C. S. Lewis, Spinner of Tales: A Guide to His Fiction* 147; *ibid*. 148.

11. William Griffin, *Clive Staples Lewis: A Dramatic Life* (San Francisco: Harper and Row, 1986) 341; *ibid*.

12. C.S. Lewis, *A Preface to Paradise Lost* 121.

13. The most famous example of the tamed Amazon is undoubtedly Shakespeare's Hipplotyta from *A Midsummer's Night Dream*, who must be "woo'd with the sword" of Theseus, the representative of civilization and order, and must become a "civilized" wife.

14. Karla Faust Jones, "Girls in Narnia: Hindered or Human?" (*Mythlore: A Journal of J.R.R. Tolkien, C.S. Lewis, Charles Williams, and the Genres of Myth and Fantasy* 49 [Spring 1987]:15–19) 15. For a thoughtful analysis of the role of the unusual narrator in the *Chronicles*, ee "He Looks As Though He'd Make It

Come Out All Right" in Peter J. Schakel's *Imagination and the Arts in C. S. Lewis: Journeying to Narnia and Other Worlds*, 70–88. For more on Lewis's ideal of knighthood, see Walter Hooper's *Past Watchful Dragons* (New York: Collier Books, 1971) 88. Susan serves as a foil for Lucy's strong and well-rounded character. Although Susan is a better archer than her sister, she suppresses her skills in favor of being "an ordinary grown-up lady" who no longer rides to the wars (*HHB* 176). Susan is always depicted as being eager for adulthood. As Polly later says, twenty-one-year-old Susan refuses to actually grow up: "I wish she *would* grow up. She's wasted all her school time wanting to be the age she is now, and she'll waste the rest of her life trying to stay that age" (*LB* 135). Even in childhood, Susan downplays her skill as an archer in her shooting match with Trumpkin the dwarf and feels guilty about shooting a wild bear, even though it is attempting to kill Lucy: "She hated killing things" (*PC* 116).

15. Evan K. Gibson, *C. S. Lewis, Spinner of Tales: A Guide to His Fiction* 149.

16. Using last names only was also a common practice in all-male boarding schools of the time, but when Lucy refers to her friends at school (*VDT* 132) she uses their first names; Though the narrator of the *Chronicles* is clearly an omniscient third person, according to Peter J. Schakel in *Imagination and the Arts in C.S. Lewis: Journeying to Narnia and Other Worlds,* the stories are "for the most part related from the perspective of one of the girls, an intriguing choice for an author generally more comfortable around men than women" (Columbia: University of Missouri Press, 2002) 74.

17. Jill is also described killing another man and the talking bull and wolf that had joined the Calormenes. The bull and wolf are appropriate opponents, with their connotations of male aggressiveness and lust. Jill, like Britomart, is consistently triumphant over such forces; though Jill

dresses in armor that "doubtless belonged to a page in the train of one of their Tarkaans" (*LB* 54), and darkens her face to appear Calormene, there is no serious attempt to mask her gender; Tirian addresses her as "lady" to the Dwarfs, who call her "Missie" (73).

18. The repellant appearance of the undisguised Duessa seems to indicate a disgust on Spenser's part with the female body. However, the same covering of women occurs throughout *The Faerie Queene*. Una is veiled through most of the first book. Her disguise, unlike Duessa's, masks her beauty. Britomart's armor is another example of this covering technique. When the disguises are removed, the characters' real natures are revealed. For Una and Britomart, their true natures are even more beautiful. With Duessa, however, her true nature is filthiness and perversity. Rather than disgust, Spenser seems to be operating from a sense of mystery about women, a sense in which good women are concealing the extent of their goodness for the eyes of only a few, and bad women are attempting to hide the extent of their hideousness. This is frequently sexual (i.e. chastity or depravity) because of Spenser's cultural views on the duality of the female body and its power to produce new humans or to "lure" unsuspecting males; Lionel Adey, *C. S. Lewis: Writer, Dreamer, and Mentor* (Grand Rapids, Michigan: William B. Eerdmans, 1998) 74.

19. Evan K. Gibson, *C. S. Lewis, Spinner of Tales: A Guide to His Fiction* 197.

20. Walter Hooper and Roger Lancelyn Green, *C. S. Lewis: A Biography* (New York, Harcourt, Brace Jovanovich, 1974) 242; Green and Hooper propose that the depth of Lewis's female characters may have been due, in part, to the presence of Maureen Moore who, along with her mother, became Lewis's responsibility as a result of the promise he made to his friend Paddy Moore during WWI: if one of them died in combat, the other would care for

the dead man's family. Lewis took his promise seriously, and while there has been much discussion of his relationship with Mrs. Moore, most of it is lurid speculation and not appropriate to the present discussion. It is important simply to understand that though Lewis did not originally have any sisters, he did inherit one from Paddy Moore; C.S. Lewis, *A Preface to Paradise Lost* 121.

## Chapter IV

1. Jerry L. Daniel, "The Taste of the Pineapple: A Basis for Literary Criticism." (*The Taste of the Pineapple: Essays on C.S. Lewis as Reader, Critic, and Imaginative Writer*. Ed. Bruce L. Edwards. Bowling Green, OH: Bowling Green State University Popular Press, 1988. 9–27) 23; Peter J. Schakel, *Reading with the Heart: The Way into Narnia* (Grand Rapids: William B. Eerdmans Publishing Company, 1979) 3; Colin Manlove, *Christian Fantasy: From 1200 to the Present* (Notre Dame: University of Notre Dame Press, 1992) 230.

2. C.S. Lewis, *Of Other Worlds: Essays and* Stories (Ed. Walter Hooper. New York: Harcourt, Brace and World, Inc., 1966) 37; C.S. Lewis, *On Stories and Other Essays on Literature* (Ed. Walter Hooper. San Diego: Harcourt Brace Jovanovich, 1966, 1982) xvi; C. S. Lewis, *A Preface to Paradise Lost* (London: Oxford University Press, 1979) 7.

3. C.S. Lewis *The Allegory of Love: A Study in Medieval Tradition* (Oxford: Oxford University Press, 1958) 310; Spenser often goes to great lengths to explain the contemporaneous existence of classical figures, including gods whose worship faded in the early Christian era, with the early medieval figures of Arthur and Merlin, and, of course, the Faerie Queene herself, Elizabeth I. In the end, however, readers must simply accept the chronological paradox as another unique characteristic of Spenser's world, meant to inspire delight

and wonder, rather than confusion and disbelief.

4. Thomas Howard, *The Achievement of C.S. Lewis* (Wheaton, Illinois: Harold Shaw, 1980) 23.

5. Walter Hooper, *Past Watchful Dragons* (New York: Collier Books, 1971). 32; Paul F. Ford, *Companion to Narnia* (New York: Macmillan Publishing Company, 1986) xxxv; Evan K. Gibson *C. S. Lewis, Spinner of Tales: A Guide to his Fiction* (Grand Rapids, MI: Christian University Press, 1980) 194; Peter J. Schakel provides an extensive and thoughtful analysis of the books' order in Chapter 3: "'It Does Not Matter Very Much'—Or Does It: The 'Correct' Order for Reading the Chronicles" in *Imagination and the Arts: Journeying to Narnia and Other Worlds* (Columbia: University of Missouri Press, 2002) 40–52. Lewis did once respond to a young reader that it really didn't matter in what order one read the books. He was probably reassuring the child that whatever order he read them in would be fine, and that he would not be "wrong" for reading them in either publication or chronological order. Lewis's agreeing with the boy's choice to read them chronologically may have had much more to do with his desire to encourage and support a young reader rather than any real desire to re-number the books. However, the latter possibility is exactly how the comments have been interpreted, leading to an unfortunate and strict re-numbering that Lewis did not ever officially endorse, although he would have had ample opportunity to do so within his lifetime. Additionally, as Schakel asserts, the renumbering is restrictive, particularly in editions that put all seven books in one volume, implying that one *may not* read the books in any other order, as readers who are, for example, familiar with the Harry Potter books, think that numbered order means the books should be read that way and no other. (Certainly this is the best way to read the Potter books, discovering Rowl-

ing's beautifully laid surprises for maximum enjoyment.) Schakel does not completely condemn the re-numbering, but asserts that "it is definitely unfortunate the publishers did not indicate that a different arrangement existed in earlier versions, remains an alternative order for reading the books, and is preferred by a number of Lewis scholars.... It is a decision that detracts from, not enhances, recognition and appreciation of the artistry and meaning of Lewis's best known books" (51–52). Walden films, in choosing to produce its film of *The Lion the Witch and the Wardrobe*, rather than beginning with *The Magician's Nephew*, also seems to have endorsed the original order in which the books appeared, while at the same time reverting to the original British texts in areas that differ from the American versions; for example, Fenris Ulf's name is changed to Maugrim. One hopes that the immense popularity of the film will help potential readers become aware of an alternate, and, in most cases, better, order than the one which the publishers currently endorse. The clever hints from *The Magician's Nephew* woven into the film (*i.e.* the carving on the wardrobe depicting scenes from Digory and Polly's adventures, the Professor's tobacco box in the shape of a silver apple, the Professor's reaction when he hears what piece of furniture Lucy has climbed into) also hint at the enjoyment of only later finding out who Professor Kirke really is, while also connecting with readers who read *The Magician's Nephew* before reading *The Lion, the Witch, and the Wardrobe*.

6. Kort, Wesley A. *C.S. Lewis Then and Now* (Oxford: Oxford UP, 2001) 144; Peter J. Schakel, *Reading with the Heart: The Way into Narnia* (Grand Rapids: William B. Eerdmans Publishing Company, 1979) 27.

7. There is also the distinct possibility that Lewis's song creation was influenced by the *Ainulindale*, or Great Music, that brought Tolkien's Middle Earth into

being. Though *The Silmarillion* was not published until 1977, long after Lewis's (and Tolkien's) death, it is possible that the two friends discussed the song-creation motif, or that Tolkien read portions of the sequence to Lewis. However, considering Tolkien's dislike of and inability to accept the *Chronicles*, it is doubtful that Lewis consulted with him on the passage, and Lewis did not read aloud his Narnia stories to the Inklings (Carpenter 226). Milton is thus a more likely candidate for source material. See also Charles A. Huttar's chapter on Milton in *Reading the Classics with C.S. Lewis* (176).

8. Genesis 1:24 NIV; Charles A. Huttar, "Milton." *Reading the Classics with C. S. Lewis* (Grand Rapids, MI: Baker Academic, 2000. 161–186) 176; Charles A. Huttar also suggests additional possibilities for the creation sequence in which animals burst from the ground in his chapter on "Milton" in *Reading the Classics with C. S. Lewis*, 176 and 182 n.

9. Both Milton and Spenser doubtless were reflecting the image drawn by Christ in his description of Himself as the shepherd of a flock: "The man who does not enter the gate, but climbs in by some other way, is a thief and a robber. The Man who enters by the gate is the shepherd of his sheep" (John 10:1–2 NIV). Though Jesus was not describing Eden's wall, both Lewis and Milton use the image of the enemy as a wall-jumper and a thief.

10. Lewis's strong opinions on Spenser, and subsequent critics' problems with them, are well documented. In particular, see Margaret P. Hannay's "Provocative Generalizations: The *Allegory of Love* in Retrospect" in *The Taste of the Pineapple* (58–78) and Doris T. Myers's excellent chapter on Spenser in *Reading the Classics with C. S. Lewis* (87–104).

11. C.S. Lewis, *Spenser's Images of Life* (Ed. Alastair Fowler. Cambridge: Cambridge University Press, 1967) 121; *Ibid.* 123.

12. C.S. Lewis, *Spenser's Images of Life*

(Ed. Alastair Fowler. Cambridge: Cambridge University Press, 1967) 121.

13. Both Lewis's friend, J.R.R. Tolkien, and one of his favorite authors, George MacDonald, used underground realms filled with goblins. (Tolkien began calling them orcs in *The Lord of the Rings*, but in *The Hobbit*, they are referred to as goblins.) In both these texts, the goblins crowd together, much like ants in an anthill. Lewis's gnomes, however, are revealed as good creatures that have been enchanted, unlike the wicked creatures that eat the Dwarfs' ponies in *The Hobbit* and try to kidnap Princess Irene in *The Princess and the Goblins*.

14. The idea of cave-phobia relating to misogyny is directly connected to the bad mother/ devourer archetype. The earth, as a mother, can devour humans in the grave and in caves. Therefore the cave embodies fears of being eaten by the earth, or being destroyed by the feminine.

15. Peter J. Schakel *Imagination and the Arts: Journeying to Narnia and Other Worlds*, 59.

16. C.S. Lewis, *The Allegory of Love*, 326; *Ibid.* 330.

17. Corbin Scott Carnell, *Bright Shadow of Reality: C. S. Lewis and the Feeling Intellect* (Grand Rapids, MI: William B. Eerdmans Publishing Company, 1974) 128.

18. Wesley A. Kort. *C.S. Lewis Then and Now* (Oxford: Oxford UP, 2001) 57.

19. Evan K. Gibson, *C. S. Lewis, Spinner of Tales: A Guide to His Fiction* 147.

20. The concept of "further in" actually has its first appearance in *The Lion, the Witch, and the Wardrobe*. Lucy enters the wardrobe for the first time, going "further in and found that there was a second row of coats ... she kept her arms stretched out in front of her so as not to bump her face into the back of the wardrobe. She took a step further in — then two or three steps ... going still further in..." (5–6). Thus the books, when read in their original publication order, are framed by *two* structures whose insides are bigger than their outsides: the wardrobe and the stable. In both cases, it is Lucy who easily accepts the paradox and tries to show the inner world to others. While her brothers and sister do eventually see the "further in" of the wardrobe, the Dwarfs in *The Last Battle* refuse to be "taken [further] in." In addition, Mr. Beaver, when he first meets the children, urges them to come into a thick grove of trees where he can confirm his friendship with Mr. Tumnus and tell them of Aslan's imminent arrival: "Further in, come further in. Right in here. We're not safe in the open! (*LWW* 62). While Edmund, later to turn traitor, mistrusts the Beaver, Peter and Lucy immediately know he is trustworthy and have no compunctions in following him.

## Chapter V

1. Evan K. Gibson, *C. S. Lewis, Spinner of Tales: A Guide to His Fiction* (Grand Rapids, MI: Christian University Press, 1980) 170; Corbin Scott Carnell, *Bright Shadow of Reality: C. S. Lewis and the Feeling Intellect* (Grand Rapids, MI: William B. Eerdmans Publishing Company, 1974) 192; Evan K. Gibson, *C. S. Lewis, Spinner of Tales: A Guide to His Fiction*, 216.

2. Evan K. Gibson, *C. S. Lewis, Spinner of Tales: A Guide to His Fiction*, 166.

3. C.S. Lewis, *Surprised by Joy* (New York: Harcourt, Brace, and Company, 1955) 228–9.

4. Matthew 10:29; Matthew 10:16; Matthew 10:34; Evan K. Gibson, *C. S. Lewis, Spinner of Tales: A Guide to His Fiction*,142; *Ibid.* 143.

5. C. S. Lewis, *Surprised by Joy* (New York: Harcourt, Brace, and Company, 1955) 231; Mary R. Bowman, "A Darker Ignorance" (*Mythlore* 24 [Summer 2003]: 62–80. Infotrac. 30 September 2003. Rpt. 1–12) 3.

6. C.S. Lewis, *A Preface to Paradise Lost* (London: Oxford University Press, 1979) 76.

7. H.S.V. Jones, *A Spenser Handbook* (New York: Appleton-Century-Crofts, Inc., 1958) 155.

8. Paul F. Ford, *Companion to Narnia* (New York: Macmillan Publishing Company, 1986) 304.

9. Philip Pullman has been one of the most vocal in condemning Lewis's treatment of Susan. However, his vitriolic criticisms are well refuted in Mary R. Bowman's article "A Darker Ignorance: C. S. Lewis and the Nature of the Fall," which appears in the Summer 2003 issue of *Mythlore.* Although Pullman and other critics are bent on equating Susan's absence in *The Last Battle* with her being sent to Hell, Lewis makes no such connection. In fact, he wrote to a young reader, concerned about Susan's fate, that although the silly and conceited Susan has been left alive in her own world, "there is plenty of time for her to mend, and perhaps she will get to Aslan's country in the end — in her own way" (C.S. Lewis, *Letters to Children.* [*Letters to Children.* Eds. Lyle W. Dorsett and Marjorie Lamp Mead. New York: Touchstone, 1995.] 67). Thus, though Susan has missed out on the glorious reunion in Narnia, there is no need for the situation to be permanent. Just as one hopes the stubborn and irascible dwarfs clustered around the Stable door will eventually discover that they have entered Aslan's Country and enjoy its beauties, one hopes that Susan's arrival in the new Narnia is only delayed, rather than prevented, by her poor choices; Evan K. Gibson, *C. S. Lewis, Spinner of Tales: A Guide to His Fiction,* 160; Lionel Adey, *C. S. Lewis: Writer, Dreamer, and Mentor* (Grand Rapids, Michigan: William B. Eerdmans, 1998) 174; C.S. Lewis, *A Preface to Paradise Lost,* 116.

10. Evan K. Gibson, *C. S. Lewis, Spinner of Tales: A Guide to his Fiction,* 167.

11. John Warwick Montgomery, "The Chronicles of Narnia and the Adolescent Reader." (*Myth, Allegory, and Gospel: An Interpretation of J.R.R. Tolkien/ C.S. Lewis/ G.K. Chesterton/Charles Williams.* Minneapolis: Bethany Fellowship, Inc. 1974. 97–118) 97; Jackie F. Eastman, "C.S. Lewis's Indebtedness to Edmund Spenser: The Labyrinth Episode as Threshold Symbol in *The Lion, the Witch, and the Wardrobe.*" (*Proceedings of the Thirteenth Annual Conference of the Children's Literature Association.* Ed. Susan. R. Gannon and Ruth R. Thompson. Kansas City: University of Missouri, 1988. 140–143) 142.

12. C.S. Lewis, *On Stories and Other Essays on Literature* (Ed. Walter Hooper. San Diego: Harcourt Brace Jovanovich, 1966, 1982) 12.

# Conclusion

1. Evan K. Gibson, *C. S. Lewis, Spinner of Tales: A Guide to his Fiction* (Grand Rapids, MI: Christian University Press, 1980) 181; Corbin Scott Carnell, *Bright Shadow of Reality: C. S. Lewis and the Feeling Intellect* (Grand Rapids, MI: William B. Eerdmans Publishing Company, 1974) 92.

2. George Sayer. *Jack: A Life of C.S. Lewis* (Wheaton, Illinois: Crossway Books, 1994) 312.

# Bibliography

Adey, Lionel. *C. S. Lewis: Writer, Dreamer, and Mentor.* Grand Rapids, Michigan: William B Eerdmans, 1998.

Alpers. Paul J. *The Poetry of* The Faerie Queene. Columbia: University of Missouri Press. 1982.

Bowman, Mary R. "A Darker Ignorance." *Mythlore* 24 (Summer 2003): 62–80. Infotrac. 30 September 2003. Rpt. 1–12.

Brooks, N. S. "C.S. Lewis and Spenser: Nature, Art, and the Bower of Bliss." *Essential Articles: Edmund Spenser.* Ed. A. C. Hamilton, Hanover, CT: Archon Books, 1972.

Carnell, Corbin Scott. *Bright Shadow of Reality: C. S. Lewis and the Feeling Intellect.* Grand Rapids, MI: William B. Eerdmans Publishing Company, 1974.

Carpenter, Humphrey. *The Inklings: C. S. Lewis, J.R.R. Tolkien, Charles Williams, and their Friends.* Boston: Houghton Mifflin, 1979.

Champagne, Claudia M. "Wounding the Body of Woman in Book III of *The Faerie Queene.*" *Literature, Interpretation, Theory (LIT)* 2.2 (November 1990): 95–115.

Christensen, Inger. "Thy Great Deliverer": Christian Hero and Epic Convention in John Milton's *Paradise Lost* and C.S. Lewis's *Perelandra.*" *Excursions in Fiction.* Eds. Andrew Kennedy and Orm Overland. Oslo: Novus Press, 1994. 68–87.

Christopher, Joe R. *C. S. Lewis.* Boston: Twayne Publishers, 1987.

Como, James. "C.S. Lewis in Milton Criticism." *Bulletin of the New York C.S. Lewis Society* 3.12 (1972): 5–6.

*C.S. Lewis: An Annotated Checklist of Writings about Him and His Works.* Comp. Joe. R. Christopher and Joan K. Ostling. Kent State: University Press, n.d.

*C.S. Lewis: a Reference Guide.* Ed. Susan Lowenberg. New York: G.K. Hall and Co., 1993.

Daniel, Jerry L. "The Taste of the Pineapple: A Basis for Literary Criticism." *The Taste of the Pineapple: Essays on C.S. Lewis as Reader, Critic, and Imaginative Writer.* Ed. Bruce L. Edwards. Bowling Green, OH: Bowling Green State University Popular Press, 1988. 9–27.

Dunseath, T. K. *Spenser's Allegory of Justice in Book Five of the Faerie Queene.* Princeton, NJ: Princeton University Press, 1968.

Eastman, Jackie F. "C.S. Lewis's Indebtedness to Edmund Spenser: The Labyrinth Episode as Threshold Symbol in *The Lion, the Witch, and the Wardrobe.*" *Pro-*

*ceedings of the Thirteenth Annual Conference of the Children's Literature Association.* Ed. Susan. R. Gannon and Ruth R. Thompson. Kansas City: University of Missouri, 1988. 140–143.

Filmer, Kath. "The Masks of Lilith: A Comparison of C.S. Lewis's Reading of George MacDonald's Lilith and *Till We Have Faces*." *Bulletin of the New York C.S. Lewis Society* 19 (January 1988): 1–5.

Ford, Paul F. *Companion to Narnia*. New York: Macmillan Publishing Company, 1986.

Frongia, Terri. "Archetypes, Stereotypes, and The Female Hero: Transformations in Contemporary Perspective." *Mythlore: A Journal of J.R.R. Tolkien, C.S. Lewis, Charles Williams and the Genres of Myth and Fantasy* 67 (Autumn 1991):15–18.

Gardiner, Katherine. "C.S. Lewis as a Reader of Edmund Spenser." *Bulletin of the New York C.S. Lewis Society* 16.11 (September 1985): 1–10.

Gibson, Evan K. *C. S. Lewis, Spinner of Tales: A Guide to His Fiction*. Grand Rapids, MI: Christian University Press, 1980.

Gibson, Lois Rauch. "Beyond the Apron: Archetypes, Stereotypes, and Alternative Portrayals of Mothers in Children's Literature." *Children's Literature Association Quarterly* 13 (Winter 1988): 177–81.

Glover, Donald E. *C. S. Lewis: The Art of Enchantment*. Athens, Ohio: Ohio University Press. 1981.

Griffin, William. *Clive Staples Lewis: A Dramatic Life*. San Francisco: Harper and Row, 1986.

Guroian, Vigen. "Faith and the Journey to Aslan's Kingdom." *Modern Age* 37 (Fall 1994): 54–62.

Hannay, Margaret Patterson. "Provocative Generalizations: The *Allegory of Love* in Retrospect." *The Taste of the Pineapple: Essays on C.S. Lewis as Reader, Critic, and Imaginative Writer*. Ed. Bruce L. Edwards. Bowling Green, OH: Bowling Green State University Popular Press, 1988. 58–78.

_____. *Rehabilitations: C.S. Lewis' Contribution to the Understanding of Spenser and Milton*. Diss. State University of New York at Albany, 1976.

Hart, Dabney Adams. *Through the Open Door: A New Look at C.S. Lewis*. Tuscaloosa: University of Alabama Press, 1984.

Holner, Paul L. *C.S. Lewis: The Shape of His Faith and Thought*. New York: Harper and Row, 1976.

Hooper, Walter, ed. *The Collected Letters of C.S. Lewis, Volume 1: Family Letters 1905–1931*. San Francisco: HarperCollins, 2004.

_____. *Letters of C.S. Lewis*. Revised and Enlarged Edition. San Diego: Harcourt Brace and Company, 1993.

_____. *Past Watchful Dragons*. New York: Collier Books, 1971.

_____, and Roger Lancelyn Green. *C. S. Lewis: a Biography*. New York, Harcourt, Brace Jovanovich, 1974.

Howard, Thomas. *The Achievement of C.S. Lewis*. Wheaton, Illinois: Harold Shaw, 1980.

_____. "Moral Notes from Fictional Landscapes." *Modern Age* 37 (Fall 1994): 39–45.

Huttar, Charles A. "C. S. Lewis, T. S. Eliot, and the Milton Legacy: The Nativity Ode Revisited." *Texas Studies in Literature and Language* 44 (Fall 2002): 324–349. Infotrac. 30 September 2003. Rpt. 1–13.

\_\_\_\_\_. "Milton." *Reading the Classics with C. S. Lewis.* Grand Rapids, MI: Baker Academic, 2000. 161–186.

Irwin, W.R. "Christian Doctrine and the Tactics of Romance." *Shadows of the Imagination: The Fantasies of C.S. Lewis, J.R.R.. Tolkien, Charles Williams.* Ed. Mark R. Hillegas. Carbondale: Southern Illinois University Press: London: Feffer and Simmons, Inc., 1979. 139–49.

Jacobs, Alan. *The Narnian: The Life and Imagination of C.S. Lewis.* San Francisco, HarperCollins, 2005.

Johnson, William C. And Marcia K. Houtman. "Platonic Shadows in C.S. Lewis' Narnia Chronicles." *Modern Fiction Studies* 32 (Spring 1986): 75–87.

Jones, H.S.V. *A Spenser Handbook.* New York: Appleton-Century-Crofts, Inc., 1958.

Jones, Karla Faust. "Girls in Narnia: Hindered or Human?" *Mythlore: A Journal of J.R.R. Tolkien, C.S. Lewis, Charles Williams, and the Genres of Myth and Fantasy* 49 (Spring 1987): 15–19.

Kilby, Clyde S. *The Christian World of C.S. Lewis.* Grand Rapids: William B. Eerdmans Publishing Co., 1964.

Kort, Wesley A. *C.S. Lewis Then and Now.* Oxford: Oxford UP, 2001.

Lewis, C.S. *The Abolition of Man.* New York: Touchstone, 1996.

\_\_\_\_\_. *The Allegory of Love: A Study in Medieval Tradition.* Oxford: Oxford University Press, 1958.

\_\_\_\_\_. *The Collected Letters of C. S. Lewis: Family Letters 1905–1931, vol. 1.* Ed. Walter Hooper. San Francisco: HarperCollins, 2004.

\_\_\_\_\_. "Edmund Spenser." *Fifteen Poets.* London: Oxford University Press, 1951.

\_\_\_\_\_. *An Experiment in Criticism.* Cambridge: Cambridge University Press, 1965.

\_\_\_\_\_. *The Four Loves.* New York: Harcourt Brace and Company, 1988.

\_\_\_\_\_. *English Literature in the Sixteenth Century Excluding Drama.* New York: Oxford University Press, 1954.

\_\_\_\_\_. *The Horse and His Boy.* New York: Scholastic Inc., 1988.

\_\_\_\_\_. *The Last Battle.* New York: Scholastic Inc., 1988.

\_\_\_\_\_. *Letters to Children.* Eds. Lyle W. Dorsett and Marjorie Lamp Mead. New York: Touchstone, 1995.

\_\_\_\_\_. *The Lion, the Witch, and the Wardrobe.* New York: Scholastic Inc., 1988.

\_\_\_\_\_. "Literary Impact of the Authorised Version." *Selected Literary Essays.* Ed. Walter Hooper. Cambridge: University Press, 1969. 126–145.

\_\_\_\_\_. *The Magician's Nephew.* New York: Scholastic Inc., 1988.

\_\_\_\_\_. *Mere Christianity.* New York, HarperSanFrancisco, 1952, 2001.

\_\_\_\_\_. *Of Other Worlds: Essays and Stories.* Ed. Walter Hooper. New York: Harcourt, Brace and World, Inc., 1966.

\_\_\_\_\_. *On Stories and Other Essays on Literature.* Ed. Walter Hooper. San Diego: Harcourt Brace Jovanovich, 1966, 1982.

\_\_\_\_\_. *A Preface to Paradise Lost.* London: Oxford University Press, 1979.

\_\_\_\_\_. *Prince Caspian.* New York: Scholastic, Inc., 1988.

\_\_\_\_\_. *The Silver Chair.* New York: Scholastic, Inc., 1988.

_____. *Spenser's Images of Life.* Ed. Alastair Fowler. Cambridge: Cambridge University Press, 1967.

_____. *Studies in Medieval and Renaissance Literature.* Collected by Walter Hooper. Cambridge: Cambridge University Press, 1966.

_____. *Surprised By Joy.* New York: Harcourt, Brace, and Company, 1955.

_____. *They Stand Together: The Letters of C.S. Lewis to Arthur Greeves (1914–1963).* New York: Macmillan Publishing Co., 1979.

_____. *The Voyage of the "Dawn Treader."* New York: Scholastic Inc., 1988.

_____ and Don Giovanni Calabria. *The Latin Letters of C.S. Lewis.* Trans., ed. Martin Moynihan. South Bend, Indiana: St. Augustine Press, 1998.

Lindskoog, Katherine. *The Lion of Judah in Never-never Land.* Grand Rapids, MI: Eerdmans, 1973.

Lobdell, Jared. *The Scientification Novels of C. S. Lewis: Space and Time in the Ransom Stories.* West Jefferson, NC: McFarland, 2004.

Loris, Michelle Carbone. "Images of Woman in Books III and IV of Spenser's *Faerie Queene.*" *Mid-Hudson Language Studies (MHLS)* 8 (1985): 9–19.

Manlove, Colin. *Christian Fantasy: From 1200 to the Present.* Notre Dame: University of Notre Dame Press, 1992.

Manlove, C.N. *The Chronicles of Narnia: The Patterning of a Fantastic World.* Twayne's Masterwork Studies. 127. New York: Twayne Publishers, 1993.

_____. *C.S. Lewis: His Literary Achievement.* New York: St. Martin's Press, 1987.

Martin, Thomas L., ed. *Reading the Classics with C. S. Lewis.* Grand Rapids, MI: Baker Academic, 2000.

Matheson, Sue. "C.S. Lewis and the Lion: Primitivism and Archetype in the Chronicles of Narnia." *Mythlore: A Journal of J.R.R. Tolkien, C.S. Lewis, Charles Williams and the Genres of Myth and Fantasy.* 15 (Fall 1988): 13–18.

McBride, Sam. "C.S. Lewis's *A Preface to Paradise Lost,* the Milton Controversy, and Lewis Scholarship." *Bulletin of Bibliography* 15.4: 317–331.

Milton, John. *Paradise Lost.* Ed. Scott Elledge. New York: W.W. Norton and Company, 1993.

Montgomery, John Warwick. "The Chronicles of Narnia and the Adolescent Reader." *Myth, Allegory, and Gospel: An Interpretation of J.R.R. Tolkien/ C.S. Lewis/ G.K. Chesterton/Charles Williams.* Minneapolis: Bethany Fellowship, Inc. 1974. 97–118.

Patterson, Nancy-Lou. "'Halfe Like a Serpent': The Green Witch in *The Silver Chair.*" *Mythlore: A Journal of J.R.R. Tolkien, C.S. Lewis, Charles Williams and the Genres of Myth and Fantasy* 11.2 (Autumn 1984): 37–47.

Piehler, Paul. "Visions and Revisions: C.S. Lewis's Contributions to the Theory of Allegory." *The Taste of the Pineapple: Essays on C.S. Lewis as Reader, Critic, and Imaginative Writer.* Ed. Bruce L. Edwards. Bowling Green, OH: Bowling Green State University Popular Press, 1988. 79–91.

Price, Meredith. "'All Shall Love Me and Despair.' The Figure of Lilith in Tolkien, Lewis, Williams, and Sayers." *Mythlore: A Journal of J.R.R. Tolkien, C.S. Lewis, Charles Williams and the Genres of Myth and Fantasy.* 31 (Spring 1982): 3–7.

*The Quotable Lewis.* Eds. Wayne Martindale and Jerry Root. Wheaton, Illinois: Tyndale House Publishers, 1989.

Sammons, Martha C. *"A Better Country:" The Worlds of Religious Fantasy and Science Fiction.* New York: Greenwood Press, 1988.

_____. *A Guide Through Narnia.* Wheaton: Harold Shaw Publishers, 1979.

Sayer. George. *Jack: A Life of C.S. Lewis.* Wheaton, Illinois: Crossway Books, 1994.

Schakel, Peter J. *Imagination and the Arts in C.S. Lewis : Journeying to Narnia and other Worlds.* Columbia: University of Missouri Press, 2002.

Schakel, Peter J., ed. *The Longing for a Form: Essays on the Fiction of C.S. Lewis.* Kent State University: Kent State University Press, 1977.

_____. *Reading with the Heart: The Way into Narnia.* Grand Rapids: William B. Eerdmans Publishing Company, 1979.

_____ and Huttar, Charles A., eds. *Word and Story in C.S. Lewis.* Columbia: University of Missouri Press, 1991.

Shippey, Tom A. *J.R.R. Tolkien: Author of the Century.* New York: Houghton Mifflin, 2000.

Simmons, Courtney Lynn and Joe. *"The Silver Chair* and Plato's Allegory of the Cave: The Archetype of Spiritual Liberation." *Mythlore: A Journal of J.R.R. Tolkien, C.S. Lewis, Charles Williams and the Genres of Myth and Fantasy* 66 (Summer 1991): 12–15.

Spenser, Edmund. *Edmund Spenser's Poetry.* Ed Hugh Maclean. New York: W.W. Norton and Company, 1982.

_____. *The Faerie Qveene.* Ed. A. C. Hamilton. Text ed. Hiroshi Yamashita and Toshiyuki Suzuki. London: Pearson Education, 2001.

Tanner, John S. "The Psychology of Temptation in *Perelandra* and *Paradise Lost*: What Lewis Learned from Milton." *Renascence: Essays on Values in Literature* 52 (Winter 2000): 131–141. Infotrac. 2 July 2003. Rpt. 1–10.

*A Taste of the Pineapple: Essays on C.S. Lewis as Reader, Critic, and Imaginative Writer.* Ed. Bruce L. Edwards. Bowling Green, OH: Bowling Green State University Popular Press, 1988.

Triep, Mindele Anne. *Allegorical Poets and The Epic: The Renaissance Tradition to Paradise Lost.* Lexington: University of Kentucky Press, 1994.

Walker, Julia M. *Milton and the Idea of Woman.* Chicago: University of Chicago Press, 1988.

Yolen, Jane. *Tam Lin.* Illus. Charles Mikolaycak. New York: Harcourt Brace Jovanovitch, 1990.

# Index